What We Really Know About Child Rearing

What We Really Know About Child Rearing

SCIENCE IN SUPPORT OF EFFECTIVE PARENTING

Seymour Fisher

AND

Rhoda L. Fisher

Basic Books, Inc., Publishers
New York

76

CAMROSE LUTHERAN COLLEGE
Library

Library of Congress Cataloging in Publication Data

Fisher, Seymour.
  What we really know about child rearing.

  Bibliography: p.
  Includes index.
    1. Children—Management.   2. Parent and child.
  1. Fisher, Rhoda Lee, 1924–   joint author. II. Title.
  HQ772.F49   649′.1   76–21736
  ISBN: 0–465–09135–0

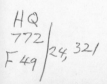

To our parents and our children

✦ PREFACE ✦

WE LOOKED FORWARD for some time to doing this book, and spent a number of years gathering material before we started to write. Our conviction that there was a need for such a book grew out of our roles as psychologists and parents. We repeatedly found ourselves frustrated because we wanted to apply to practical situations what was known scientifically about children and their mothers and fathers, but we could not find such knowledge assembled in usable form in one place. However imperfectly, we have tried to remedy this difficulty. We have examined endless pages of scientific literature in our attempt to come up with dependable ideas that would be helpful to parents and others who deal with children. It has been surprising how clearly the scientific findings point to certain conclusions in some areas. But it has also been disappointing to find how little is known in other areas. We have tried to be broad and fair in our interpretations of what various researchers have championed. While we have not hesitated to offer our own opinions about various problems, we have been careful to label them as impressions rather than fact.

Our search for information in the scientific literature made enormous demands on the library facilities of the Medical School of the State University of New York at Syracuse. We would like to express our warm appreciation for the expert and friendly help we received from the library staff. We would also like to express special thanks to Mary McCargar, who typed this book as it went through its successive stages.

~CONTENTS~

CONTENTS

CHAPTER 6

CHAPTER 7

CHAPTER 8

CHAPTER 9

What We Really Know About Child Rearing

Introduction

WHAT REQUIRES more skill than being an effective parent? What is more demanding and complex? A list of all the problems facing the average mother or father would be endless. Every day, you, as a parent, have to make decisions about such issues as: how much freedom to allow your child; whether to punish or not punish; whether to be protective or give a nudge toward independence; whether to expect loyalty to your values as compared to more "modern" ones; and how much information to transmit about sex, human frailty, and the secret recesses of the body. It would seem reasonable to have as much help as possible in making such tough decisions. This is evident in the energetic way most parents have read books offering advice about child rearing. Parents have also, by the thousands, enrolled in courses that would presumably make them wiser about how to cope with their children's problems. Each year, too, great numbers consult child treatment centers and various clinical experts for help in dealing with seemingly overwhelming difficulties that plague their relations with their children.

We have written this book to provide information and guidance to mothers and fathers that will help them approach more sensibly the tricky dilemmas they face each day. We are a wife-husband team who has collaborated on a variety of scientific projects. We are both psychologists, and we have worked in clinical research settings with children and parents. One of us, Rhoda Fisher, devotes her full time to treating children and parents with problems. Not the least of our qualifications for writing this book is that we have raised two children of our own and therefore have had intensely personal reasons for understanding what goes into the parent-child drama.

To an extent, we started this project in a spirit of protest and even indignation. We were astounded at the way self-styled experts offer courses and books to the public about how to raise children that are founded on little more than personal opinions and experiences. Several widely disseminated books giving detailed and confident advice to parents have lacked elementary scientific credibility. Numerous authors have urged that we swallow their prescriptions for child care purely on their say-so. They assure us, on the basis of their private speculations or vignettes from their clinical experiences, that they are in a position to give us sound information. It is surprising—and perhaps a measure of the prevailing hunger for guidance—how many parents have been willing to adopt new ways of dealing with their children in terms of such fragile assurances.

We feel that in a matter as important as shaping the lives of our children, we should want to act only in the light of information known to be dependable. We would go farther and say that the seal of dependability must ultimately come from scientific study. We therefore set ourselves the goal of bringing together in this book whatever meaningful information and advice can be offered to parents from the accumulated scientific research. We tried to translate scientific conclusions so that they could provide guidelines in dealing with common child-rearing puzzles. It is true that there are gaps in our scientific knowledge about parent-child relationships, and some of these gaps are embarrassingly large. We will acknowledge these and be honest about them.

One question we have pointedly asked ourselves is: can giving parents information and advice in book form really help them? Can parents absorb such information and apply it in practical situations? There are those, especially of a psychoanalytic persuasion, who would argue that parental behavior is determined by unconscious motives and attitudes, acquired early in life, that are almost impossible to change— except by extraordinary methods like experiencing several years of psychoanalytic psychotherapy. No real evidence exists for this pessimistic position. If it were true, it would represent a unique state of affairs. There is no other area of human behavior in which giving people increased meaningful information does not help them to make more rational decisions. Actually, more and more evidence has come to us that people with specific problems (for example, a child who repeatedly has temper tantrums, or a child with toilet training difficulties) can cope better with them when simply given pertinent information and direct advice. There is now a considerable literature showing that parents will often alter their responses to their children when they can see that improved relationships are likely to follow. Scientific publications dealing with behavior therapy and parent-training procedures attest to this. While unconscious feelings no doubt play a sizeable role in what parents do, their behavior is also affected by how well they understand the consequences of different courses of action.

We have sifted through the scientific literature concerned with parent and child and have matched this information against the chief recurrent questions that parents ask themselves. A wide range of topics will be taken up. We aim to unravel what is known about such matters as: the effects of different kinds of discipline; the way to raise children who are like ourselves and yet sufficiently different to be real individuals; and the attitudes that foster emotional stability in our sons and daughters. We also pull together the facts concerning other matters, such as what determines the ability of a child to achieve in school; the factors shaping the child's masculinity or femininity; and the impact of a mother or father being away from the family for long periods of time.

Most books about raising children start out by setting the stage with "The Parent" and "The Child." They portray you, the parent, as being somewhere in your home; nearby is your offspring, who is somehow troubling you or creating a problem that needs to be solved. They treat the situation as if you and your child existed in virtual isolation—as if there were just the two of you in a domestic vacuum. The advice they offer is often strongly colored by this view. They give the impression that the parent's individual decisions pretty much determine what will happen to the child. The way in which such books set the stage with "The Parent" and "The Child" does sound fairly plausible. After all, you do repeatedly find yourself in situations in which there are just you and your child, whose behavior calls for a decision or judgment. But we think there has been too much slick oversimplification of the nature of the parent-child relationship. This has led not only to a good deal of unrealistic action, but also to senseless guilt on the part of parents.

There is now convincing scientific information indicating that the behavior of both parent and child is strongly influenced by the family system of which each is a part. Psychologically, neither parent nor child ever really acts as a self-contained unit. The way in which you deal with your child cannot be well understood without seeing both of you as members of a family, in which there is delicate interdependence and mutual influence. Further, you and your child are members of a larger community, and your behavior may at times be sharply affected by what is happening "out there." The assassination of President Kennedy set off shock waves that were likely felt in almost every household in the United States. There is scientific documentation that the event increased anxiety in many families and confronted parents with the task of clarifying for their children the meaning of violence and death. It is also obvious to parents that the TV set is a channel that constantly brings messages and images to their children that can affect them. Parents who had to get up in the middle of the night to soothe a child frightened because he or she couldn't shake off the vision of a TV monster understand the power of outside influences on their children only too well.

It is also insufficiently understood that the special setting in which fate has decreed you must raise your children will have a powerful effect on how you deal with them. If you live in a crowded apartment, you will have different problems than those who live in a large roomy house. If numerous members of your extended family, like aunts and grandparents, are around a great deal, your relationships with your children are bound to be different from what they would be if you live isolated from all relatives. The religious and social characteristics of your neighborhood have been shown to influence the behavior of your offspring. Numerous other things, such as the state of the economy or whether it is a time of peace or war, create a framework within which you and your children have to adapt.

But what we would especially like to emphasize is that what happens between parent and child reflects not only what is going on directly between them but also the roles each is playing in a larger family drama. Numerous studies of familes have shown that they are tight little organizations with a network of rules and values that impinges upon its members more than they know. Each family member is "assigned" a role within the organization, and these roles go beyond just being labeled as "mother," "father," or "child." In some familes that are particularly preoccupied with issues of power and competition, you may be assigned a role on the basis of whether you are strong or weak. For example, father and the boys may be designated the strong ones, and mother and the girls may be the weak ones; just the opposite pattern has also been observed. In other families in which there is much concern over matters of guilt, virtue, and evil, certain members may find themselves designated either as sinners or virtuous ones.

The role assigned to an individual by the family can become a guiding force. A girl who is defined as weak by a family because of her sex will probably learn a great variety of ways to fulfill her role. Unless she does so, the family will reject her and make life painful. The child assigned the position of scapegoat since birth, because the family feels some great guilt that needs to be disowned and loaded onto someone else, will learn to act in the way scapegoats are supposed to. The individual parent gets caught up in these family dramas and finds himself or herself making decisions about the children in terms of a family script. A mother may punish her son with unusual severity after a minor infraction because she is responding not so much to the specific infraction as to the scapegoat role the family has tattooed on his hide. She may be puzzled by her own severity, react with guilt, and even lean over backward for a while to make up to the child for her unfairness. But in the long run she will find herself acting out the family's need for a scapegoat. She may determinedly decide to treat her scapegoat child more fairly, but this will prove difficult unless she makes an effort to change the attitudes that pervade the whole family. For example, if she begins to be "nice" to the scapegoat, the other family members may see her as allying herself with him and begin to treat her as another scapegoat. Her husband may become angry at her because she does not inflict on the scapegoat child the punishment he supposedly "deserves." The "virtuous" children in the family who have been protected against punishment by the much more visible badness of the scapegoat may feel indignantly threatened by mother's change in attitude and begin to address her with unfriendly, accusatory intonations. In short, her position in the family can be threatened if she tries to react to the "bad" child as if all that were involved was a transaction between the two of them.

In a very real sense, any parent has to balance his or her responses to each child in the family in the context of the rules and roles governing that particular family. With rare exceptions, the concept of "The Parent" dealing with "The Child" is a fiction. We do not mean to imply that parents are completely programmed by the nature of their family situation and can do little as individuals to modify the behavior of their children. We merely want to point out that when you are the member of any group you lose some of your autonomy and freedom of action. Quite analogously, during the hours that you are at work, you know that there are many things you can't do and others you must do. Families differ in how much rigid predictability they actually impose on their members. In some, a parent has a fairly fixed script and in others he or she is much freer to improvise. But to some extent, all families limit individuality. Rarely can you fully understand the actions of a parent toward his or her children without knowing the matrix of family rules in which that parent operates. A father who is treated by his family as not worthy of respect will respond differently to poor school achievement by his child than will one who is acknowledged to be strong; such a father may secretly prefer failure rather than success for his children because they will then be less of a threat to his self-esteem. A mother who sees her daughter as having a more affectionate closeness to her husband than she herself does may put special pressure on the daughter to cultivate a social life outside of the family.

In this introduction we have deliberately focused on the almost bewildering complexity of what happens between ''The Parent'' and ''The Child.'' We do not want the reader to forget that a parent's transactions with a child cannot be grasped through simple slogans or concepts. It is misleading to suggest otherwise. But that is all the more reason to acquire as much dependable information as possible about how parents and children live together.

Finally, before beginning our book, we would like to call attention to certain recent developments that have made it especially difficult for parents to define their relationships with their children—and therefore have made it equally difficult to render and enforce decisions concerning them. There has been a powerful movement to democratize the family and to label all members as equal. This is a reflection of the political values of our time. But is also derives from other things. There is a new emphasis on the importance of reason and logical justification. Less and less willingness exists to accept the statements of authority figures, unless they can stand up to the scrutiny of intellect and logic. Similarly, the power of mother and father is less accepted as ''given.'' Parents are more and more expected to prove in meaningful ways that they have the right to command respect and be listened to. This is not an easy thing to do. The well-informed adolescent is often more charged up with intellectual information than are his or her parents. The child who has learned the "new math" in school is not impressed with the intellectual prowess of parents who can only respond blankly to requests for help with math homework. Parents have to work harder to carve out a respected niche for themselves. Further, they have to be cleverer and more flexible in devising ways to motivate their children to do what the paents think is "good for them." The decreased potency of authority in the family has created crises for millions of parents. They are looking for principles and knowledge to guide them in these new circumstances. They have fresh incentives to stock up on information about what shapes their dealings with their children.

⚜ CHAPTER 1 ⚜

---

*The Child's Emotional Security**

SURVEYS INDICATE that most parents devote a lot of thought to the emotional security of their offspring. They watch to see if the children are anxious or unhappy. They wonder if they will be able to stand up to life's strains. At times they worry about the children's vulnerability to neurotic symptoms, delinquency, and even more serious breakdowns. Rarely do parents completely escape such worry. It is magnified when there has been a good deal of parent–child conflict and the child is obviously distressed by the tension. Parents not infrequently ask themselves whether they have been unreasonable in a damaging way. They ponder whether they have pushed too hard. They question whether they have, by some action or decision, put their children off balance. They have an investment in finding out what will strengthen them.

Considerable attention has been directed to this matter by researchers. Hundreds of studies have been undertaken to track down the

---

* A brief description should be offered about the way in which references are cited in the pages that follow. In the reference section, there is a list of the most important scientific papers and books that were used to arrive at conclusions and recommendations. These references are cited within chapters by number. In most instances citations are given only for major points and topics. It was decided that any attempt to document each specific point and each study mentioned would detract from the readability of the text and tend to make it look like a telephone directory.

things parents do that either preserve or disable their children psychologically. We have distilled these studies and have tried to grasp their message. We were pleasantly surprised to find certain principles emerging that fit well with common-sense notions. One may begin by saying in a general way that the same conditions that encourage friendly and happy contacts among adults apply also in adult relationships with children. The world that you and your children build at home is in many ways governed by the same psychological rules that apply to the interchanges of people "out there." This is true despite the fact that members of a family share a special, probably unique intimacy.

Sensible Communication

We were greatly impressed with the evidence that *distortions in parent communications* contribute strongly to disturbances in children. With few exceptions, scientific studies have found that members of disturbed families have trouble telling each other what they want, feel, and intend (1, 2, 4, 37, 43). When meaningful communication between people breaks down, they become uneasy, mistrustful, and unsure of the future of their relationship. If you are a three-year-old child and you find that your parents—upon whom you are wholly dependent—keep expressing themselves in ways too vague or contradictory to decode sensibly you become scared. You experience your ties with them as tenuous and fragile. If your life is literally hooked onto the whims of people who fill their messages to you with blanks and undecipherable stuff, not only will you misunderstand them, you will also see your transactions with them as mixed up. In time you will begin to feel equally mixed up. If parents fail to maintain adequate communication, they can cause their children distress and drive them to troublemaking and unusual compensations. There is reason to believe that poor communication can affect a child's ability to think logically, that it can make him feel isolated and alone, and that it can arouse unbearable anger in him. It seems to be able to make him feel so unwanted that he refuses to eat or runs away or balks at doing what is expected of him in school. It can simply make him feel so unattached and adrift that he is painfully frightened.

We do not know a great deal about what causes parents to communicate inadequately with their children. There are probably many reasons, ranging from limited intelligence to unconscious wishes to escape responsibility. But we suspect that one reason is that many parents simply are not aware how important such communication is to the child. The child comes into your life as a being capable of little communication. He cannot talk. It takes a relatively long time before he can construct meaningful sounds and gestures. He can grasp only a small fraction of the rich information you are capable of offering him. Under such circumstances it is easy to develop the notion that you and your child are able to have only a limited amount of interchange. Habits of bland and simplified communication evolve and harden into rituals. Parents are lulled into believing that it is unnecessary to put much energy into how they tell their children what they are thinking and intending. They likewise discourage their children from trying to tell clearly what their own thoughts are. We would suggest that if parents were truly impressed with the role of good communication in a child's emotional security from the day of birth, they could be inspired to do a better job in this sphere.

What is meant by poor communication between parents and children? The term covers a wide territory. As just noted, it can simply refer to the condition of parents investing minimal effort in what they say to their children. A mother's communications to her child may too often be brief and scarce in detail. She may not get around to saying enough to convey the real nature of what she expects of her child or to cover fairly the complicated things going on between them. She may use "short-hand" phrases that are difficult to pin down. Interestingly, studies have shown that the phrases and sentences produced by parents of disturbed children are harder to follow than those emanating from parents of normal children (4, 10, 16, 38). Persons who have raised disturbed children seem to use words vaguely, and they are also inclined to wander off the point. They start as if they are headed toward a conclusion about a certain issue, but then go off on a tangent about something else.

Here is an example:

CHILD: Are we going on vacation next month?
PARENT: We sure do need a vacation. I am tired myself. It would be a good idea to get away. How long is it since we took our last trip?
CHILD: Do you think we will go next month?
PARENT: If we do, we should go to a nice place. I am so tired of the

weather here. It's hard to decide when is the best time to get away. When I was a kid we didn't take vacations very often. We didn't have enough money.

The parent seems superficially to be dealing with the question the child has raised, but will not get to the point. Instead, his responses grow more rambling and tangential. The child necessarily gets the impression that he can't make contact or make himself understood.

There are other forms of inadequate parent-child interchange. Poorly communicating parents are often impatient with their children when the latter are trying to express themselves. They have been observed to interrupt them and to signal that they don't really want to hear from them. They discourage them by the use of sarcasm and criticism. The child who finds that his parents react negatively almost every time he wants to make a meaningful statement eventually gives up (although some children keep trying bravely for a long time). He concludes that his parents do not really want to know what is on his mind. We have seen cases in which worried parents have brought children in for clinical evaluation because they acted as though they were mute, although they seemed to be of at least average intelligence. We have found in every one of these cases that the parents were, at heart, uninterested in hearing from them. They did put on a thin facade of sociability with the child. But even when they seemed to be talkatively mixing it up with him, they were simply stringing words together for the sake of appearance. When such parents are made aware of their attitude and the emptiness of their messages, they sometimes begin to respond more sensibly. It is surprising how even a slight improvement on their part results in higher verbal output from the child.

So devalued may communication become in a family that the members learn to "tune each other out." Even when they appear to be listening to each other, they are selectively not attending. A child may, from his family experiences, learn to listen to one parent and not listen to another. A striking study literally demonstrated that if a child is asked to listen to tape recordings of conversations in which his mother and father took part, he may consistently be able to tell you in detail what one of his parents said and be unable to give more than a sketchy account of what the other said. He obviously has learned to tune out one parent, but not the other. In one instance where "tuning out" was a frequent cause of trouble, a mother described a family dinner during which she noticed that her husband was obviously not listening to her or to what their children were saying. She became concerned that the children would be disturbed by the father's unresponsive attitude, so she began to talk rapidly, to pour out words to cover up his silence. This caused the children to listen only to her and resulted in the noncommunicative father being even more isolated. This incident could not help but puzzle the children and leave them feeling troubled.

Another form of poor communication occurs when a parent shifts back and forth to different levels of discourse in a bewildering way. The following version of a parent–child conversation illustrates this:

CHILD: What should I wear to school today?
PARENT: Anything you'd like. Well, your red dress is pretty. So is your green one. Why don't you make up your own mind? I do really like the red one.
CHILD: I guess I'll wear the red one.
PARENT: I think you should wear that one more often. It's so pretty. Sometimes I think you're shy about wearing bright colors.
CHILD: I better hurry. I am going to be late for school.
PARENT: Yes, let me help you. You will look very pretty. Let me button that top button for you.

The parent in this case keeps shifting from the business at hand—the decision as to what dress the child should wear that morning—to very personal issues such as the child's presumed overdependence and shyness. The overdependence and shyness may be legitimate issues for the parent to bring up on some occasion, but it is only confusing to interject them in a situation where time limitations require an immediate practical judgment. We do not mean to imply that the parent should not place the burden for the decision upon the child. But this would merely require a straightforward statement like, "It's up to you. Pick any dress you'd like." Such a message would be crystal clear. But instead the parent pours out a mess of statements touching on everything from the immediate practical choice to the child's personality. It is bewildering to carry on business with someone who won't stick to the subject and who insists on peppering you with a lot of unrelated thoughts at the same time. This is especially difficult for a young child who has still not mastered the mechanics of integrating and making sense out of diverse chunks of information.

Still another example of confusing communication is the so-called "double bind." This means, for example, telling the child that you approve of something but at the same time intimating that you really don't. Examine the following conversation:

CHILD: I put on the new shoes you bought me yesterday. How do they look?
PARENT: They're fine. I am glad you put them on. By the way, what happened to that other pair of shoes that we bought about a month ago? They are my favorites.

The child has been given two contradictory messages: (1) that he should wear the latest pair of shoes that the parent purchased; (2) that he has really displeased the parent, who would have preferred he wear a different pair. A second, rather humorous example of the double bind involves a son who comes to dinner wearing one of two ties his mother purchased for him and who is greeted with the rebuke, "What's the matter, didn't you like the other tie I bought you?" Such trick communications are obviously mean. If repeated with any consistency, they indicate a hostile, depreciating stance on the part of the parent. However, we suspect that they can also occur because of carelessness or a lack of sophistication about such exchanges. That is, as the result of a day of crowded events, parents may have multiple messages saved up to deliver to a child. Some of these messages may be contradictory, but instead of taking care to sort them out, the parents issue them all at once. They become careless about contradictions simply because they are tired or flustered or distracted. Actually, it is a fact of life that we do entertain potentially contradictory feelings and expectations toward intimates. We want them to be supportive and close, but we don't want them to be intrusive or to interfere with our independence. We want them to be successful but we don't want them to be "better" than we are. We usually monitor ourselves and keep these contradictions from appearing simultaneously when we talk with them. But there are some people who are simply without insight regarding such things. They have not cultivated adequate sensitivity in this area. Perhaps their sensitivity could be increased if the problem were pointed out and they were shown how to monitor contradictions in their responses.

Intellectualization and "glossing over" are among the most prominent forms of blocked communication. A parent may repeatedly respond to the things his child says by recasting them in words that take the heart and emotion out of them. He reduces them to a stage of vague generality. Here is an illustration:

CHILD: I am worried about the spelling test we're having tomorrow. I failed the last one.
PARENT: Words are so complicated. They don't follow any regular rules and they don't spell the way they sound.
CHILD: I just can't get them right.
PARENT: Learning how to spell is really hard. You have to learn all the special rules and exceptions.

The child is trying to tell his parent about his anxiety and his concern about failing. But the parent sidesteps his intent and translates his communiqué into a dissertation on the formal properties of spelling. The emotion in the child's communiqué is eradicated and replaced with some bland talk. In this way the parent can avoid getting involved. He can, like so many parents, take the pathway of least energy input. But the scientific literature suggests that in the long run the saving in energy is only temporary. Eventually, repeated incidents of poor or blocked communication are likely to result in a disturbed child, and coping with such a child becomes a serious and draining task.

Returning to the sample conversation just cited, how could the parent have responded more communicatively to the child? Let us replay the interchange from a new perspective:

CHILD: I am worried about the spelling test we're having tomorrow. I failed the last one.
PARENT: You're worried about failing this one? Why are you having trouble?
CHILD: I am not sure. I guess I don't like spelling too much.
PARENT: Maybe you find it so unpleasant because you haven't been putting in enough time to be really sure you know all the words on your spelling list.

In this idealized replay the parent and child are talking directly to each other. This permits a more realistic exploration of the problem troubling the child.

It is important to emphasize at this point that good communication is not synonymous with being a smooth talker. It is not necessarily the verbally fluent parent who rarely hesitates in his speech who is giving the clearest messages. Someone who speaks awkwardly can still transmit a lot of meaning and be clear in what he intends to convey. In fact, one study found that in normal, well-adjusted families there was a tendency for the members to be informal as they addressed each other and also to interrupt each other frequently. As new ideas and feelings arose, each member felt free to introduce them into the stream of the discussion. Instead of being formally smooth in the sense that a well-prepared speech is, the interchange had a jerky, ebb-and-flow quality that reflected the flexibility of the members in telling each other what seemed to be important at the moment.

We think it is worth mentioning, too, that some parents get into the habit of casting most of their messages to their children in negative terms. In disturbed families the parents are inclined to focus on their differences with their children and to highlight things that will create tension and disruption. They are less likely to talk about the things children do or say that are friendly or promote family solidarity. By focusing on what is negative, the parents give the children an increasing feeling that the family cannot be a place where happy things occur. They also give the impression that they will show interest in their children only when they have a suitable negative target upon which to comment. It is not surprising, then, that many children embark on careers of making trouble for their parents because this is the only sure way to evoke their "interest." Obviously, persistent negative response by parents has its roots in their anger. However, it may be that they permit themselves to become so extreme in their focus on the negative either because they are not aware of how disruptive this is or because they have their own private theories about the value of negative messages in shaping their children properly. We will merely note that several scientific studies indicate that a "negative feedback" stance by parents has a long-term disorganizing impact on family relationships.

We have skimmed through several of the important ways parents interfere with the exchange of information and emotion between their children and themselves. We would speculate that each parent has his own favorites among these. There are those who specialize in simply saying as little as possible, others who talk a lot but who rarely get to the point, and trickier specialists who introduce so many complexities and misleading contradictions into their statements that even a sophisticated computer would not be able to track them accurately. The parent who wants to improve communication with his child probably can, if he is of at least average intelligence, observe and detect his own interfering strategies. There are those who would dispute whether this is possible. But we think there is good scientific evidence that if someone is highly motivated and willing to monitor his own behavior honestly, he can put two and two together. We would repeat again that there is also reason to assume that a parent who clearly recognizes and strongly wants to change some aspect of his behavior has a fighting chance to do so, at least in part.

The "Good" Relationship

It goes without saying that the way you interact with your children reflects not only your own individual habits of communication and your willingness to invest real effort in getting through to the children, but also how you feel about them. We want to discuss now the kinds of parental attitudes that have been found to foster security and stability in children. Some of the things we will say are obvious, but they are worth repeating as part of an effort to give you a rounded picture of what is known about the impact of parental behavior.

A key finding in the research literature is that parents of disturbed children give great priority to their own wishes and preferences over those of their children (14, 29, 52). Parents of disturbed and nondisturbed children have been studied in their own homes and in the psychological laboratory. Also, their attitudes and feelings have been analyzed by means of psychological tests. Further, studies have been done to find out how the children in the two types of families actually feel about their parents. From these sources it has become evident that parents who get too selfishly absorbed in their own goals and wishes are headed for trouble with their kids. If a child finds that his interests are usually expendable when they conflict with those of his parents, he feels he is being treated like an object rather than a person. He develops mistrust of his parents and casts them in the role of opponent rather than friend. Even more fundamentally, he begins to doubt the security of his family world.

How do parents show their children that they consider them to be secondary—that they are capable of acting unfairly if it serves their own ends? Some do so in very obvious, unmistakable ways. The "battered child" bears witness to this (20, 52). As has been widely publicized, there are parents who brutally attack their children for the slightest infraction. Their openly announced orientation might be paraphrased as follows: "I am unconcerned about how you feel. You will fulfill every wish or request I impose on you. If you resist I will hurt you. It makes no difference to me how much you suffer as long as I can make you behave the way that suits me."

The open unfairness of parents who "batter" their children is paralleled by the only slightly disguised unfair behavior of parents who demand that their children conform to extremely strict standards of performance. Extremes of strictness are often seen in parents' expectations concerning toilet training. They not only demand unusually early control of the anal and urinary sphincters by the child but severely punish lapses in control. The research and clinical literature is full of examples of well-educated parents who figuratively put their children on a toilet-training rack. Some of these parents are simply victims of erroneous theories of child development. They have grossly inaccurate ideas about how quickly a child can learn to control his sphincters. (By the way, there is evidence that a parent may be very strict about toilet training but be nondemanding about other aspects of child training such as weaning, freedom to move about, and so forth. However, there is a tendency for parents to be consistently strict versus nonstrict in a variety of situations.) The super-strict approach to toilet training frequently leads to rebellious complications. Research has shown that children who continue to have difficulty in controlling their urination and defecation have often been trained in an overly demanding and intrusive fashion.

Many parents learn to conceal unfairness in skillfully camouflaged ways. They employ all kinds of devices to conceal what they are, in fact, doing. Take the common example of the parent who is so invested in himself that he simply refuses to spend more than token time with his children. He will justify his behavior as necessary because of his business or other conditions "beyond his control," and his elaborate rationalizations can sound pretty convincing. Even so, his children will, in time, correctly sense that his behavior means that they are of limited importance to him. Another, more concealed example is provided by parents who repeatedly manage to block their children from doing the things they would like to do—but always with a fancy justification that adds up to "I am doing this for your own good." Perhaps the hardest to detect in their unfairness are symbiotic parents who try to merge the identity of their children with their own. They hover closely to them and devote endless time and energy to them. But their devotion is directed to making sure the children do not accomplish anything on their own or develop any ability to be separate persons. In so doing, the parents convert the children into extensions of themselves, incapable of originating anything that would conflict with their views. This is one of the most unfair and disabling of the "put-down" strategies parents are known to employ.

A "good" relationship between parents and children has many of the same qualities that mark any friendly contact. There is a feeling of closeness, of fairness, of interest, and of warmth. Repeated studies have affirmed that disturbed children experience their parents as basically unfriendly to them (29, 48). They experience them as manipulative. One investigator characterized such parents as Machiavellian. The well-adjusted child is more likely to see his parent as supportive of him when the going gets tough, able to empathize with his feelings, and willing to accept him as an individual in his own right. A parent who finds that he is chronically irritated with his child can be sure that his negative feelings are reciprocated. If you feel really distant from your child or are forever telling him that he can't do most of the things he would like to do, you can be fairly certain that something is wrong. The quality of friendliness as compared to unfriendliness is easy to identify. Feelings of warmth and closeness, or their absence, are also obvious. Any moderately sensitive person can, with some careful introspection, estimate how "good" his relationships with his children are. In fact, one study has demonstrated that parents are rather good judges of how their children feel and, indeed, how vulnerable they are to future disturbance. Parents should take seriously their own intuitions about what is going on between their children and themselves. If there is an extended period of interreaction that "feels" unfriendly, it would be sensible to do something about it. In many cases this would mean the parents should do some soul searching and try to discover in what way they are being exploitative or unfair.

Parents in Balance

Another major factor associated with child disturbance is living in a family where the parents are out of balance with each other. Parents are the managers and coordinators of the family group. They often have to work together and pool their knowledge in coping with problems. If they cannot coordinate, this sends disorganizing vibrations through the family. The same sort of thing happens in any organization where the top leadership is divided or in conflict. Many large institutions spend a good deal of money each year to bring in consultants who will detect imbalances among their key executives and try to straighten them out. They know from sad experience that all sorts of difficulties evolve from such imbalances.

Husbands and wives in families with disturbed children are often in conflict (2, 3, 48). They differ from each other in their slant on things. They are inclined to disagree and to make interpretations that are "out of phase." If you assign a task to them to perform jointly in the psychological laboratory, you find they have trouble coordinating their efforts. If you ask them to discuss one of their children, they express unlike opinions about him. It has also been found that they have different ideas about the goals of their family and how family decisions should be made. Therefore, they become a source of contradictory demands upon their children. The husband may direct the children along a certain path, only to have the wife suggest a complete about-face. We are acquainted, in a treatment context, with a husband-wife pair finely tuned to take the opposite sides of practically every issue. Their child, consequently, has had a hard time building up a unified sense of identity. The opposing views of his parents have become part of his own personality. He no sooner tries to make a decision than he feels pulled in two different directions. He is frequently in conflict within himself, puzzled, and indecisive.

The imbalance between parents can show itself in many ways. Since they have unlike ideas about family goals, they also disagree as to when the child is "right" and "wrong." They disagree about when he should be punished. They disagree, too, about the kind of punishment to be employed and how severe it should be. They likewise disagree about when he should be rewarded and what proper rewards are. Inconsistency becomes a dominant theme and introduces a sense of unpredictability. The child rarely knows what to expect. The only thing he can be certain about is that there will be no consensus and no clearcut definition of what he is supposed to do. In this kind of setting we have observed that it is not unusual for the child to drift into the role of becoming a mediator between his parents. He is so often *in between* them that he begins to feel responsibility for reconciling their differences. He becomes a special referee and a bearer of messages from one side to the other. He does this not only because he cannot stand the conflict between his parents but also because they gradually find that it is convenient to have such a concerned and dedicated mediator to buffer their differences. The parents can become dependent on using such a child mediator to maintain a semblance of equilibrium between them. The child may find that his best rewards come when he is playing the referee.

The following conversation involving a child and his parents depicts how the child does his best to intercede between his "out of balance" mother and father:

FATHER: It makes me mad that you spent so much on new clothes this month.

MOTHER: You're so stingy! You never want me to buy anything for myself.

CHILD: My teacher got mad at me today. She said that I made too many mistakes on my homework.

FATHER: Why don't you be more careful?

MOTHER: Don't watch TV so much and you'll have more time for your homework.

While it may not be immediately obvious, the purpose of the child's self-critical remark ("My teacher got mad at me today") is to set himself up as a target and, in so doing, divert his mother and father from attacking each other. If he can turn their anger in his direction, maybe they will forget their differences with each other. We have repeatedly seen children who were willing to sacrifice themselves in this fashion in order to encourage some semblance of harmony between their parents.

Children do learn to become highly expert "bridges" between their parents. However, this is a great and really unfair responsibility to place on the shoulders of any child. He feels that it is his fault if things do not go smoothly between his parents. He blames himself for tensions and disagreements. Such a load is enormous. It represents a reversal of the usual parent-child relationship. Instead of being supported and nurtured by his parents, he is forced to put the best part of himself into helping them. The child bridging between his parents is prematurely expected to give up his childhood and to take on an adult-level job. As a result, he grows angry and feels that he is being treated unfairly. He wants to escape and to find a place where people will take care of him. We have noted that when the child who has served as a "bridge" between his parents does become sufficiently emotionally upset so that his parents have to seek treatment for him and put up with his "symptoms," he gets a sense of satisfaction at having turned the tables and given them a taste of what it is like to carry a heavy burden. Incidentally, in line with our wish to clearly distinguish scientific fact from anecdotal observation, we must note that what we have just said about the "bridging" child is based on clinical reports rather than scientific evidence. We offer this material in a speculative spirit, to provide one illustration of how parents who are in conflict with each other may possibly cause trouble for their children.

Especially damaging to their children are parents who behave in conflicting or nonsynchronized ways when it comes to sexual identity. If mother wants to be more masculine than father or father wants to be more feminine than mother, confusion builds up in the offspring. This is a difficult matter to discuss because of our radically changing standards as to what is properly masculine or feminine. There is a strong movement among feminists to abolish all distinctions in sex role, so any consideration of this topic gets into supercharged issues. We will simply call attention to a few implications of what the research literature has uncovered. One of the clearest research findings is that children get upset when there is a reversal of conventional male-female power roles in the family. If mother acts more powerful than father, this seems to cause trouble (2, 3). We are not, on this basis, arguing against reversals of usual sex roles if spouses are so inclined. Each family has to make its own decisions about this matter in terms of its own aims and information (1). We do know that a core part of each person's identity (his concept of who he is) is built around his classification as male or female and the meanings he ascribes to being masculine or feminine. If you grow up in a family in which mother and father act as if they cannot distinguish any differences based on sexual structure, or in which they drastically challenge widely accepted models of masculinity-femininity, you will have some very special problems in spelling out exactly who you are supposed to be. It is especially true that a boy living with a father who abdicates his masculine role to mother will feel that he does not understand manliness or the part it is supposed to play in his own self-definition.

The balance between mother and father with respect to sex role is tested in a hundred different ways every day. Numerous decisions have to be made in which parents reveal their attitudes about the usual standards of masculinity-femininity. Children pick up their parents' attitudes in this area in terms of such things as competition for power or dominance, amount of investment in activities usually considered to be masculine or feminine, and the manner in which they dress and deal with their own bodies. They also have many opportunities to witness how each parent responds to the sex-role behavior of the other. Does father seem irritated when mother does something like ride a bicycle or throw a baseball? Does he seem negative when she chooses not to wear the stereotyped "feminine" mode of clothes? Does she seem disapproving when he encourages their son to be aggressive? Does she get uncomfortable when he seems to prefer doing things that have conventional feminine connotations (for example, being passive and quiet)? If their parents are out of phase with each other in their ideas of womanhood and manhood, it soon becomes apparent to the children.

Confusion about sex role can trigger extreme responses. For example, we have fairly good evidence that the angry assertive behavior of many delinquent boys represents a defensive denial of doubts about their masculinity. Male delinquents not infrequently come from families in which an imbalance has exposed them to an atmosphere in which there was feminine dominance. They have grown up in situations in which they experienced magnified feminine influence and a minimum of male decision making or interest. This can happen in a variety of ways. Commonly, it reflects either the complete absence of the father from the family or his presence in the role of someone who is a failure in the sense that he cannot carry his fair share of the family load. But in some cultures it simply reflects the extreme amount of intimacy mother has with her son, as compared with the amount of time father has available to spend with him. The boy who feels that he is getting too much feminine input becomes alarmed that he will not be able to achieve an acceptable image of manhood. So, he is drawn to do things that will dramatize his masculinity. He hopes by means of violent and aggressive behavior to correct his sense of masculine-feminine imbalance. He advertises his manliness and in so doing calms his doubts about himself (12, 25, 43, 51, 55, 57). We have seen little boys as young as three or four years of age who were doing violent things like setting fires and committing mayhem on other children in a desperate attempt to bolster the masculine part of their self-concept. Relatedly, we have seen girls who were painfully puzzled because they could not get a balanced message from their parents about how to be girlish and who were therefore driven to histrionic ways of mimicking femininity. For example, they dramatized their weakness and cultivated passivity in order to imitate the stereotyped image of a woman as someone who is dependent and compliant. One little girl who was referred to us for evaluation did this by fainting whenever unpleasant things happened to her in school.

In general, we would say that what typifies parents who are "in balance" is that they form a coalition. They combine their talents and fill in for each other's deficiencies. They agree on goals and support each other in getting to them. They give up some of their individualism for the advantages of the alliance.

Too Close—Too Distant

Too much closeness can make you uneasy. We have all had the experience of finding that another person has put his body too close to ours or asked an intimate probing question, making us feel almost as if we had been invaded. But we have all felt anger and loneliness, as well, because certain people refused to come close and stood off at a distance. Most of our long-term relationships with others fluctuate back and forth through different stages of closeness. This certainly applies to parents and children. Day in and day out, their level of intimacy shifts. In some families there may be a distinct pattern. Closeness may gradually become greater or less as the child grows older.

Studies of disturbed families suggest that they are characterized by erratic changes in closeness versus distance (21, 26, 29). Parents may approach their children unusually intimately one day and be coldly detached the next. Indeed, they may shift their closeness in an unpredictable way even from minute to minute. Note the fluctuations that take place in the following interchange between a parent and child:

MOTHER: You look sad today. Is something bothering you?

CHILD: I don't know. I am sort of tired. I don't feel good.

MOTHER: You should get more sleep. I give up. I've been telling you for weeks you should go to bed earlier.

CHILD: (Begins to cry) Nothing is going right. Some of the kids in school have been picking on me.

MOTHER: That's terrible. I won't stand for that. They can't do that to us. (Reaches over and tightly embraces child)

CHILD: (Cuddles against parent and cries intensely)

MOTHER: Everything will work out. (Remains silent for about a minute) My gosh, it's getting late. I better get back to work or we won't have any dinner tonight.

In the course of this encounter the mother first invites closeness by making a very personal comment ("You look sad today"). But then when the child begins to talk about his upset feelings, she seizes upon the peripheral remark ("I am sort of tired") to put herself into a distant hostile stance ("I've been telling you for weeks you should go to bed earlier"). The child is not fazed and opens up even more. The mother is moved by the child's emotional display and draws him into intimate closeness by embracing him. The child draws as close to mother as he possibly can. At that point the mother apparently becomes uncomfortable and tells the child that she wants to pull away ("I better get back to work"). In a brief period she has shifted from the pole of closeness to distance and back again repeatedly. It would be amazing if such behavior did not have an unsettling effect. How can you sustain a relationship with someone who is here one moment and gone the next?

It is difficult to spell out exactly what kind or amount of closeness children need with their parents. Obviously this will be influenced by a variety of things. Children may want more or less closeness depending upon such factors as their stage of development, the toughness of their immediate problems, and the availability of friends of their own age. Because we know so little about this matter, parents simply have to use their own best judgment about how to conduct themselves. But we do have enough scientific information available to say that parents who are either too extremely close or too extremely distant disconcert their children. The "distant" parent can walk the stage in many costumes. He can be the one who rarely interacts with his children and gives them the message that he does not want to get intimately involved with them. He can be the one who seems to want to be close when he is around, but whose work (for example, being a traveling salesman) results in his being away from home for long time periods. He can be a sick parent who is too preoccupied with his symptoms and pain to have much energy available for anyone else. Of course, there are great numbers of families in which one of the parents is "distant" in the ultimate sense that he is dead, or absent because of divorce, separation, or desertion. There are findings suggesting that the earlier in life that a child loses one of the parents (who is then permanently distant), the more likely he is to develop signs of psychological distress.

Parents may not be aware of the more camouflaged strategies they employ to keep their distance. One parent we know maintains his distance from his children by presenting himself as an extreme believer in equality and democracy. He insists that almost all decisions in the family be made by what amounts to a vote. He remains rather aloof from this decision-making process on the grounds that he does not want to bias anyone's opinions. He has an elaborate rationalization to justify why he will not involve himself. Another parent we have observed talks a great deal to his children and spends quite a bit of time with them. He appears to be seeking closeness, but when we listen to what he says to them we discover that the content is largely egocentric. He is always talking about himself, and his children get so bored and irritated with him that they hardly listen to his words. He is, in actuality, light years away from them psychologically. The elaborate disguises used by parents, to hide from themselves the fact that they are really evading closeness with their kids, are a measure of how guilty most people feel about not being a good "close parent."

Parents who are overly close to their kids, on the other hand, do not usually feel guilty, since parent-child closeness is defined as good and natural. But there are various ways in which parents can, through special forms of closeness, create problems for their offspring. One form that almost everyone knows about has to do with making your child overly dependent. There are parents who follow their children around and keep them from ever learning how to do anything on their own. They watch and scrutinize; they issue a stream of suggestions; they "help." They seem fervently dedicated to protecting and helping,

27

but it is apparent that they are actually preventing their children from learning independence. They give them the repeated message, "You can't do things right on your own. You need me to get a job done. You'd better be scared and passive when I am not around to prop you up." Parents who shape their children into such dependence are probably deeply motivated by fear. They see the world as a dangerous place and they believe their kids have to be protected every step of the way. We know, too, that some parents impose intense closeness on their children because they themselves feel the need to be hooked to someone. They doubt their own ability to survive as separate persons, and so they attach themselves defensively. The tendency to "hook on" in this fashion is encouraged in families where the parents do not support each other and feel unusually alone.

We have been astounded at the ingenuity of parents in devising ways to keep their children closely bound and, in that sense, to interfere with the children building their own boundaries. We have dealt with one family in which the mother and father seem outwardly to encourage independence in their children. But if you listen to the things they tell them day after day, you are struck with the focus on fear-inspiring themes. They keep emphasizing how uncertain life is, how easy it is to get hurt, and how difficult it is to get by on your own. They feed their children a stream of images that amount to saying, "You will find the world out there very dangerous. You'd better stick with us so that we can protect you." In another family we know, overdependence is encouraged by what at first sight appears to be arrogance and a sense of superiority. The parents give their children the message that they belong to a socially superior family and that there are few people outside of the family with whom they ought to associate. They picture others as largely of inferior stock. This has resulted in the children perceiving themselves as isolated and having no one to relate to except their parents. They feel they must count on their mother and father, and no one else, for human contact. In still another family we studied, the dependence of the children is maximized by erratically exposing them to unpleasant doses of independence. In the name of teaching their very young children to be independent, the parents suddenly and irregularly go off on extended excursions. The children are not prepared for such departures; furthermore, nothing is done to deal with their anxieties. They become highly sensitive about whether they can count on mother and father being around when they need them. Their concern about possible parental loss results in their clinging to their parents more and more. Incidentally, this clinging behavior angers the parents and gives them a rationale for embarking on more excursions in the name of "independence training."

The extreme example of the parent who takes over his child through over-closeness is provided by the phenomenon of "projective identification" (53). This refers to a parent seizing upon his child as a vehicle for expressing some very strong need or goal of his own. He converts the child into a replica of something he has in mind. He may "see" in his child a chance to fulfill a longstanding ambition. Or he may, in a more negative way, find that he can free himself of certain bad sensations if he can load them onto the child. He may get rid of his own guilt or feelings of inferiority by converting his child into a scapegoat whom he permanently casts in the role of "the bad one." The child has little chance under these circumstances to develop an identity of his own. He becomes a creature of his parent's imagination and is therefore strongly bound to him. While the evidence is incomplete, there are observations in the literature suggesting that some children who show antisocial behavior are really acting out "bad" roles their parents have projected onto them. Strangely, their antisocial behavior usually results in their becoming alienated from their parents, but at the same time it reflects a special form of over-closeness to them.

While the causes of over-closeness and distance are subtle and complex, we would propose that it is possible for parents to examine their own behavior to see if they are going to either extreme. One direct approach is to introspect and check out your own feelings. Do you usually *feel* that your children are at a distance from you? Do you *feel* as if you are avoiding emotional involvement with them? Or do you *feel* that you are fused with your children and that neither you nor they have any privacy from each other? Do you *feel* as if your time is completely monopolized in monitoring them? Do you *feel* as if what is happening to them is, in a sense, happening to you?

At another level, you can look for signs in the behavior of your children to tell you if they are experiencing you as overly distant or close. Do they seem to avoid you? Do they cling to you and act as if every separation were potentially catastrophic? Do they abruptly and erratically draw close, move away, draw close again, and so forth? Do they act as if you were intruding upon them? Do they seem to be chronically lonely? It would be helpful to point out here that children's feelings about closeness-distance not infrequently surface in their attitudes about going off to school. For example, some children seem scared when they have to leave in the morning. They may, in some instances, simply refuse to go to school. Such behavior has been referred to in psychiatric circles as a "school phobia." Although there is still disagreement about the cause of the "school phobia," there are solid indications that it may stem from being overly close to parents, especially mother. The child who is reluctant to go to school seems to experience his mother as fused with him, and he doubts that he can get along if he is separated from her. He cannot picture himself as a separate person. Interestingly, the mother of such a child seems to have a similar problem in conceiving of herself as an individual distinct from the members of her family.

Children who are struggling to resolve closeness-distance problems with their parents are likely to show special distress when confronted with events such as having their parents go away on vacation or being sent to summer camp, having to go to the hospital, having to live with visitors in the home for extended periods, or the birth of a new brother or sister. In each of these instances, the child has to adjust to being away from his parents or to getting less attention from them than before. By watching their children's behavior in such critical situations, parents can be tipped off as to whether changes are needed in their style of relating to them. We think this sort of sensitive and understanding awareness of critical situations which may reveal potential problems is basic to mother and father being able to help their children cope with them before they get out of hand. The help may take the form of thinking through what each is doing that may be destructive, and jointly exploring how their own immediate difficulties with each other may be adding to the problem. Further, they may want to call in professional consultation to obtain a more detailed understanding of what is out of balance.

Social Skills

Getting along with people calls for skill. There are complicated things you have to learn in order to understand others and to convey your intentions to them persuasively. The child who is having difficulty adjusting to life is often one who is socially awkward. He may be unusually shy or he may be inappropriately aggressive. He has trouble coordinating smoothly with people. He fails to grasp the right cues. He does not understand or is misunderstood by others. Studies have shown that poorly adjusted children are inclined to have parents who lack social skills (23, 49). This has been particularly well shown with reference to their mothers. If a child's parents lack social competence, he will probably have trouble picking up the right information about how to relate effectively to others. His parents will provide inadequate models. They will not reward or punish him appropriately as they see him trying out different approaches to people. We have witnessed numerous instances in which parents did not seem to know that their children were doing things that rubbed people the wrong way. They were not in a position to correct their children, because they simply did not know the children's behavior was inappropriate.

What are some social skills that seem to be lacking in children who are not adjusting well? We wish to specify that we can answer this question only impressionistically, in terms of the disturbed children we have personally observed. Here are a few of the deficits in skills that we would list:

1. They do not seem to know what is the "right" amount of communication to address to others. They either do not talk enough or talk much too much.

2. Relatedly, they do not have a realistic idea about how aggressive to be. They either let people push them around or they are too forceful in their own approach.

3. They often lack experience in dealing with a wide variety of people. They have not learned what to expect and therefore find it disconcerting when they get into situations that force them to encounter many people.

4. They have not had enough practice in coping with social situations in which they may be criticized. They do not know what to do when publicly brought under attack or ridiculed.

The child who is not early given the chance to acquire important social skills will repeatedly have bad experiences with people. Their behavior toward him will be puzzling and, all too often, disappointing. What we are saying here is that a child's sense of stability depends in part on how well he has acquired a competent repertoire of social acts. If this is so, it would mean that parents could find it profitable to take note of how their children behave in various social situations. They could observe what difficulties their children have that might be due to lack of knowledge or to too narrow a range of contacts, and then take steps to give them the extra training needed. Children can be explicitly advised about whether they talk too little or too much when they are in groups. They can be given hints about what to say when someone criticizes them publicly. They can be taken into a variety of social situations so that they can learn what it is like to meet many types of people. It is interesting, in this respect, that some of the techniques developed to help psychologically troubled people are based on giving them the chance to practice social skills that they will need in meeting people, applying for a job, and so forth.

Addiction

Feelings of defeat and catastrophe surge up in parents who discover that their offspring have become hooked on drugs. Some parents also get alarmed when they discover that their offspring have become hooked on alcohol—and even cigarettes. It should be added that addiction to overeating is another common problem. Much effort has been devoted to find out what drives adolescents and young adults to become dependent on the repeated intake of certain substances. No one cause has been isolated. Many factors seem to contribute (24, 27, 28, 44). Certain addictions are more common in particular religious groups, in specific socio-economic classes, and even in urban as compared to rural regions. There is an apparent—but very indefinite—tendency for persons who are addicted to be more psychologically anxious than nonaddicted persons. A similar trend has emerged indicating that the addicted are more likely to come from troubled families than are the nonaddicted. Their parents are more often people who are psychologically uncomfortable, who are in conflict with each other, or who lack clear-cut family values.

However, what should be of most direct practical significance to parents is the observation that the addictive behavior of the child is often an imitation of similar addictive actions he has witnessed in his own parents. Alcoholic parents are more likely to point their children in the direction of excessive drinking. Parents who smoke increase the probability that their children will smoke. Parents who are big overeaters encourage similar overeating in their children. It is interesting too that young people who get hooked on hard drugs are more likely to have come from families in which the parents were inclined to use chemical props. Such parents are more likely to take minor drugs (like aspirin and tranquilizers) to relieve pain, to control anxiety, to alter mood, to control appetite, and so forth. They may, further, be quick on the trigger to use "medicines" to soothe and make their children more comfortable. In other words, they give their children the message that imbibing chemicals is an effective method for coping with life's difficulties. The verbal denunciation of drug addiction by parents is drowned out by the respect they show for drug substances by chronically using them in various ways. Parents have to face up realistically to the fact that they set the tone for drug usage in the family. Their actions day by day will significantly affect the chances of their children becoming addicted as they enter adolescence.

We would like to add, more speculatively, that recent research has suggested that addiction is sometimes a substitute for a sense of being powerless. Somehow, the injection of a drug or the puff on a cigarette or the swallowing of alcohol may generate sensations that counteract feelings of weakness and inferiority. Some of the research findings bearing on this issue of power are quite convincing. One study that followed persons from the time they were children until they were adults was able to show that males who became alcoholics were struggling with conflicts about inferiority versus strength in their early years of development. This certainly suggests that addiction may have something to do with how adequately parents handled power issues in the family. We wonder whether parents who give their children a vision of life as a place where you usually fail to achieve what you want—by habitually putting the children down, for example—are not encouraging a future addictive solution.

The Disturbed Parent

Parents who are extremely upset or who have a hard time surviving psychologically tend to bring up children who are unstable (29, 34). Reliable information indicates that a child of a schizophrenic individual has a higher than average probability of getting into trouble psychologically. This is also true for the child who has an alcoholic parent. If both parents are in serious psychological trouble, the children have an even greater likelihood of becoming psychological casualties. Even individuals who do not show any clinical signs of psychological distress but who experience a lot of strain and uncertainty in the course of bringing up their kids will magnify disturbances in them. We can add that parents of poorly adapting children have from time to time been found to be characterized by such negative qualities as low self-esteem, indecisiveness, and the inclination to be self-deprecating. If life is extremely upsetting to you, some of your distress will probably rub off on your children. The correlation is far from one-to-one, and it is true that many children with disturbed parents go on to live rather happy, effective lives. Indeed, some children who manage to survive in an unusually stormy and conflicted family develop particularly complex personalities with special creative potential. But if one thinks in terms of probabilities, there is an increased chance of a disturbed parent ending up with a disturbed child. Since this is so, it would seem sensible for persons who know that they have been feeling distressed for a long period of time to monitor the condition of their children sensitively. They should be realistically prepared to secure extra support or guidance for them. The value of early detection of psychological stress cannot be too strongly underscored. At least one long-range study has demonstrated that if early detection is followed up with special counseling and psychological support, the chances for attaining a tolerably comfortable adjustment are significantly increased.

What We Don't Know

Parents construct theories of their own about what will keep their children sound and stable. Having committed themselves to one of these theories, they will invest tremendous effort in implementing it. This they will do despite the fact that they rarely have any solid evidence for knowing whether the theory is valid. There are so many procedures and rituals that parents pursue purely on the basis of some untested belief that these practices will protect their offspring. If you look around, you will see parents willing, purely on faith, to undertake time-consuming and self-denying activities in order to fortify their children. Think of the mother who decides to breast feed rather than bottle feed her baby because it will be psychologically "better" for him. If she were to consult the scientific literature she would find little support for her decision. Some mothers and fathers rarely leave their children with baby sitters because they believe that the more time they spend with their offspring, the more emotionally sound the children will be. They go to great lengths to prevent their children from ever feeling alone or "deserted." But except for the extremes of parents who are almost never available, there is no proof of a positive correlation between children's security and the amount of time parents spend with them. One can name many other analogous, unvalidated things that parents do to "help" their children, such as: always picking them up as soon as they cry; not allowing them to read certain kinds of material that would presumably be too threatening or upsetting; and imposing special regularities such as always going to bed at the same time or eating only at specified intervals.

The truth is that we do not know whether any of these parental plans and procedures do anything for the emotional security of their children. They may or may not. It is even possible that some of them have negative effects. There is no way at present to get around such ambiguity and uncertainty. Parents obviously have the right to develop their own theories and try their own little child-rearing experiments. However, they should more realistically evaluate the evidence they have for what they are doing. They should watch their children to determine whether they are actually responding as if they were being strengthened or helped. They should be prepared to alter their approach if that seems advisable. In short, parents must avoid rigid commitment to approaches the validity of which is actually untested. Someone has pointed out that the most destructive acts people have committed in the past against other people have been in the name of some theory or rigid doctrine. Some of the worst child abusers have justified their behavior in terms of a punitive child-rearing theory which they felt was unquestionably true. When people respond to others directly, in terms of feeling and of the evidence apparent to their eyes, they are less likely to crush others in a ruthless mold.

We will emphasize again and again in this book that parents need to be conscientious observers and to analyze what is actually happening. They need to "investigate" as soon as they notice that unpleasant feelings and tensions are building up in the family. They must be prepared to change their behavior if it seems to be damaging to their children. It is our impression that millions of parents do make such flexible changes every day, and that this is what keeps their families in workable balance.

CHAPTER 2

Control and Discipline: Reasonable and Unreasonable

IT DOES NOT take long for new parents to discover that one of their most demanding problems is to get their child to do what they want him to do. Even in dealing with a newborn baby, mother and father quickly find that they want to control him and are often puzzled about how to proceed. They may hope to get the child to stop crying so much or to stop waking up so often in the middle of the night. Their thoughts turn to possible means of "persuading" him to do what they expect. They may consider staunchly refusing to respond when he cries, or saying something that sounds disapproving. They may even entertain fantasies about inflicting a few well-placed taps on his behind to give him a strong message that he is doing the wrong thing. It is a rare parent who does not feel uncertain about how to discipline. Fundamental questions come up every day. Is praise better than punishment for motivating a child? Is spanking likely to have bad long-term results? Should you spontaneously use any discipline you feel like administering, and hope that your natural parental instincts will result in your doing the right thing? Or should you plan in advance what sorts of disciplines you will

37

use with respect to different kinds of acts? Should discipline be applied differently to boys as compared to girls? Endless queries of this sort cross every parent's mind.

[It is our impression there is value in systematically thinking through such matters. If you limit your judgment-making so that it occurs mainly under the pressure of crisis situations, you are more likely to do irrational and even silly things] We have worked therapeutically with families in which the parents were able to reduce levels of tension dramatically in a short time by planning in advance what discipline they would probably use if certain transgressions occurred. This enabled them to respond more reasonably. It was the difference between thoughtful anticipation and the reliance on impulsive decision making. There are some who might label planning of this sort as too deliberate and impersonal—but they might reflect that there are few times in the affairs of the world at large when it would be considered inappropriate to give careful advance consideration to potential difficulties.

Influential Parental Attitudes

Different parents treat their children in infinitely different ways. The combinations and permutations are endless. But researchers who have examined the attitudes of large numbers of parents toward their children have found that they cluster around a fairly small number of issues or themes (16, 20, 32, 53). First of all, there is an underlying theme of acceptance versus rejection. It is a fact that some parents like their kids a lot and some don't like them very much at all. Liking and not liking are as much a part of parent-child feelings as they are in any other human encounters. There are parents who communicate to their children that they have great love for them and who invite closeness. There are others who unmistakably give the message that they find contact with their children unpleasant and who ward off closeness. Children judge how accepting or rejecting their parents are in terms of such signs as the amount of love they show, how much they listen with interest, how proud they are of their achievements, how much time they spend with them, and their willingness to discuss problems and worries.

In actual fact, few parents are at either extreme. The majority have mixed feelings of both liking and disliking. While parents who are negative or positive toward a child are inclined to maintain that stance over fairly long periods of time, it is also true that large shifts can occur as the child passes through different stages of development or as the parents' life circumstances fluctuate. We know a family in which a father had for a long while felt negatively toward his son, whom he considered to be in alliance with mother against him. When the father and mother were able to resolve some of their anger and disagreement with each other, the father and son were likewise able to settle some of their differences. The father experienced an upsurge of positive, loving affect toward his son that had long been submerged. In another family, a mother who had felt negatively toward her children because their presence signaled her bondage to what she regarded as a stereotyped mother-housewife role, became considerably more positive toward them when she obtained a job outside of the home that was more satisfying. We have also seen the reverse process, in which positive feelings were transformed into negative ones. We observed a family in which the mother was brightly positive toward her children until her husband had a severe disabling accident which threw most of the family responsibilities onto her shoulders. She became overwhelmed by the load and more and more began to see her children as burdens who were making her life miserable. It did not take long for her children to sense this change in her attitude.

We cite these examples to emphasize the point that the positive or negative feelings you have about your children are not fixed forever. While in most families there is probably moderate long-term stability in this liking-disliking dimension, quite a bit of variation can also occur. It is painful to most parents to become aware that they can feel dislike toward their own "flesh and blood." They react with guilt and see themselves as villains. There is no doubt, however, that experiencing various amounts of dislike toward one's children is a common occurrence. In any case, we would like to note that how positively or negatively you feel toward your children is a persistent backdrop to how you discipline them. It will permeate all of your transactions with them and they will quite accurately sense your feelings. This in turn will affect how your children respond to your efforts to control and influence them.

A second important theme in parental behavior has to do with how much intrusive control parents impose on their children. Scientific surveys have consistently shown this dimension to be an important one. As everyone knows, some parents keep reaching into their children as if they wanted to control their very thoughts, while others give them an amazing amount of autonomy. Children judge the intrusiveness of their parents in terms of such things as whether they seem always to want to change them, constantly inquire about everything they do, interfere with their making their own decisions, always ask who has phoned them, keep telling them they are not grateful enough, and do not let them forget their misdeeds. Nothing stirs more dispute among parents than the question of how much individuality kids should be allowed. While mothers and fathers show moderate consistency in how intrusive they are, it is also true that they may be more intrusive about some things than others; furthermore, their attitudes may shift as the child moves into different phases of his life. The mother who feels she must monitor and control her baby's body processes (such as eating or urinating) almost as if they were her own may, when that child reaches adolescence, be quite nonintrusive in her attitudes toward his body. Incidentally, one study has shown that the earlier in childhood a mother begins to control her children intrusively, the more likely they are to turn out to be inhibited and dependent in their long-term behavior.

There is evidence that parents' anxieties play a big part in how controlling they are. A person wants to control and regulate what he fears. Just as you are likely to double-check whether the doors and windows of your house are securely locked when there has been an epidemic of burglaries in your neighborhood, you are also likely to check carefully the behavior of your kids when it involves issues threatening to you. If you are afraid of aggression and the consequences of being too hostile, you will inspect your children carefully and try to anticipate when they show too much anger. If you have been brought up to regard toilet functions as dirty and bad, you will be extremely watchful to make sure your kids regulate their sphincters and "keep clean." You may monitor your children like a determined wire tapper because you want to keep certain things from happening that make you uncomfortable or perhaps even scare you. The procedures open to parents for invading their children are too numerous to describe. They vary from severe spanking to seductive offers such as "If you do what I ask I will love you forever."

The highly concealed strategies that may be used by parents to invade their kids in a controlling way are illustrated by the following interchange:

CHILD: John hit me and I am going to get even. I am going to hit him in the nose as hard as I can.

MOTHER: Don't let John push you around. Fight back.

CHILD: The next time I see him I'll really hit him.

MOTHER: Be careful if he tries to hit you with one of those big stones in the field where you play with him. You could get badly hurt. It's all right to fight but you don't want to end up in the hospital.

This exchange depicts a mother who gives the initial impression that she approves of her child expressing his anger toward someone who has wronged him. But her own anxieties about hostility finally drive her to conjure up an awful, bloody image of what the expression of anger can lead to. This image has the effect of scaring the child and preventing him from doing the aggressive thing he would like to do. It is a way of getting inside of him and dominating him.

Interestingly, several psychoanalysts have described examples of parents using equally subtle means to "get" their children to do things that are considered bad or wrong. Apparently there are parents who, after long denying themselves the right to do something tempting (for example, express hostile or sexual impulses), influence their children to do that tempting thing. The parents thus derive vicarious satisfaction from their children, in the same way as they might from watching a movie in which the central character does things they have always been afraid to attempt. How do they influence their children to act out bad stuff? One observer described a mother who was righteously puritanical about sexual matters, but who insisted after each of her daughter's dates that she describe in exquisite detail everything that had happened. She was especially insistent that anything with sexual connotations be minutely elaborated. Her daughter sensed her deep interest in her sexual adventures and took this as encouragment to have sexual experiences—to provide indirect stimulation for mother. Another observer told of a family in which the father kept urging his son to be conforming and obedient but who got obviously excited and "high" when his son described his delinquent escapades. In so doing, father was indirectly encouraging his son to be delinquent. He was, in his own way, directing his son to get involved with exciting "bad" activities. Because children are so dependent on their parents, they become keen experts in picking up signals from them and going in the direction they point. Parents also become very expert at giving such directive, motivating signals, in some instances even denying to themselves what they are actually telling the child to do.

A third global aspect of parental behavior that has been isolated relates to how firm or lax parents are in enforcing the rules they lay down for their children. This does not have to do with intrusiveness. Rather it concerns how much parents feel that their children are obligated to operate within a system of rules or standards. Children judge this in terms of such things as whether parents will let them *not* complete work that has been assigned; allow them to spend money as they please; let them go where they please; can be easily talked into things; neglect to punish misbehavior; and seldom insist that they do anything. Firm parents have to work harder than lax ones. They have to remain alert to whether their kids are obeying the rules. Also, if the kids are not doing so, they have to be motivated to get back on the track. It is obvious that your whole approach to discipline and control will be affected by how firm your standards are.

Scientifically, not a great deal is known about the effects of treating children at the firm extreme as compared to the lax extreme. There are a lot of theories in this area, but little solid information. Some have suggested that rather firm and consistent enforcement of rules is important to the child if he is to build up a stable set of standards of his own. It is said that if he grows up in a world in which the rules are not clearly enforced, he will feel confused. His world will presumably lack structure and definiteness. The point has also been made that a child who is reared in a lax atmosphere may come to feel that his parents are really uninterested in him. He may interpret their easygoing attitude as an unwillingness to get seriously involved with him. One study reported that lax parents were likely to shape children who had low self-esteem. But, on the other hand, a lax approach has been viewed by some as having the advantages of not subjecting children to chronic frustrating pressures and of giving them the freedom to develop in their own truly individual way.

Our main purpose in outlining the three major dimensions described above that seem to run through parental behavior is to provide a framework for the information dealing with control and discipline that we will take up in this chapter. Your approach to disciplining your children takes place in the broad context of how much you like or dislike them, how much you intrude or "get into" their decision making, and how strict your standards are. We would suggest that parents ought to give a fair amount of thought to these three basic dimensions and arrive at an estimate of where their own behavior falls in relation to them.

Positive or Negative?

What is the most effective way to motivate your children to do what you consider to be right or proper? Is it by offering tempting rewards? Should you make frequent use of punishment? In the psychological laboratory it can be shown that both rewards and punishments have strong effects on behavior. They are both capable of motivating children to work faster and more accurately at a variety of tasks. It is our impression, based on a survey of the pertinent literature, that there is no simple formula based on scientific findings to tell you when reward as compared to punishment should be applied (6, 8, 10, 11, 21, 29, 31, 33). More and more sophisticated studies of parents and children indicate that the impact of rewards and punishments depends upon the context. A warm and friendly mother who spanks her child produces a different effect than a cold and distant mother who administers the same punishment. An angry, irritable father who offers his son money for having completed a chore will obviously have an effect unlike that of a relaxed, friendly father who does the same thing. A child who on a particular day has already been severely spanked once will respond to a second spanking quite differently than if he had not been punished at all for several days. Punishment by father may, in some families, convey meanings quite unlike those associated with mother administering punishment. There is no end to the things that may affect the impact of discipline. Just to highlight the relativity of it all, we would like to mention two studies that discovered that parents (especially fathers) high in anxiety are more likely than those low in anxiety to get an effective response from their kids when they administer punishment. No sensible explanation for this finding has been offered. It is simply a curious observation that dramatizes the fact that discipline is applied by people with feelings, and you have to know something about these feelings to predict what the discipline will do. Anyone who tells you that you can base your discipline of your children on a few simplistic rules is out of touch with the real facts. Broad statements such as "One should never spank" or "Showing too much affection spoils the child" are only misleading.

How Do People Discipline Their Children?

Parents are richly ingenious in concocting discipline. They employ an amazing gamut of techniques. In reviewing with one mother her disciplining behavior during a day with her children, we discovered that in a space of about twelve hours she had done the following:

1. Criticized her son for being late for breakfast.
2. Praised her daughter for her good eating manners.
3. Administered a brief spanking to both kids for getting into a noisy fight.
4. Offered to make her son's favorite dessert if he got a high mark on a test he was going to take in school the next day.
5. Reminded both kids that their allowances would be paid to them at the end of the week if they performed their household duties.
6. Given her daughter an angry glance for making too much noise while she was talking on the phone.
7. Told her son he could watch television for only one hour because he needed to study more to improve his grades.
8. Become increasingly silent and cold in manner when the kids did not get ready for bed at the usual hour.
9. Bubbled with reassuring love and affection when her daughter, as she was going to sleep, confided something that was worrying her.

This is merely a resume of the highlights of what she did in that twelve-hour period to get her kids to conform to her standards. She praised, punished, rewarded, withheld friendliness, and bestowed affection. She was busy dispensing multiple forms of discipline.

It cannot be too greatly emphasized that your approach to discipline will have tremendous effects on your child's personality. It can influence how authoritarian he will be. It can affect his ability to be active and aggressive. It can affect his habitual level of anxiety. It can leave a mark on how positively or negatively he views himself. There is evidence that it can play a role in how he deals with life problems. For example, one study demonstrated that parents who inflexibly stick to one form of discipline are inclined to produce children who turn away from their problems and rely on denial to ease their anxieties. Another interesting study has demonstrated that when mother has a monopoly on administering discipline in the family, her kids tend to be intropunitive. That is, they are inclined to be hostile and depreciating toward themselves.

⟨Note that discipline usually occurs under conditions of tension and disturbance.⟩ It is a time of trouble, and it gives children a chance to witness how their parents behave when in an upset state. They are, again and again, presented with a model of how to act when one feels angry and frustrated. Parents who become overwhelmed by their anger and seem to lose control of themselves are offering their kids a model. They are, whether they like it or not, telling their kids that they don't expect them to exercise much self-control. This is the real message, no matter what they may say verbally to the contrary. Similarly, parents who seem scared, blocked, or indecisive about how to cope with disciplinary dilemmas are offering their kids a model to imitate. It is dramatic sometimes to see how even a very young child will incorporate into his own behavior what he has learned about his parents in the heat of disciplinary battles. We were asked on one occasion to evaluate a five-year-old boy who was rather dramatically making all kinds of serious threats against his brothers and sisters. He would, with some fanfare, grab a knife and act as if he might stab one of them. Or he would light matches and broadly hint that he was going to start a fire. When we got to know his family well we discovered that his father was accustomed to administering discipline in a highly dramatic fashion. He treated every infraction of his rules as if it were of monumental import. He shouted and screamed. He threatened and his voice quivered with passion. He became terribly absorbed in himself as a central figure in an emotional spectacle. It was therefore not illogical that his son should adopt a similarly dramatic, drum-pounding role when he became disturbed and frustrated.

Many of the child's notions about how strong emotion should be expressed are probably picked up in disciplinary struggles. Often, the moment of truth for children is when they watch their parents operate at the pitch of strain and anger. Also, of course, it gives them the optimum chance to find out how their parents feel about them when their guard is down.

It is helpful, when discussing discipline, to get some perspective on the major varieties parents have devised. A number of researchers have surveyed these varieties and broken them down into what appear to be sensible groupings (32, 44). One major distinction that has been widely accepted concerns using love-oriented as compared to power-oriented approaches. The love approach relies on affection to enlist the child's cooperation and obedience. It is exemplified by parents praising or kissing or admiring the child for something he has done. The power approach is based on the use of force and intimidation to control the child. Examples of power expression are spanking and shouting angrily. Further, it is possible to break down the affection and power approaches into subdivisions. Affection can be used to control in either a positive or a negative way. On the positive side, you can motivate your children to do something by showing love or friendliness. On the negative side, you can control them by threatening to withdraw your love if they are not obedient. They quickly learn that if they are not obedient you become distant and are unlikely to say anything friendly. A favorite, related technique used by parents involves isolating the child. The "bad" child is often told to go to his room and is not permitted to communicate with anyone. This cuts him off from any friendly input. He is impressed with the fact that he has been exiled and has lost the normal chances for getting warmth and attention. All forms of reward and deprivation, like giving money for a good report card or cutting off a kid's allowance because he has been bad, are really indirect ways of bestowing or withdrawing love and approval. As for the more power-oriented approaches to discipline, they can be subdivided into, first, the use of physical punishment and, second, various kinds of verbal threats that imply potential physical attack. They are built on the premise that the parent is bigger and more powerful than his child and can do things to hurt and scare him. The fact that a power-oriented method is being used by a parent can sometimes be fairly well concealed, but it is still there. Humor, rationalization, and blaming someone else may be pressed into service as a cover-up. Consider the following interchange:

CHILD: I don't want to go to sleep yet.
PARENT: It's time. You know that.
CHILD: No, I want to stay up.
PARENT: Oh, come on. (In a half joking, smiling way, picks the child up firmly and carries him to his room, laughing and kidding as he carries his squirming child.)

Although this entire maneuver is camouflaged by the parent as if it were just humorous fooling around, he is, in effect, using force to make the child obey.

Consider still another example of such semi-concealed use of power:

CHILD: I don't want to go to sleep.

FATHER: It's time. You know that.

CHILD: No, I want to stay up.

FATHER: I don't really care, but you know that your mother will get angry and spank you if you don't get to bed soon. (Spoken in a kindly "Don't blame me" tone of voice.)

The father threatens the child with spanking but pretends that he has nothing to do with the threat.

Parents do develop fairly strong preferences for particular disciplinary methods. Some are especially inclined to use affection as a motivator, and some consistently employ spanking * and threats. Such preferences have been found tied to social class: middle-class parents are more likely to rely on affection; the so-called lower classes are more attracted to power techniques. There have also been claims that fathers resort to physical punishment more often than mothers do, but there are observers who claim just the opposite. It does seem to be true that parents use discipline based on offering or withholding love more often in their relationships with their daughters than in those with their sons. This is an interesting difference that we will discuss in more detail later.

BEING TOUGH AND PUNITIVE

Although it is very complex, the scientific literature does offer certain useful guidelines about discipline. We would suggest, first of all, that there is good evidence that harsh punitive discipline will eventually create a lot of trouble for parents (44, 47, 52, 58). If you frequently use severe spanking and if you often approach your children with a fierce

* One interesting study asked over 300 mothers of five-year-old children to describe "How much good does it do?" to spank. About half thought spanking "does good" and half had serious reservations as to what it accomplished. A majority said their child usually responded to spanking with "hurt feelings," and a much smaller percent said their child's response was to be made "cross or angry." It is not surprising that the parents who thought spanking "does good" were also the ones who employed it most frequently.

determination to make them feel pain for their misdeeds, it is likely that you will link their development—in a lopsided way—to matters of hostility and aggression. One common result of parents being too punitive and tough is that they breed similar toughness in their kids. The child who finds himself again and again harshly disciplined becomes increasingly angry and resentful. He sees his parents as enemies. He also begins to model his behavior in the direction of the aggressive example they present. He learns to act punitively; if he has been on the receiving end of a good deal of physical punishment, he will be inclined to express himself through physical aggression. He learns to hit in the same way that his parents hit him. Tough parents are likely to create miniatures of themselves. Their punitive attitudes return to haunt them. Aggressive, delinquent adolescents have not infrequently been reared in homes in which brutal discipline was common. But it is also true that harsh parents can completely subdue their children and render them submissive. They can shape children who are timid, scared, and preoccupied with being squelched. This is especially probable when girls are exposed to controlling punitive discipline. Maximal aggressive acting-out in children seems to be encouraged by a family setting with parents who are harsh in punishing what they consider to be wrong but who make few attempts to control subsequent outbursts of hostility. That is, their punitive style stirs up a lot of resentment, but they do not seem interested in regulating how the resentment gets expressed.

The amount of power and punitive force that parents put into their discipline is influenced by the general family atmosphere. Some families are committed broadly to an authoritarian attitude. They are invested in power and the show of strength. Authoritarian parents may not only apply tough discipline to their children but also be hard in their dealings with each other and outsiders. One study reported that husbands who push their wives around encourage them to rely on punitive methods in dealing with their children. In short, a wife who gets pounded on may relieve some of her frustration by pounding on the kids. Such violence is a pervasive theme in some families. It is also true that there are families in which power and violence are so much feared that discipline is rarely enforced. Sometimes both extremes occur in a family. An interesting study discovered that the delinquent child not infrequently comes from a family in which there is a tradition of extreme force. But it also noted that as the delinquent grows older, he may learn to intimidate his parents to such an extent that they are afraid to discipline him. They learn to lean over backwards in order to avoid trouble with him. In certain families there is simply a fear of all aggression. No one in the family feels comfortable about being assertive. The super-polite and mild-mannered ways that typify them from day to day make aggressive child discipline methods appear to be inappropriate.

It is difficult to pin down whether the effects of harsh punishment result from the punishment itself, or whether they are due more to the underlying attitudes that stimulate the use of harsh techniques. Punishing parents are usually angry ones. They are typically mad at their children. The children's perception of their anger may be more frightening than the actual punishment administered. To experience your parents as antagonistic must, in and of itself, be deeply threatening. There are indications that parents who are perceived by their children as friendly and reasonable can, within limits, employ spanking and other power forms of discipline in effective ways that are not damaging.

One of the most surprising things that research has uncovered about harsh discipline is that it seems to work against the development of a reliable conscience and consistent moral values (21, 31, 33). A common rationale used by the severe parent is that he wants to make sure that his child will turn out to be a law-abiding, conscientious person. Even in the sophisticated realm of psychoanalytic theory, it has long been thought that tough parents were the ones who raised the child with the strongest conscience or superego. This assumption does not fit the facts. Repeated studies have shown that friendly, warm, nurturant parents are those most likely to stimulate loyalty to moral standards and values. Their attitudes persuade the child to identify with them and to "take in"—interiorize—their values. The severely punished child is inclined to experience his parents as alien and to reject making anything with which they are identified a part of himself. He sees them as enforcers who stand over him to make sure he will do the "right" thing. He sees them as taking the major responsibility for his conforming to proper standards. By way of contrast, the child with nurturant, nonpunitive parents is persuaded to adopt their standards and to assume the responsibility for checking on his own behavior. He becomes the enforcer, rather than expecting his parents to play such a role. He learns to monitor and check himself as a way of pleasing his mother and father.

Parents who are intensely punitive have good practical reasons for examining their own behavior. Unless they do so, as part of a process of trying to act more reasonably toward their kids, they will have to cope

with extremes of aggressive or submissive action from them. It is obvious how extreme aggressiveness can cause trouble. But equally serious
trouble may be caused by the child who won't assert himself, won't take
responsibility, and passively waits to be guided. He is unlikely to be a
raving success at anything that calls for verve or initiative. One of the
prime questions that highly punitive parents should ask themselves is
"Why am I so angry at my kids?" They need to become aware of the
extent to which unreasonable anger energizes their disciplinary approach. We suspect that it is the parent who is oblivious of how angry
he feels and who justifies his toughness in a self-righteous way who has
the greatest destructive potential. We worked therapeutically with one
family in which the mother had been cruelly put down and humiliated
by her parents and who seemed to have a similar need to humiliate her
own children. Even for mild infractions she would spank them and force
them to kneel for painfully long periods of time. Her anger toward them
made her feel so justified that she had no idea how extreme her discipline really was. But when we simply made her aware of how often
she initiated her discipline because the children angered her, rather than
on the basis of her child-rearing principles, this created enough self-
conscious doubt (and also guilt) to cause her to start curbing her extreme
practices. For example, she stopped forcing them to kneel. This, in
turn, resulted in their behaving less oppositionally and decreased her
temptations to clamp down on them. But a more fundamental change in
her behavior toward them evolved only after she had worked through
her irrational assumptions that there are only two possible roles in the
world: the dominating victor, or the exploited victim. Her actions had
been guided by the notion that if she did not subdue and dominate her
children, they would eventually get her down.

We do not want to leave the impression that parents should not at
times be tough and punitive. There are misbehaviors that may well
merit a tough response. *Parents need to know how to use power-
oriented discipline when it is appropriate.* We have warned only against
excessive use of power. Actually, if parents are *afraid* to use power-
oriented discipline, their kids will detect the fact and share in their anxiety. They may very well, on the basis of such a model, become inappropriately inhibited about using power in their contacts with other kids.
Their fear of power behavior may put them at a disadvantage because it
will interfere with their being normally aggressive and assertive. Someone has suggested that an open confrontation between parents and chil-

dren from time to time may help the children to define themselves. Presumably, they are made acutely aware that it is possible for them to stand in one place and their parents in another. They can deeply savor what it is like to be sharply separated from their parents on a particular issue. This may help them to define the boundaries of their selfhood. Children who are shielded from ever experiencing angry differences with their parents may have trouble in learning how to be separate individuals. These are only speculations, but they are interesting to consider. Incidentally, there are several studies of delinquent children which conclude that when the children angrily defy their parents, they may be trying to prove they do have individuality. They may be trying to show dramatically that they are not puppetlike extensions of their parents.

GIVING IT MEANING

Another important principle suggested by scientific work is that acts of discipline should, whenever possible, be well explained (6, 32, 44). This means that when you punish your children for something they have done, it should be made crystal clear to them why you are doing so. In the heat and confusion of the moment that you spank or threaten, it is all too easy for children to miss the real point. They may not grasp why you are down on them. Let us illustrate what we mean. Suppose that two of your children get into a lively argument as to which of them owns a certain toy, and in the course of their fight they smash your favorite vase. You become angry and spank them. You may think it is quite obvious that they are being punished for breaking the vase. But they may have different perspectives. They may decide you were really angry because they were competitive and dared express anger so boldly and openly. They may think you are against anything that creates noise and disorder in the house. Or they may wonder whether you are against defining the property rights of each member of the household and would prefer a communal sharing spirit to prevail. Of course, there is always the possibility that their interpretation is more correct than your own. You may think your primary reason for spanking them was the breaking of the vase. Actually, you may have just become fed up with their aggressive competitiveness. But assuming that you really do have an accurate idea of your own motivation, you need to explain it. In the instance above, you would tell your children in understandable language that you spanked them because they allowed their anger to become so extreme that it resulted in the damage of something you value highly. You would give them the message that it is okay to fight and disagree, but that at the same time they are obligated to control their destructiveness.

Our own experiences with parents and children have persuaded us that when parents are deceptive in their explanations of why they have punished, their children inevitably detect this. A few dramatic encounters soon give them enough information so that they can spot the fact that they are not being told the truth. In fact, we have generally been amazed at how sharply and accurately children perceive the motivations of their parents. Again and again we have been surprised to find that even when parents are not aware of why they treat their kids in certain unreasonable ways, the meaning gets through to the kids themselves. They may not be able to verbalize directly what they understand. But one can, by means of subtle psychological tests or interview techniques, ascertain that they do have images of their parents that portray them in their true light. For example, a father who felt competitive with one of his children and who covered up his often unfair behavior by being apparently "close" and "nice" was depicted in the child's representations of fathers, in imaginative stories, as demanding and hostile. A mother who acted as if she were willing to let her children make their own decisions and express their own individuality, but who actually kept tight moment-to-moment control over them, was visualized in an imaginative fantasy by one of her children as having the relationship of a "Siamese twin."

When punishment is administered without clear explanation, it is less effective. It is more likely to produce diffuse rage. It is less likely to shape the child's behavior in a direction the parents intend. It is less likely to lead to the child building up internalized moral values and standards. Interviews with parents have shown that those who do explain why they are punishing feel that their discipline has been more effective than those who rarely offer such explanation.

CONSISTENCY

In adding up the accumulated facts, it seems safe to say that parents ought to be consistent in their discipline (1, 4). If you punish a child today for not coming in when you call him to dinner but you fail to do so for the very same act tomorrow, this will diminish your effectiveness as a disciplinarian. There are all sorts of ways parents can be inconsistent in their approach to discipline. They may, as just mentioned, punish an act at one point in time but not another. They may differ in their standards. Father may punish his son severely for staying out late and mother may have only a mild negative reaction. This obviously exposes the son to two contradictory reactions to his behavior. Inconsistency is evident, too, when parents punish a certain act if it is committed by one of their children but not when it is committed by another child in the family. Similar messages of inconsistency are implicit when parents disapprove and punish what a child does but engage in such acts themselves.

A particularly confusing form of inconsistency occurs when parents punish an act but simultaneously give secret signals that they really approve of it. Let us illustrate what we mean. On one occasion we worked with a family in which a teen-age son refused to come home when he was expected, stayed out very late, disappeared at odd hours during the night, and sometimes vanished for an entire day. His parents employed a variety of severe punishments to stop this behavior. When we studied this family we found that the boy had been an unwanted pregnancy, that his parents rather consistently favored his brothers and sisters over him, and fairly obviously considered him to be a pest. They punished him for running away but simultaneously made it clear that they did not want him around the house. Therefore their punishment was meaningless to him and ultimately ineffective. The protests of youth groups in many different countries were focused on this kind of double-message contradiction. They protested the fact that they were taught by "the Establishment" that certain things were right or wrong, whereas at the same time respected members of that Establishment gave them opposing messages by the examples they set. They were outraged because they were punished for acts that brought rewards when committed by authority figures.

We do not have any statistical evidence, but it is our impression that the most frequent disciplinary inconsistencies result from conflicting parental views. Parents take contradictory positions not only because they come from different backgrounds but also because the values of the male and female in our society are often divergent. Masculine and feminine orientations about right and wrong and about what is adequate punishment may be quite contrasting. Furthermore, several studies have shown that inconsistencies between fathers and mothers are likely to be accentuated as they cope with the contrasting problems of the boys and girls in their families. Mothers have special problems with daughters that they may not have with sons. Fathers may be more hard put to cope with their sons than their daughters. So, it is not surprising that mothers and fathers may have quite different ideas about whether sons or daughters are misbehaving and what kinds of punishment they deserve. The negative effects of disciplinary inconsistency have been fairly well documented. There is scientific evidence that delinquents and criminals come from families in which such inconsistency was prominent. Relatedly, inconsistency has been observed to intensify conflict in children and to stimulate them to be overly aggressive.

It should be underscored that consistency does not mean rigidity. Parents who set up fixed, unchanging penalties for misbehavior and who do not take circumstances into account in their discipline are mocking the idea of consistency. It is reasonable to take into account the conditions surrounding a child's breaking the rules before one makes disciplinary decisions. For example, if a father has been engaged in rough-and-tumble wrestling with his young son that stimulates the son to a high pitch of excitement and the son then hits his brother, this act should probably elicit a different disciplinary response than if it occurred in a quiet, less provocative context. Or consider two children, both of whom defiantly refuse to go to school on a particular day. While one may be simply testing the limits and flexing his muscles, the other may have failed a test the day before and be struggling with sensations of failure. Quite obviously, each of these children should be dealt with differently. One of them is really asking for a disciplinary confrontation, but the other is only secondarily being disobedient. The parent who deals with the refusals of these children to go to school as if they deserved the same disciplinary response is only demonstrating unreasonable insensitivity.

LOSS OF LOVE

Once parents have set up a loving relationship with a child, they make use of it to influence and guide him. Since he wants to retain their friendship, they learn that they can exert pressure by showing displeasure. The displeasure gives the child the message that he has momentarily fallen out of their favor and that he probably will not regain it until he does what they expect of him.

A typical and obvious way in which loss of love is used as leverage is portrayed in the following exchange:

MOTHER: James, you've been fighting with your baby sister all morning. I want you to quiet down and stop it.

SON: It's her fault. She keeps teasing me. Tell her to stop. (His angry tone clearly shows that he is going to keep pressing the onslaught on his sister.)

MOTHER: You're not acting like my little boy. Mommy doesn't like you when you are so mean.

SON: (Starts to cry.)

Mother announces, in effect, that she will suspend her usual affectionate ties with her son until he shows more obedience.

The threat of loss of love is one of the most powerful means of disciplining children (21, 31, 33, 53). Middle-class parents are especially likely to employ it. Congruent with common sense, studies have shown that threats of loss of love are most effective when made by parents who are usually warm and affectionate. The child with warm parents is much more likely, when they show displeasure, to feel he will really lose something than does the child whose parents have not bestowed much friendliness. There are a thousand different ways in which mothers and fathers bring such pressures to bear, from direct statements like "I don't like you when you act that way" to very indirect, subtle hints. We have been struck with the way in which parents develop codes, almost unrecognizable to the outsider, that tell their children that they had better do what is expected or take the chance of losing love. Children can be trained to respond to such codes with radar-like sensitivity. Consider what happens in the following transaction between a child and her mother.

MOTHER: Would you please wash the dishes? We're expecting visitors in a little while.

DAUGHTER: (Sits unresponsively watching TV and acts as if she had hardly heard what her mother said. Murmurs a few words that suggest she probably will not do the dishes until the TV program is over.)

MOTHER: (Feels annoyed at her daughter's response but does not want to have a direct confrontation about the issue. She remains silent for a little while and then finally makes what appears to be an irrelevant remark.) It's been a tiring day. I feel worn out. I really wish that I could go to sleep right now.

CHILD: (Seems strangely mobilized by these remarks and after a few minutes gets up and does the dishes.)

What an outsider would not understand is that the mother's reference to being so tired is her coded way of declaring that she is at that moment fed up with her daughter's refusal to fulfill her request. It is also a threat, well understood in terms of many previous exchanges, that if the daughter continues in her refusal the mother will be angry and will drag her feet the next time the daughter wants something from her. The mother is declaring in her coded way that she will be "too tired" to give her daughter any friendliness or support.

Let us analyze still another example of coded communication about loss of love.

FATHER: When you get a chance will you take the garbage out?

SON: O.K. I don't have much time now. I'll do it later. (Said in a reluctant tone that means the task has been indefinitely postponed.)

FATHER: (Feels hesitant and frustrated. Does not, for various reasons, want to create an acute conflict situation. Finally after several minutes he responds in a half-cynical and half-resigned tone.) You're so busy these days! Pretty soon you'll be going away to school [college] and then we'll hardly ever see you.

SON: (Looks at his father uncomfortably.)

The father, who was irritated with his son because he balked at doing what had been requested, expresses his feelings by conjuring up an apparently innocent image that depicts the son going away and being separated from the family. This "separation" image can be viewed as a concealed way of hinting at the possibility of losing the support or love of your parents.

We think it is important to make parents aware that they do, at times, deliver messages in such subtle, concealed ways. The less open and direct the lines of exchange are between parents and children, the more often are sneaky, coded communiqués employed. It is the refusal to face the fact that such sneaky things are going on that causes a great deal of trouble in some families.

A number of studies have suggested that parents who rely strongly on loss-of-love discipline make their children dependent and unusually sensitive about whether people will like them. There is proof, too, that parents are more likely to use loss-of-love strategies in dealing with their daughters than their sons. Psychological tests and interviews have consistently shown that girls in our society are more preoccupied than boys with the possibility of losing love. For example, if you have them create imaginative stories, the girls will more often introduce themes about people who are deserted or have to separate or cannot get together despite their great love for each other. It seems to be a core aspect of Western culture to make girls highly sensitive to the possibility of losing love. This may play a part in producing what have long been labeled as feminine traits (21, 32, 53). It seems to encourage conformance to the conventional image of the somewhat dependent and clinging female. We are not offering any value judgment about this matter. We are simply calling to the attention of parents the knowledge that exists about this issue.

The greater use of loss-of-love discipline with daughters than with sons is only one example of quite a number of other, related sex differences that have been described. The literature abounds with reports about how particular forms of discipline may influence sons and daughters differently. Just consider a few illustrations. One researcher found that boys from punitive homes were unusually responsive to signs of social disapproval, but it was girls from nonpunitive homes who were most sensitive to disapproval. Another researcher observed that for boys it is an absence of sufficient discipline that impairs dependability, whereas for girls it is an "overdose" of discipline that has such an effect. Still another investigator reported that if a mother was strict and used physical punishment a lot, her daughter behaved very aggressively. But in the case of a son, it was likely he would be nonaggressive if his mother was strict (especially if she did not favor physical punishment).

The widely accepted norms about what is proper behavior for boys as compared to girls necessarily results in different patterns of response to the same disciplinary practices. There is a definite trend for boys to respond in a more feisty and assertive way to discipline than do girls. Similarly, girls will more often settle for passive modes of adaptation. They will less often seek open conflict and confrontation (21). We have witnessed many instances in which the same disciplinary practices in a family were very disturbing to a child of one sex but not to that of the other sex. A father who is tough and harsh may make life miserable for his son, whereas his daughter may assimilate his toughness without much evidence of disturbance. Of course, it is always debatable in such instances whether the father was really as tough with his daughter as he was with the son. Actually, it is likely that changing standards about masculinity-femininity will gradually reduce sex-difference effects. But the process will be slow, because the differentiations are so deep rooted. While everyone knows that parents respond in unlike ways to sons and daughters, few realize how early this begins. Even in the first few weeks of life, mothers already deal with the sexes differently. This shows up, for example, in the amounts of touching and smiling they direct to boys as compared to girls. Very early, too, they begin to restrict girls more than boys with respect to motility and movement in space.

The Targets of Discipline

Up to this point we have largely discussed the kinds of discipline parents employ. But we would like to shift and get into the matter of how parents target their discipline. What sorts of things stir them to "corrective" action? A number of surveys (for example, 53) have revealed that certain standard problems are especially likely to galvanize parents of younger children into action. They will be briefly reviewed:

1. Parents spend a lot of time in the early years disciplining children so that they will avoid life-threatening situations. They try to impress them with the dangers of crossing streets, wandering away from home, eating foreign substances, and so forth.

2. Parents labor mightily to get their kids to respect the many objects and gadgets in the home. This means they have to be "taught" that they cannot destroy household property. Relatedly, they are given many instructions about keeping the house neat and orderly.

3. In many families there is also a focus on the major issue of obedience itself. Parents want to be able to feel that they can count on their children doing what they tell them to do. Tough encounters are especially likely when parents want "instant obedience" or the elimination of the slightest sign of resistance or delay when a request is made. One study found that about 25 percent of the parents interviewed were really quite strict in the kind of obedience they expected. But it is also interesting that about 20 percent were willing to put up with a lot of resistance and delay when they made requests.

4. Control of anger and aggression is another prominent issue that often elicits discipline. Parents chronically struggle to curb the hostile encounters among their children and also to limit the ways in which anger gets expressed when frustrations occur. The key frustrations are often those associated with doing things on time (for example, going to sleep when expected); being restricted in movement ("You can't go out now"); performing assigned tasks ("Take out the garbage"); being regulated as to how much noise is allowable ("Stop screaming so loud!"); and sharing the available facilities (such as not being able to watch a favorite TV program because someone in the family wants to tune in on a different program).

5. Finally, a whole series of things having to do with the child correctly regulating his own body should be mentioned. Great importance is placed on children controlling their urinary and anal sphincters, keeping clean, eating in certain ways, and adhering to regimens that are supposed to keep one in good health.

In later years, as the child develops, disciplinary concern shifts to other issues like school behavior, how much time can be permissibly spent away from home, how fast emancipation from parental authority can occur, and the acceptable pathways to becoming sexually active. We chose to list these points even though they are obvious to any moderately experienced parent. It is helpful to have a miniature schematic map of the situations that most often make demands upon mothers and fathers to become disciplinarians.

One of the things that has been learned from observing normal (and also disturbed) families is that children detect what is important to their parents not only in terms of what they do discipline, but also what they do not discipline. They sensitively scan the things that elicit unusual disciplinary reactions from their parents. They note that certain acts on their part always get them an angry spanking. But they note, too, that they can usually "get away" with certain behavior in a surprising way. Further, they note that there are acts that evoke inconsistent discipline, sometimes getting no response and at other times an exaggerated one. They learn to decode these patterns of reaction and end up identifying with the feelings and anxieties underlying them.

Let us illustrate what we mean. In one family we studied from many angles, we knew the parents were both "uptight" about issues related to achievement. They were people who felt small and "down." They had struggled for years to prove that they were as good as, and even better than, most other people. Success and achievement were key motifs in their lives. The possibility of failure anxiously haunted them. This was

59

strongly reflected in the way they treated their children. They over-reacted to anything they did that could even remotely be associated with issues of success or failure. They frequently offered outlandish rewards and praise to the children for good school marks or competitive honors. They also could not conceal their deep disappointment about even minor failures. The threat of loss of parental love was obvious to the children in such instances. In addition, as these parents watched themselves and saw how much they were overreacting to achievement events, they cyclically went to the opposite extreme and tried to act completely nonchalant. They would then neither reward nor praise their children's successes and failures. These extremes and confusions in disciplinary behavior registered. The children took over their parents' anxieties in this realm. They became convinced that this was a special, scary part of life with which they could not cope. The family came to our attention when the parents sought therapeutic help for one of their children who was failing badly in school. This child, whom we found with a standard test to be above average in intelligence, was so scared and sensitized about achievement that he had convinced some of his teachers that his I.Q. was sufficiently low that he should be assigned to a special class for slow learners.

It is the irrationality in parents' disciplinary practices that eventually tells their children what they fear and are mixed up about. There is a powerful "contagion" effect, and gradually the children find themselves struggling with the same issues that plague their parents.

We were disappointed in how few general rules we could tease out of the scientific literature dealing with discipline. Careful analysis of hundreds of publications gave a small harvest. It is impossible, at least at this stage, to give parents more than a handful of guidelines about how to apply discipline. There are too many exceptions and too much relativity. Again and again one finds that the effects of a specific kind of discipline vary, depending upon whether it is administered by mother or father, whether the recipient is a son or daughter, whether the parents are friendly or unfriendly, whether they are middle or lower class, and so forth and so forth. It is clear that disciplinary decisions have to depend largely on the wisdom of individual parents. While we did spell out several potentially useful ideas suggested by previous work, they have only modest value. Perhaps the most important guiding idea to keep in mind is that extremes of any form of discipline seem to have negative repercussions. The overly aggressive and the overly "nice" parent are both asking for trouble. We see the discipline administered to a child as the distilled end product of a great many elements. It reflects anger, rule definitions, and a lot of things going on in his family. It often expresses the mother's and father's life values—their concepts of what binds people together and what it takes to influence others.

CHAPTER 3

The Body: Intimacy, Eating, Body Openings, Sickness

MOST PARENTS are amazed at the craft and ingenuity that have gone into the construction of their child's body. Coming into close quarters with a newborn is quite an experience. The miniature human being is so complexly put together, so surprisingly strong, and yet so potentially fragile. Anyone who takes on the care of this miniature person becomes involved in an intimacy with its body that exceeds anything else he or she has likely ever experienced before. Of course, the average mother has already had the special intimacy of containing the child's body within her own. But this is different from the vivid encounter you have with your child's body when you simultaneously see, hear, feel, and smell it—and realize that its existence depends on your efforts. Every parent has the difficult task of coming to terms with his or her child's body. He has to make sense out of it and learn to be comfortable with the way it functions. Parents who are uncomfortable with the workings of their child's body are headed for complications in their relationships with that child. By the way, it is also true that, from Day One, children try to make sense out of their own body experiences. Hunger pangs, skin sensations, pressure feelings, and a thousand other body experiences confront them as a blooming confusion. They will have to learn to sort out such experiences and to give them meaning. But, as we will discuss later, they have to achieve this while bathed in the powerful biases of mother—and father—toward various aspects of the body.

The unusual psychological closeness of the child's body stirs up intense responses in parents. These responses range from over-identification to cold retreat. Some parents who have had limited opportunities for intimacy with other people become keenly involved with this new chance for closeness. They revel in the good "feel" of the child's warmth. They stroke, kiss, squeeze, and tickle. Others, who have grown up in families in which the body is an object of suspicion and a source of guilt, are frightened by their child's naked presence. They keep his body covered as much as possible, touch him minimally, and entangle the care of his body needs in a network of do's and don'ts. Dealing with the child's intake and discharge needs is often especially threatening. Some women and most men have, up until the time they became parents, rarely or never had contact with such body substances of another individual as vomited-up food, feces, urine, and even tears. They are suddenly and starkly confronted with aspects of another individual's body that are usually considered to be dirty and disgusting and therefore kept concealed. Parents are often embarrassed and even made anxious by having to deal with the child's genital organs. In the course of cleaning and handling the child, they repeatedly touch and inspect its genitals. Some discover that this requires big changes in their attitudes about modesty and privacy. It must play a part in the known fact that mothers respond differently to the body of their newborn son than to the body of their newborn daughter.

Part of the threat of the unique intimacy parents experience in relating to the child's body can be understood within the framework of the concept of the "buffer zone." It is pretty well established that each person has standards about how close he wants other persons to get to his own body. In order to protect his own sense of integrity and privacy he wants a buffer zone of a certain size between himself and others (9, 21). Obviously this buffer zone will differ in terms of whether he is relating to a friend, an enemy, or a lover. But many people have difficulty in permitting closeness even when it involves someone they love. They are uneasy when *anyone* draws too near. A woman who is accustomed to keeping others at a certain distance (including her husband) may find her constant bodily closeness to her newborn child rather unsettling. Intellectually, the closeness makes sense to her, but the buffer-zone standards of a lifetime are not so easily given up, even when it is your own child that is involved! To care for your child's body is to be faced with all the raw things about bodies that society usually camouflages. It is helpful to parents to be aware of this fact and to be prepared to cope with the feelings that will, as a result, be stirred up. It is not helpful simply to reassure yourself that since you are dealing with your "own child's body" you have no reason to feel negative or disgusted or anxious. The fact is that it is not unusual to experience such feelings, and it may take a while to come to terms with them. They do not occur in a vacuum. You will find that they influence how you deal with your child and how you deal with your spouse in situations that involve the child's body. Most important of all, your feelings will get communicated to your child. There are suggestions in the scientific literature that a baby can sense whether adults are handling his body positively or negatively—with warmth as compared to reluctance.

It is known that people adopt attitudes toward their own bodies that symbolize how they feel about themselves. The equation of your body with yourself makes it a convenient target to which to attach feelings about self. Studies have shown that a man who feels he is a failure may unrealistically see his own body as too small or unmanly or inadequate. A woman who feels she is not really feminine may unrealistically see her breasts as too small or assume her face is unattractive (8, 9). Similarly, because your child's body is so psychologically close to you, you will be inclined to attribute to it certain of your feelings about yourself. You can unload onto the child's body what you find distressing in yourself. A mother who regards herself as unfeminine may falsely perceive her daughter's body as deficient in femininity. A father who regards himself as a failure may inaccurately get the impression that his son's body is on the small side or not robust enough. There are a thousand different ways in which parents can illogically attribute things to their child's body that are not really there. The child will gradually detect how his parents view him and will assume they are right. He will come to view his body in the same ways they do. He may then develop unusual defenses, such as body rituals or rigid clothing preferences, in an attempt to cope with the unpleasant things he assumes to be true of himself.

Let us consider some illustrations of this process. In one family that we were asked to help with a problem there was an adolescent boy who wore a heavy leather jacket from the moment he got up in the morning until he went to bed at night. He insisted on wearing the jacket even when it was uncomfortably hot. We discovered that his parents were anxious, uncertain people who expected life to be a series of catastrophes. They regarded their son's body from the day of birth as terribly fragile and likely to be seized at any moment by a virulent ailment. He, in turn, had been more than convinced by their attitude. He too regarded his body as fragile. He wore his leather jacket to protect himself. It represented armor that bolstered his body walls and prevented invasion by alien stuff. In another family we encountered a five-year-old girl who refused to uncover any part of her body in the presence of others. She would only wear dresses with long sleeves and refused to don a bathing suit. An analysis of her mother and father revealed that they were both preoccupied with feelings of being dirty and unworthy. They had projected these feelings onto her body and treated it as if it were a dirty thing. This was especially true when they had to deal with its excretions. The child perceived her own body as such a despicable object that she was ashamed to show it to anyone. She kept it covered to hide its dirty qualities. Interestingly, as soon as her parents came to grips with the fact that they were treating her as a disreputable object, she radically changed her clothing habits. She no longer insisted on keeping herself covered and was quite willing to wear a bathing suit. In still other families we have seen children who were forced by their parents' unreasonable attitudes to resort to such body compensations as achieving supermuscular perfection; adopting stooped-over, pathetic-looking body postures; and refusing to eat any but a small number of "special" foods.

The child builds an image of his body in the context of how his parents regard him (8). It is not widely recognized how complicated it is to make sense of your own body. This task is no less difficult than it is to give meaning to all the things that occur outside of your body. Each child is bombarded with millions of messages from his body. He receives input from his skin, his internal organs, the front and back and right and left sides of his body, his face, his genitals, and so forth. He has to "put it all together." He has to learn that his body can be truly separate from that of his mother and that it belongs to a specific sex. He has to learn the uses of his various body parts. He has to come to terms with the fact that his parents focus a lot of anxious concern on his urinary and anal sphincters. He has to make sense out of the fact that certain substances that come out of the interior of his body are regarded as dirty and disgusting, while at the same time substances that go into his body, such as food, are treated as good and desirable. He also has to come to grips with the fact that his body can be completely uncovered under certain conditions but not others, and that it can be hurt and eventually will cease to exist. As adults, we take all this learning for granted and are oblivious of how difficult it actually is. Only when we encounter retarded or brain-injured or psychotic children who are grossly unable to interpret certain body experiences do we realize what normal children have had to master. There are disorganized kids who literally do not recognize where the boundaries of their body are, who cannot distinguish the right and left body sides, who feel that parts of their bodies do not belong to them, and who are unsure whether they are male or female (8).

The way a child pictures his body is only vaguely related to its real characteristics. A boy with a strong physique may feel that he is weak. We have seen a number of girls and women who are physically beautiful but who felt they were unattractive. One actually believed she was ugly. She had grown up in a home with a mother who was rather unattractive and jealous of her good looks. This mother had been antagonistic and competitive. She had consistently given her daughter a message that she did not like her and that she was unpleasant to have around. This made the daughter feel that she was an ugly thing, and even the sight of her own pretty features in the mirror would not banish this feeling. There are many individuals who struggle from early childhood to come to terms with the negative and contradictory things their parents have communicated to them about their bodies. To realize the seriousness of this problem, one has only to look around and see how dissatisfied great numbers of people are with their appearance and how preoccupied they are with hypochondriacal complaints and the urge to bolster themselves with a thousand different patent medicines. Clues are beginning to appear in the scientific literature about how parents contribute to body anxiety; we will shortly discuss these clues.

We would like to emphasize, from still other perspectives, how difficult it is for an adult to appreciate the child's very special problems in understanding his own body. As the baby grows, he is confronted with an ever-changing body. In just a matter of months his size increases dramatically, he develops remarkable new motor abilities, and his appearance alters greatly. In the course of the years he has to adjust to his ever-changing physique. He is aware of these changes and from time to time is pleasantly or unpleasantly impressed by them. But in the midst of it he has to maintain a stable image of who he is. That is not as simple as it may sound to an adult whose body configurations have remained fixed for a long period of time. Consider, too, some of the other special body-image problems facing the child. He is given very little information as to what his body is all about. Studies have shown that kids are puzzled about their body functions. They have only the vaguest notions of what their "insides" are like. They also tend to find that people are reluctant to communicate with them about certain parts of their bodies. They learn that their anal and genital regions are somehow mysterious, dangerous, and not to be openly discussed. They get anxious about these mysterious places. They are often not even allowed to acquire a vocabulary for thinking about such areas. Parents need to be especially aware of this issue. They should not only make it clear to their children that it is all right to talk about the body but also, by example, provide words for referring to every one of the major body parts (including the anus, penis, testicles, breasts, and vagina). No one has done a formal study to demonstrate that children who receive such assistance adapt better than those who do not. Our recommendation is based on our contacts with children who seemed to be unnecessarily scared about body things because they found them to be so undefined and vague.

Still another body problem confronting children that parents overlook is the great disparity between their own size and that of adults. From surveys that have been made of children's fears, we know that they can get quite concerned about being hurt by the big things all around them. To be tiny in a world of much larger beings is to feel vulnerable and somewhat powerless. Parents sometimes reinforce this sense of being small and vulnerable by taking advantage of their own superior size and strength. For example, they do this by "playfully" overpowering the child so it cannot move, or by throwing him into the air in a scary way, or by adopting "I tower over you" postures which imply that they could control him with no effort at all. One psychologist has interestingly shown that children's fears about this matter are reflected in the frequency with which children's jokes deal with the disparities in size between themselves and adults.

Eating

The first problems having to do with the child's body often show up as his parents learn to feed him. It is a rare parent who does not see feeding as a big responsibility. Much feeling and concern are packed into every part of the feeding routine. One of the initial decisions facing every mother is whether to breast-feed her child. The large majority of women in Western countries choose not to do so. They have been reassured by physicians that bottle-feeding does not have a bad effect on the child's health. But many women are guilty when they do not use their breasts to nurture their child. They feel they are not giving the child their best. They feel they are being impersonal because they are not directly involving their body in their child's sustenance. There is a tendency for mothers who decide to breast-feed to be those who are most identified with the conventional role of mother. They seem to have the greatest need for the special "nursing" experience. A fair amount of research has been invested in trying to find out if breast-fed babies do better in any way than those bottle-fed. This research has not revealed a measurable advantage for the breast-fed (4, 11). It has not really been possible to show that they are happier or better-adjusted or friendlier or have a better relationship with their mothers. No one can, with scientific assurance, argue that a mother who breast-feeds is going to produce a better child than one who does not.

Interestingly, many women who do try to breast-feed give up the effort after just a few weeks and switch to the bottle. They do so for a variety of reasons. When questioned, they refer to the greater convenience of the bottle, their lesser anxiety about whether the baby will get enough nourishment, and so forth. But there are more private reasons that also play a part. Some women find they are embarrassed by having to expose their breasts while nursing. Others reveal that the sensations stirred in their breasts by the lips of the sucking child have an erotic-like quality that, under the circumstances, are disconcerting. They are shocked by the arousal produced by the baby's lips. One study observed that women concerned with sexual modesty had special difficulties with breast-feeding. But those women who like breast-feeding and who accomplish it successfully enjoy the accompanying close body contact and the body excitation. One psychologist obtained samples of what women think about and fantasize while they are nursing. Generally, they were found to feel fused and united with their child and were filled with pleasurable sensations. Their thoughts were on a level that minimized formal logic. They drifted and their fantasies had a wishful flavor. It is obvious that a woman's decision whether to breast-feed, and whether to continue it after she starts, will depend not only on a number of practical things such as how much time she has available but also on her attitudes about exquisitely intimate body contact and the exposure of her breasts. The average woman may be flustered by her own emotional responses to the whole matter of nursing; it could be helpful to her to realize that many other women have similar responses (such as embarrassment). The average husband may not perceive how his wife feels and may be puzzled by her ambivalent behavior with reference to nursing. It would probably make good sense for the wife to share her feelings with her husband. This would give her a chance to talk out her confusion and therefore to act more sensibly about a highly emotional matter.

Another feeding problem that develops immediately has to do with who is going to be in control. Babies can get hungry just about any time. They can signal you at any moment of the day or night that they want food. This can be pretty aggravating. They are rare parents who do not consider possible ways of setting feeding times at more predictable and convenient points. Some parents put their child on a fixed schedule. No matter how much he cries or squirms, they will give him nourishment only when the clock hands point to predetermined numbers. Other parents go to an opposite "self-sacrificing" extreme and provide nourishment at the slightest sign the child is hungry. It is interesting that at each of these extremes, parents can offer what they consider good reasons for their feeding strategies. Most parents fall in between the extremes. They try to feed at certain major times, but they are willing to bend to the will of the child if he shows that he is fairly determined to eat either earlier or later than they would like him to.

Modest evidence exists that mothers who insist on a rigid feeding schedule feel less warm and affectionate toward their babies than do those who are more flexible (36). Mothers who adopt the rigid approach seem also to be more insecure about the whole matter of taking care of a baby. It may be their lack of confidence in their ability to care for the baby correctly that leads them to seize on a method of feeding that, once set up, requires no further decision making: you simply feed your child at a certain predetermined time, and you don't have to think about all of the complicated signals he sends you concerning his wishes. While no one can say with assurance at this point that feeding a baby on a rigid schedule is bad for him, there are a few studies that do hint this may be so. The rigid schedule may produce a more dependent organism, less capable of arriving at its own decisions. This possibility should be kept in mind by those who are tempted by the superficial easiness of doing things by the clock.

Still another major issue in early feeding of the child is that of when and how to wean him. At what age do you stop offering the breast or the bottle and insist that he eat solid food? From a purely physiological point of view, great latitude is possible. Some cultures begin to wean as early as the first few months, while others delay it until a couple of years have passed. But are there psychological effects tied to such differences? The answer is that we are still pretty much in the dark about the matter (4, 11). There are a number of studies implying that *extremes* in weaning produce repercussions. If weaning is demanded very early (before the age of six months) or if it is attempted only after the child has spent an unusually long time (24 or more months) relying on sucking for nourishment, this seems to be especially frustrating. Sometimes the frustration registers in the child's need to keep sucking things, such as his thumb. The extremes in weaning times do seem to have a sizeable impact on the child, in the sense that correlations have been found between them and the development of certain traits in early and late adolescence. The nature of this impact can only be vaguely defined, but behavior having to do with dependence, optimism, and perhaps impulsivity is probably influenced by it. One cannot, however, declare that such and such an approach to weaning will directly encourage dependence or any other particular trait. The problem is that the child's adaptation is so complex to anything done to him. He can, for example, react to long-delayed weaning by becoming unusually passive and dependent, but he can also react against the passivity that has been encouraged in him and try hard to be proudly independent.

Freud and other psychoanalysts suggested years ago that early feeding relationships with the parents might affect the individual's personality. A careful review of the research literature (11) indicates this is probably true to a small or moderate extent. Anthropologists have examined differences among cultures that approach feeding of the child in various ways. They have found that the more severe and anxiety-provoking the early feeding and nurturance practices are, the more often the adults in such a culture see the world in aggressive rather than benevolent terms. Also, when these adults get sick, they are more likely to assume that it was caused by eating bad substances. In other words, if things go wrong with their body, they assume the cause has to be bad feeding. Further, they seem to be more inclined to consume a lot of alcohol. It is reasonable to caution parents that they are in error if they assume that their early feeding practices will not affect their children's psychological future. What they do may well stir reactions that will echo for years to come. As already mentioned, the reactions revolve particularly about matters of dependence and independence.

In our work with families we have noticed that some parents are tempted to use eating times like breakfast or dinner to impress their authority on their kids. They tell them what to eat and how much to eat. They spell out what they consider to be "good table manners" and even define the right way to sit "at the table." They create the impression that a family meal is primarily an occasion when parents scrutinize their kids and issue edicts to them about how to manage their bodies. The family meal becomes an arena for combat rather than an occasion for nurturance. This can happen, too, as mother and her newborn baby evolve their feeding relationship. It can become a battle for dominance. Mother may set out to prove she is "in charge" and that the baby will have to fit his hunger needs into the framework of her convenience. Not infrequently he will resist and show his frustration by crying, being irritable, vomiting, and so forth. We have seen several instances in which young adolescent girls were so desperately angry about the way food (and its symbolic equivalents) had been used by their parents to control them that they determined to stop eating. They were willing, with suicidal intensity, to risk death from starvation in order to defy their parents.

There is probably no one or two or even three proper ways to feed and wean young children. A psychologist who reviewed the scientific material bearing on this matter decided that what counts is how much satisfaction, rather than distress, your feeding approach brings to your child. It is long-continued frustration that is most likely to produce maladaptive symptoms. Any parents of average intelligence can, if they are willing to look, make a pretty good estimate of whether their child likes the way they are feeding him. They can certainly tell if he is frightened or angry or painfully discouraged by their feeding methods. It obviously does not make sense to persist in such methods if they are causing a lot of distress. Once again, the important point is not to deal with your child in a fixed mechanical way, but to keep watching and gauging how he is experiencing what you are doing.

Only a vague understanding exists as to how children develop special food likes and dislikes that sometimes continue through adolescence and even into adulthood. It is known that parents' attitudes toward various foods play a significant part. For example, youngsters raised in Italian families usually prefer Italian food, or those raised in Jewish families favor Jewish cooking. But it remains a mystery why a child will suddenly take an intense dislike to eggs or a particular vegetable. In families we have studied, unusual food habits are encountered fairly often. In one family a six-year-old would eat only hot dogs. In another, a child repetitively ate only hamburgers and nothing else. In still another, an adolescent girl went through a phase when she refused to eat anything solid. She would eat only foods that could be reduced to a semi-liquid state. Some adolescents suddenly declare that they can no longer tolerate eating meat and become devout vegetarians. There are suggestions in the scientific literature that finicky attitudes toward food reflect anxiety about other issues. Several studies have noted that those who are unaccepting of many foods are more likely to get high scores on tests measuring neuroticism (23). We have, in a clinical way, been able to trace some extreme food attitudes in children to particular conflicts. In one instance where an adolescent girl rather suddenly felt revulsion toward meat and would eat only vegetables, we detected that she was so intensely angry toward her parents that she entertained unconscious fantasies of attacking and hurting them. She was so overwhelmed by fear and guilt at having such feelings that she became supersensitive to anything linked to violence or death. She associated meat with the killing of animals, and her guilt was so pervasive that she was disgusted by the idea of taking into her body something that had been killed. She could not tie herself to violence even in this indirect way.

When children suddenly or dramatically change their eating patterns in the direction of giving up a whole group of foods, this is often a way of trying to cope with a serious personal problem. Parents should give careful thought to what might be involved. The renunciation of food is a traditional way of expressing feelings and dramatizing ideas. It is a fundamental ritual in all the major religions. A child who decides to renounce a class of foods may be telling you that he feels dreadfully guilty, that he is angrily protesting the way you treat him, or that he wants to shake you up and draw your attention to him. He may be announcing that he does not like the role you have assigned to him in the family and that he intends to embark on a new course of life.

Another frequent eating issue has to do with whether children are eating too much or too little. There are children who eat so greedily that they become obese, and there are others who do not eat enough to sustain themselves. Little is known scientifically about such extremes in eating behavior. There are suggestions that they stem from anxieties about affection and love. The child who endlessly fills himself with food may be trying to convince himself that he need not worry about being cut off from the "supplies" his parents are supposed to provide. Food is often associated with affection and nurturance. The obese child may feel it necessary to keep stocking up because he perceives his parents as undependable providers of support. He may assume they could let him down at any moment, and he ravenously fills himself to neutralize his anxiety. The child who resists eating and who chronically looks half-emaciated is even less well understood than the obese one, but several clinical reports suggest that he may, in part, be expressing his resistance to his parents whom he feels are trying to use food (and love) to control him. He experiences food as something that parents stuff into him to prove they are in charge, and to dramatize that they are giving him something for which he must feel indebted and therefore must be willing to be obedient. We would underscore that this explanation is based on a limited amount of evidence; it is probable that there are also lots of other reasons why children balk at eating.

Let us illustrate the difference between parents who use food to gain intrusive control over a child and those who do not by citing the following parent-child exchange:

MOTHER: Time for lunch.

DAUGHTER: (Eats a few bites and then makes it clear she does not want to have anything more to do with the food.) I'm not hungry.

MOTHER: I thought you would like what I made today. I prepared your favorite lunch. I made a special trip to the store this morning to get what you like.

DAUGHTER: (Looks uneasy and embarrassed, but even more determinedly shows that she does not intend to eat another bite.)

In this exchange, the mother tries to make the child feel guilty. She associates the food with her having made the sacrifice of going on a special trip to the store. She is clearly trying to make the child feel indebted to her, and she is associating food with indebtedness. The child quite sensibly rejects her ploy and refuses to eat what is really a hostile offering. Note the following replay of the mother-daughter exchange in which the mother has no special intent to use food for controlling purposes:

MOTHER: Time for lunch.

DAUGHTER: I'm not hungry.

MOTHER: All right. I'll put the food in the refrigerator and you can have some later if you get hungry.

DAUGHTER: O.K. (She does not experience any strong emotion about what is happening because she and her mother are just talking about a variation in her appetite and there are no camouflaged strategies to gain control over her.)

The spirit in which parents give food and other forms of nurturance may well be of more importance than the specific practices they favor. A mother may wean her baby early but do it in a kind, concerned way; another mother, who weans late, may do so in a spirit of indifference and coldness. A mother may, in her apparent generosity, heap food on a child and yet make him feel terribly guilty about every bite. A father who urges his kids to finish every bit of the food on their plates so they will grow up "big and strong" may really be reminding them that they should not waste what he had to work so hard for. Only parents themselves can look inwardly and judge their own real motives. We are not suggesting that parents should live in a constant state of guilty self-scrutiny. However, we do not think it is unreasonable to expect them to scan themselves periodically, especially if they are getting a lot of "static" from their kids that they do not understand.

Urinary and Bowel Training

Probably one of the toughest jobs parents take on in the early years is teaching the child to control the openings in his body that provide outlets for waste products. One big difficulty is that it involves dealing with stuff usually labeled as dirty and even disgusting. Also it requires that the child learn, for the first time in his life, to take the initiative in regulating a natural rhythm in his own body. Instead of allowing his bladder or intestine to empty itself whenever he has impulses to do so, he must take the responsibility for blocking such impulses and waiting for the proper time. In a sense, he has to be trained to interfere with the natural inclinations of his own body. This calls for strong convincing. The child has to be given good reason for doing so. He is skeptical and resists the idea of fitting his body to an outside timetable, so he gets into battles with his parents about who will boss the urinary and anal sectors of his anatomy. Parents use all sorts of techniques to convince him it is better to control than not to control. They praise, reward, punish, and spank. Ultimately, they usually prove to him that he has a lot to gain by curbing his body. He finds out that his parents won't love and accept him unless he makes his sphincters behave properly.

There is no end to the disputes about what is the best way to "toilet train." You can find all varieties of advice about the best time to start it and how to enforce it. You can also find a good deal of speculation in the literature about the influence of toilet-training methods on how the child's personality will develop. Surveys have shown that parents differ widely as to when they institute bowel training (4, 11). Some begin as early as the first three or four months, while others do not start until after two or three years! Some take one or two months to complete the process fully and others require well over a year. It is roughly true that the majority in the United States begin to expect bowel control at about six months. Bladder control is achieved by the majority of children between the ages of two and three years. Some parents never punish for "slips," while others use painful retaliation for lapses. Children also show unbelievable variations in how they respond to toilet training. Some attain almost perfect control in relatively few weeks. Others continue to have control problems for years. There are individuals who remain bedwetters into adulthood.

Freud thought the experiences children have in the course of learning bowel control are crucial in their character formation. He suggested that unreasonable over-rigid toilet training could interfere with their psychological development and "fixate" them into the pattern of the "anal character." He portrayed this character type as highly concerned about maintaining self-control and not allowing aggressive feelings, which they regard as bad, to slip out. Also, he said that "anal characters" were unusually invested in avoiding anything dirty and in being neat and orderly. Presumably, they had been so traumatized by their severe toilet training that they had to be extra sure that they did nothing "dirty" that paralleled the dirtiness of losing bowel control. Quite a number of researchers have tried to check out these assumptions (4, 11). They have discovered that while there are people who act like "anal characters," there is no good evidence that they were toilet-trained differently from others. Instead, they have discovered that the so-called anal character traits are more likely to appear in those whose parents were typified by such traits. The compulsive, super-orderly mother tends to fashion a child who is sensitively concerned about keeping his world under tight orderly control.

It is true that the way parents program toilet training will affect their children's responses to it. In general, the more that parents use training procedures that are tough, rigid, and involve severe punishment, the more their children will balk. Studies have shown that kids who cannot seem to learn bowel or urinary control have been subjected to unreasonable toilet-training demands. Their training was started at an unusually early age. They were expected to reach perfect control in a very brief period. They were severely punished for any slips. They were watched and scrutinized, and the whole process of sphincter regulation was bound up with fear and guilt. One of the better studies in this area found that the more severe the toilet training, the more the child obviously becomes emotionally upset. Mothers who use severe methods are often inclined to be tough about other areas of training, too. They more often expect their children to meet high standards in table manners, general neatness, ability to control their anger, obedience, and so forth. They also tend to be cold and to have heightened anxiety about the responsibilities of child rearing. We have consulted with numerous parents who were concerned because their children seemed unable to meet normal standards of bowel or urinary control. *Without exception* we have found that such parents treat their children intrusively. They act as if the child's body belongs to them and they have the right to manipulate and schedule it in any way they think proper. They ignore the child's natural body rhythms. They give him the message that he can expect little body privacy.

We have been amazed at the multiple ways parents intrude on the child's body. It is worth digressing for a moment to focus on this matter. One of the most obvious forms of parental intrusion has to do with their insisting that the child can eat or urinate or defecate only at the precise times they decide are right for him. They tell him, in effect, that his body has to function by their clock. This scheduling of body functions may be extended to many other things, such as declaring a precise time to go to sleep, a precise time to take a bath, a precise time to brush teeth, and so forth. No body functions are permitted to occur spontaneously. Another, more concealed form of intrusion derives from parents microscopically watching the child's body. They look him over carefully at every opportunity and instantly tell him if they detect anything out of order or out of line. They want to know the origin of every new scratch. They comment about his posture. They are quick to inform him if his hair is uncombed or if he has an excess particle of dirt on his face. They comment on whether he is eating too much or too little. They tell him whether his clothes are too tight or loose or loud or whatever. Actually, their observations may rarely be negative. They may be quite complimentary. Such parents may even be very sympathetically tuned in as to whether the child feels good or bad, has pain, or shows other body symptoms. But what impresses the child is that his body is always in the spotlight and in the public domain. This can be just as upsetting as if his parents were able to see into his brain and monitor what he was thinking. Still another way that parents intrude is by giving the child the impression that his body is so fragile that it cannot survive unless they are close by to protect it. They are forever warning him about danger. They convince him that injury is imminent and that he cannot expect to survive unless they keep their eyes on him. In other words, they make him feel that his body cannot exist as an independent thing. It is not unusual for some parents to show not only this brand of intrusion but also several others at the same time.

We have collected a representative series of statements by parents that often reflect their intent to boss the child's body. Consider the following examples in which either a mother or father is addressing an offspring:

Are you sure you've eaten enough so you won't be hungry?
Your eyes look tired. Why don't you stop reading for a while?
There is a little scratch on your face. How did it get there?
You don't look right to me. Are you sure you're feeling well?
Baseball can be dangerous. A lot of people get hurt playing sports.
Are you absolutely sure you don't have to go to the bathroom?
Hold tight to my hand. This is a tall building and you could fall.

You look so much like me. People can tell you are mine.

Why do you always wear the same pair of jeans? You have lots of other clothes in your closet.

Stop fooling around with your food. It takes you so long to eat your meal.

Don't slouch like that. Stand up straight when you walk.

Parents who find themselves issuing numerous statements of this sort to their kids should question why they are doing so. There is a good chance that they are trying to exercise control in a domain where the child should, as early as possible, feel that he is in command. If he feels his body space can be invaded at the whim of his parents, he cannot confidently claim it as his own. But without such confidence it is difficult to construct either a sense of identity or genuine individuality.

Not much is reliably known about why parents insist on inappropriately intruding into the child's body space. But we can offer several tentative explanations based on both our clinical work and research with families. First of all, there is a simple matter of inertia. The child's body is for the period of pregnancy literally a part of his mother's body. She gets used to thinking of his body as overlapping with hers. If she nurses him, this view is further extended. But even if she doesn't nurse him, she (and her spouse) learn that the child's body is an extension of their own in the sense that it cannot survive unless they service it. In a metaphorical sense, the child's body is attached to them. Mother and father do, as part of their parental responsibility, take a proprietary attitude toward the child's body for a long time. It is difficult to give up this attitude as fast as the child's growth realistically makes it logical to do so. You do not easily surrender title to what you proudly count as yours.

Fear is another powerful motive for parents inappropriately holding onto the child's body. They may see their surroundings so full of threats that they are convinced they have to keep guiding him. They assume that without their ever-present guidance of his body, he will fall victim to one of the threats. They take over his body to guard him. Of course, they end up making the child more vulnerable, because he loses confidence in his own resources. With respect to the matter of fear, we would like to mention that parents' fears for their own security may push them to be possessive of the child's body. If you are scared enough, you will cling to anything within reach. We recall one case in which a woman who had lost her husband and who felt alone and deserted ruled her child's body with an iron hand because she desperately needed to be sure that he would remain close and available as a companion. Finally, we have also seen parents who intruded on the child's body as a way of putting him down. They wanted, usually unconsciously, to make him feel weak and inadequate. They wanted him to feel as if he were merely an appendage. We have seen this in competitive families where the members choose up sides. A father may be angry at his son because he sees him as a potential ally of his wife. Or a mother may resent her daughter as a likely opponent who will be on father's side. Such parents may express their anger and suspicion by imposing unreasonable body controls. What is terribly confusing to the child is that such controls are invariably disguised as something that is being done "for your own good."

Apropos of this last point about anger, it should be emphasized that anger is a prominent feeling in parents during toilet training—and probably also in the child. The parents get tensely fed up when the child "slips" and soils himself after they have spent so much time and energy training him. It is also obvious that the child can be filled with rage at the way his parents clamp down on him when he slips. This rage often makes him terrifically resistive. He simply will not stop soiling or urinating at the wrong times. We have followed the day-by-day course of enuretic children and been impressed with how often their slips follow an angry or frustrating episode with their parents. We have seen instances in which parents quickly reduced enuretic incidents by simply deciding to be a bit less tough and demanding. But they are rarely able to produce long-term improvement with such a simple resolution (2, 25). That usually requires exploration of their motives for being so severely controlling. However, we do not want to exaggerate the efficacy of psychotherapy (applied to the child or the parents or both) in resolving toilet-training difficulties. There are many cases in which it does not work. Claims have also been made for the effectiveness of conditioning procedures, such as the use of an apparatus that awakens the child every time he urinates in bed. While these claims seem to hold up well with reference to some enuretic children, there are many for whom they do not. The harsh fact is that once parents have created the threatening hostile conditions that stimulate resistance to toilet training, it is not easy to reverse them. Interestingly, most children with toilet-training problems gradually (and after considerable suffering) adapt on their own to the cultural rules about sphincter control. We do not know why.

Perhaps the incongruity between wanting to be taken seriously as a person and the contempt directed at those who are too infantile to control their orifices is sufficiently impressive, after a while, to lead to conformity.

Clothes

In the average family a good deal of energy and concern is invested in clothes. For years, parents choose what their children will wear. Actually, mothers are the ones who do most of the choosing. In so doing they exercise much more power than most people realize. They shape how their kids will look. They can consistently dress them in bright or dark colors, in tight or loose garments, in conventional or unconventional fashions, in styles that emphasize or deemphasize their sex identity, and so forth. In other words, a mother can consistently make a child look drab, she can make him stand out from the crowd, or she can highlight the fact that he is one sex rather than the other. She can consistently present him as attractive or unattractive. Studies of clothing behavior have found that many people recall that they had a lot of conflict with their parents about what they should wear (9). They associate clothes with being controlled. It does seem to be true that parents typically cajole or command when clothes are involved. They are most likely to be concerned with why the child is so sloppily dressed, why he isn't wearing sufficient clothes to protect him from the cold, why his clothes are so dirty, or why he has on things that don't match. We do not mean to imply that parents do not also have positive and friendly communications about clothes. Many parents admire how their kids look when they are dressed up and they let their kids know this. But it is interesting that most people, in looking back to their childhood, associate clothes with parental restriction.

There is no question but that the clothing you choose for your children will affect how they are seen by others and also how they view themselves. This is well documented by research showing that the way a person dresses will influence the impressions people form of him. It may positively or negatively bias them with reference to such qualities as his intelligence, friendliness, and dependability. Most parents build up an image of the sort of appearance they want each of their children to project. It is fascinating to witness the array of effects they try to achieve. We have carefully watched some of them and can offer a number of illustrations.

1. A mother dressed her two young daughters in a way that dramatized their delicate femininity. She chose dresses made of delicate materials, in styles that would not go well with running around or playing vigorously. She frequently used the excuse that they might "ruin" their clothes as a rationale for keeping them away from outdoor activities.

2. In another instance, a mother seemed dedicated to making her daughters look as large and massive as possible. She chose clothes for them that were elaborate, wide at the shoulders, made of bulky materials, and often brightly colored. She also styled their hair in a "stand-up" expansive fashion. Interestingly, she herself was large and somewhat obese.

3. A young boy was almost always dressed like a fashion plate by his mother. His clothes were of the latest mode and meticulously kept. He stood out in any group of children as the "little gentleman."

4. All of the kids in one middle-class family projected an image of what appeared to be poverty. Although the family had a substantial income, they were dressed in clothes that looked like they had been picked up at a rescue mission. Their style of dress conveyed the impression that they were of low status and poor.

In each of these instances we were impressed that the way the children were decked out expressed a wish or need of their parents. In one case it might be a desire to assert, "We are big and powerful," and in another it might be the sentiment, "We are poor and down. Don't expect very much from us." We do not mean to suggest that the average parent is as singlemindedly devoted to shaping his children's appearance in a particular mold as would seem to be true in these examples. But we do think that there is a general theme or bias that shows up in the clothes most parents choose for their kids. We should acknowledge that what we are saying is our own impressionistic opinion. Almost no scientific research has been done with reference to this issue. We should add, though, that a few scattered studies have found correlations between personal needs and the type of clothing people prefer (9). In view of good evidence that in many ways parents do project their own personal needs onto their children, it is not farfetched to assume that the clothes they pick for them could serve such projection.

Of course, the inescapable question arises: is the image you want your children to present acceptable to them? It is probable that parents frequently run into resistance picking their children's clothes because they are trying to fit them into a preferred mold. Parents are forever plagued by their kids doing things like refusing to wear the latest clothes purchased for them, or becoming fixated on one outfit and leaving everything else hanging in the closet. Kids can stubbornly hold out for a long time against wearing what does not suit them. The revolt against parents' clothing images could not be better highlighted than by the sudden swing toward the half-poverty-stricken, half-"earthperson" image that occurred among middle-class adolescents in the 1960's. They refused to deck their bodies with the trappings of abundance and conformity that their affluent parents heaped on them.

What are some of the psychological purposes that clothes serve for children? We have just referred to one purpose. It can be a way of stating what a person stands for, as in the example of the middle-class kids who wear tattered jeans. A kid can dress in a fashion that asserts, "I am masculine and tough" or "I want to be the center of attention and I won't take a back seat to anyone" or "I am very serious and dignified and intend to obey all the rules." The use of clothes to advertise what you stand for is especially obvious in the fad for wearing T shirts that have messages and pictures emblazoned on them. At another level, kids also see clothes as a source of comfort, support, and protection. The feel of the soft texture of a garment may be soothing to a child as he is going to sleep. The tight firmness of a coat against his body wall may help a child feel that he is well protected on the way to school, in the same way that the sturdy walls of a fort provide security for those inside. It is striking how often children use clothes to give themselves a feeling of being enveloped in protective armor. We have already mentioned the boy who wore a heavy leather jacket everywhere because it made him feel securely enclosed. For him, it was like wearing a catcher's mask and chest protector all day long. It is quite common for kids to become attached to a particular sweater or hat or belt that they value because the "feel" of it has a psychological boundary-enhancing effect. In very young children, a similar feeling is sometimes gained from holding on to a favorite teddy bear or toy. We have wondered whether the average child's fascination with things like tents, sleeping bags, and other cavelike retreats does not stem from the body-encircling walls they provide. We have wondered, too, whether badges, patches, and pieces of equipment that get attached to the body may be valued, at least in part, because they make the borders of the body feel more solid. It is worth being aware of such possibilities. Your child's singleminded determination to keep using an article of clothing that you feel he has outgrown or that you consider too worn out to be exhibited to other people may reflect his need for certain reassuring sensations. It may not in any way represent an effort to defy or frustrate you. It may, on the contrary, be extremely puzzling and frustrating to a child when you insist on taking away from him something reassuring to his body. He may understand the intellectual reasons you give for so doing, but feel that you are going out of your way to stir up trouble.

The tension between parents and their children about clothes often crests at that point when the children loosen their bonds with the family and assign growing importance to their contacts with their peers. As they spend more and more time with friends, the opinions of these friends become more and more important. They begin to dress to please and attract their peers rather than to satisfy their parents. It is difficult to pinpoint any one age at which this happens. But it evolves rapidly as kids move into early adolescence. The differences between the parents' values and those of the next generation may first surface dramatically in disagreements over what is proper clothing. As children insistently introduce into the family what their friends define as the right thing to wear, the stage is set for clashes. We have seen a number of families in which the tensions between parents and adolescents first exploded into open warfare over the parents' attempts to force changes in clothing or hair styles. A father or mother will demand the removal of a beard, or that longer skirts be worn, and the adolescent responds as if invaded. Tremendous resistance flares. In exploring such trouble with adolescents, we have found two prime reasons for their outraged reaction. First, they feel that their parents' demands are an intrusion into their body space (which is supposed to belong to them and no one else). Secondly, they see these demands as a threat to their right to learn the values of their own generation and to gain acceptance as one of its members. Of course, by the same token, the reasons parents so often react violently to the clothing values their kids import into the family is that they threaten the apparent rightness of the values that have bound them to their own generation.

A few words are in order about how individuals use clothes to give themselves messages concerning proper conduct. It is pretty obvious that when a policeman is dressed in his uniform, he feels a special constraint to act like a guardian of the law. The garb of the nun conveys an unrelenting reminder to her that she must be restrained and nonsexual in her body deportment. There is an interesting study of a religious sect

(Hasidic Jews) that places great importance on wearing certain distinctive garments. It is understood in this sect that the wearing of such garments helps its members to stick to proper, moral behavior. Members who have been interviewed indicate that while they are wearing their distinctive costumes, they feel that they are under public scrutiny and therefore have to be doubly careful to do the right thing (9). Parents count on children getting similar instructions from the clothes they choose for them. The child whom mother dresses up very formally for a special occasion gets a continuing reminder from the formal style of his attire that he ought to behave in a polite, dignified way. The adolescent girl for whom mother chooses "little girl" clothes is reminded everywhere she goes that she must not yet begin to experiment with more grown-up, womanly modes of behavior. Parents react negatively when they detect certain kinds of self-instructions in their children's attire that clash with their own standards. For example, a father may become angry when he perceives that his daughter, who is about to go and meet her boyfriend, is dressed in an obviously "sexy" style. He recognizes that in her choice of clothes she has implicitly defined a sexy role for herself that evening.

It would be no exaggeration to say that clothes function as semaphore signals in most families. These signals are transmitted and received whether we consciously analyze them or not. They undoubtedly are involved in the continuing exchanges between parents and children, and parents should at least recognize this fact of life.

Being in Touch with Your Body

We are impressed with the inherent wisdom of what our own bodies tell us, if and when we listen to them. Moment by moment we are the recipients of messages from our bodies that mirror our reactions to life events. These messages are often more realistic than the intellectual, rationalized versions we construct of those events. For example, we have all had the experience of going to a party and meeting people who by reputation and social standing should be pleasant to relate to and yet, at the same time, finding ourselves disturbed by unpleasant body feelings. This produces confusion. We do not understand why we should have such unpleasant body sensations in a context we tell ourselves is good and interesting. But a close examination of the situation will usually reveal that the unpleasant body feelings are triggered by something threatening. It may be that the "nice" people at the party are conducting themselves in a competitive way, or they may be snooty and distant, or they may expect you to act in a manner that does not fit your self-concept. There are many other situations where our body sensations provide more valid accounts of what is happening than do our intellectualized accounts, which are colored by what we think ought to be true. You may recall the last time you were talking in an apparently pleasant way with a friend, but then began to notice tension building up in the back of your neck. This signaled your anger about something that was evolving between the two of you, but you probably ignored it; only later, when you analyzed the events, did you realize how angry you had been.

There are untold numbers of people who ignore what their bodies say and keep doing things that will probably hurt them in the long run. A good illustration is the executive who pushes on day after day, fighting to get to the "top." He apparently loves what he is doing but keeps getting disconcerting body feelings, such as sensations of heavy weariness or tense discomfort. Consider, too, the case of the mother who apparently cares cheerfully and maternally for her five children (and even considers bearing a sixth) but whose body is filled with disquieting tensions reflecting her basic rejection of what life is demanding of her. The body experiences of such persons signify dissatisfaction. No matter what facades these persons don, they are, in fact, uncomfortable with their roles. It seems to us that it is valuable to be able to tune in on your own body sensations and to recognize what they mean. This is related to the position we have taken that the more pertinent information a person has available, the more competently he can solve problems.

There is no doubt that the way children are reared in our society discourages grasping body cues and using them constructively (9). Emphasis is placed on what children do and how they act. Little attention is given to their body sensations and feelings unless they are of the unpleasant variety implying illness. Although there is great concern about the body in our culture, there is a widespread guilty embarrassment about being "too interested" in one's own body. There are quite a number of parts of the anatomy and body functions about which a child is not supposed to think or say much. A child usually meets concealed

85

resistance if he devotes too much attention to his body. The average mother who happens to witness her child trying, out of curiosity, to get a good look at its genitals or anal area in the mirror does not respond very favorably. There is little motivation to give children a vocabulary to describe their body states. They learn to label major emotions like joy, sadness, and fear. But they do not get training as to how to make finer distinctions about their internal sensations.

A phobic attitude toward body experience is especially encouraged in boys. Girls are given much more freedom than boys to look at and be interested in their bodies. No one thinks it strange if a girl sits down in front of a mirror and minutely scrutinizes herself as she does this or that to her skin and hair. But if a boy did something similar, he would risk being labeled a sissy or even worse. The rigid body attitudes taught to the male are reflected in the relatively narrow range of clothing styles he wears and his reluctance to experiment with his body appearance. Boys are not supposed to show much conscious interest in their bodies unless it is in the context of athletics and making oneself strong. A good deal of research has shown that not only do girls have greater awareness of their bodies than do boys, they also have a greater sense of body security. This surprises most people. The stereotype is widely accepted that because the male has a stronger body than the female, he also has more body confidence. But the scientific data show that the average male has a lot of anxiety about getting hurt (8). He is relatively uncomfortable about body things. Even in his dreams he shows more anxiety about body damage than does the female. The difference in the way males and females respond to sudden changes in the way they look was brought out in a study of college students. Males and females who were in a dark room were asked to describe their own appearance while viewing themselves in a mirror during brief flashes of illumination. Masks of various kinds were placed on their faces and they were often startled by the changes in their appearance. Some of the masks depicted a person of the opposite rather than same sex. An analysis of the mirror descriptions that were given indicated without any question that the males were more disturbed than the females by the alterations produced by the masks. They more often showed specific signs of anxiety—for example, by misperceiving and misidentifying the sex of the mask they were wearing (8).

But returning to the major point we were considering above (the reluctance of parents to allow their children to get intimately acquainted with their own bodies), we think it is valuable to say it out loud. Parents should realize that such bias exists in our culture and that theoretically they have a choice as to how far they will go along with it. However, we would add that it is not clear what the advantages and disadvantages are of raising children who are comfortable about examining their own body experiences, as compared to bringing them up with a relatively low awareness of their own body events. This is still unknown territory. There are hints that the child who learns to be sensitive to his body may, as a result, become especially capable of understanding the emotions and subtle communications of others. He may also be more capable of being creative (9). We do not know the possible negative effects of being body-sensitive. It may stimulate too much preoccupation with emotion. It may interfere with adapting to the conventional masculine role. It may lead to too much egocentricity. Such issues remain to be evaluated. We suppose that the extent to which parents should use their own body sensations in responding to their kids can also be debated. For example, if on the surface all seems to be going well between them and yourself, and yet almost every time you get near them you get sensations of discomfort (such as tension in your neck), should you look into the possibility that all is not really well? It might be a good idea. But each parent has to answer this sort of question for himself on the basis of his own experiences. He has to decide whether he is comfortable operating that way. He has to ascertain how successful he is with such a mode.

Being Sick and Hurting

Tension between parents and children surges up as soon as illness and pain appear in the family. During the early months after birth, most parents react with alarm to the slightest signs of sickness in their children. They experience all kinds of extreme emotions as they negotiate between the child's symptoms, the pediatrician's attitudes, and their own fears. They are inclined to overreact to hints of pain or discomfort in the child and to anticipate dramatically all the worst possible things that could happen. The pediatrician typically finds himself in the role of trying to keep parental anxiety within realistic bounds. Studies show that mothers who are unusually anxious about symptoms of illness in themselves repeat this attitude in dealing with the symptoms of their children. They are quick to label their kids as sick and also to take them to the doctor. One researcher found that if you know the general level of anxiety of a child's mother, you can predict how scared and uncooperative the child will be when he goes to the dentist for treatment (19). Children are highly sensitive to parental attitudes about the body and about being sick. Indeed, illness in any family member has a sizable psychological impact on all of the other members. Intense emotions are triggered. Parents with a chronically ill or disabled child make all sorts of special adaptations (5, 12, 14, 22, 24). For example, they have been found to feel psychologically closer than average to his body and to more directly relate his body attributes to their own. Similarly, children who live with one or more parents suffering from a long-term disease show more body anxiety than other children.

Complicated forms of parent-child relationships are built up around issues of illness. When children develop symptoms, parents are, first of all, confronted with the prime question of whether what they have on their hands is life-threatening. Beyond that, they find, as the child grows older, that they are repeatedly required to decide whether his symptoms call for giving him special nurturance and privileges. Every morning millions of parents ponder and puzzle whether the aches and pains of their children are serious enough to excuse them from going to school. They feel guilty about the possibility of sending a sick child off and possibly aggravating his condition. But at the same time, they are concerned about whether excusing the child from school may not encourage weakness in him and motivate him to use illness as a way of escaping responsibility. In our culture sickness is equated with being passive. It is also equated with weakness. For males it has the special connotation of being unmasculine. People are almost always highly ambivalent toward sickness either in themselves or others. They feel sympathy toward the sick one and see him as having the right to a lot of nurturant support. At the same time, they are aware of his weakness and his potential for becoming a burden. To be sick usually gets you a lot of soft attention, but it also puts you into the position of "the weak one." Children soon learn about this ambivalence whenever they tell their parents they feel sick. It is not surprising, then, that several studies have shown that children (and adults) develop a good deal of guilt about being ill. If you get inside of them psychologically, you find that they harbor an unreasonable sense of having done something wrong. It is not unusual for those with severe chronic illnesses to fantasize that they are paying the penalty for past sins or misdeeds. Anyone who has been sick for any length of time knows that one does begin to feel guilty about being a burden to those providing care.

Most parents manage to behave fairly reasonably when their kids get sick. However, we have seen families in which painful dilemmas develop because parents could not control their fears and confusions. We know families in which the mother and father are so afraid of passivity that they cannot tolerate signs of weakness in their children. They especially associate being sick with being weak. The appearance of illness in their children brings them too close to weakness. It reminds them that the same thing could happen to them, so they greet any complaints of illness with coldness and suspicion. They convey the message, "You can't be sick. It's wrong and a sign of inferiority. We won't stand for it." Their children sense that they are frightened of sickness. They also perceive that the parents are treating them unfairly. As a result, they become unusually alarmed whenever they get sick and, in addition, they are motivated to use their symptoms to make trouble. They exaggerate their discomfort, complain unpleasantly, demand extremes in support and reassurance, and use their symptoms to evade the things their parents expect of them. We do not mean they do so in a calculated way. They evolve these defenses with as little awareness of what they are doing as their parents, who set the whole process in motion.

We should explicitly note that while there is scientific evidence that parents create unreasonable guilt and confusion in their kids about being sick, little is known about how they do so. We would like, however, to mention a few of the ways we have observed. One of the most obvious involves asking questions and making comments that fairly directly imply suspicions about whether the child's symptoms are genuine. Remarks such as the following fall in this class:

Does it really hurt?
How come you didn't tell me about this when I talked to you a while ago?
Well, I guess you won't have to go to school today (uttered with cynical overtones).

But guilt can also be instilled by remarks that go to the opposite extreme and exaggerate the child's incapacitation. The parent who consistently responds to a child's symptoms as if they were much worse than they really are is, at one level, saying, "If you are less sick than I am pretending you are, you just aren't very sick, and you should be ashamed of stirring up so much distress in me." Finally, we would point out that guilt is often aroused in the sick child when he detects that his parents are frustrated by the inconvenience his condition causes them. He senses that they are angry at him because his illness makes him a burden, and he blames himself. The widespread occurrence of guilt about being ill probably stems from the fact that even the best-intentioned parents do get irritated with the problems posed by the illnesses of their children. In addition, in instances where parents are very passive people who just can't stand any extra pressures or responsibilities, they not only show anger at the child's illness but have a way of multiplying his guilt by dramatizing what a burden he is. They give the message: "Can't you see how much I am already suffering? There is no room in this family for anyone else who is troubled. If you are sick, you will make my life terribly uncomfortable." Basically, the child who dramatizes his pain and who acts like an hypochondriac is probably protesting the way such parents treat him. He may be telling them that they are too intolerant of weakness in him. His proclamation of symptoms is a way of getting even by giving the parents a large dose of the very thing they don't like. It is his declaration of discomfort and his need to get something he lacks, such as attention or devotion. Studies of persons who unrealistically keep complaining about their body have shown that they feel painfully unloved. They seem to focus complaining attention on their own body as a compensation for what they consider they have been deprived of.

We know that people get very scared by medical things. Even when they put on a brave front, they are internally pondering all the bad things that could happen. Several studies have shown that threats to the body stir up disproportionate anxiety because they are seen as potentially life-threatening—and also mutilating (9). Your child should get extra special support and reassurance when circumstances result in his or her being hospitalized (3). Interviews with children in the hospital and probes of their inner feelings by means of psychological tests and dream analysis have shown that they are in state of alarm. They are scared not only about what is going to be done to their body but also about their separation from home base. A significant part of their alarm can be dampened if their parents demonstrate that they are going to stick with them and not leave them alone for long periods with the strangers who inhabit the hospital. It is also important that they be prepared in advance for medical procedures. Unless they are properly oriented as to what is happening, they may easily see a stranger who approaches them with a long needle, and who seems intent on plunging it into their tissues, as an assailant. Children who are given good support and explanation in such crisis situations have been found to recover more quickly and with fewer complications. It should be mentioned that evidence exists that boys are really more frightened than girls by medical procedures. They may, in the name of masculine prowess, put on a more composed facade. But we know that they are significantly more scared. One study found that the dreams of hospitalized boys are definitely more filled with images of being hurt and attacked than are those of hospitalized girls. Boys are more likely than girls to interpret surgery and related procedures as potentially disabling. They see them as an attack on their manhood, and on that basis they overreact emotionally. So your male child may actually need just a bit more support when he is hospitalized than your female child does.

Parents who have a child with a gross body defect (such as a birth injury or an amputation) have to contend with a major blow to their self-esteem. They not only have to come to grips with the fact that persons with serious defects are generally regarded as devalued, but also that such depreciatory feelings exist within themselves. They will not only be inclined to perceive the child as inferior but also to see themselves, who are his producers, as sharing in the inferiority. One study reported that the child with a defect never fills the role of the favorite one in the family. Unless parents become aware of such negative attitudes and do something to master them, their flawed child will have a doubly difficult time adapting psychologically. There is evidence that the way a child with a body defect adjusts to it is appreciably influenced by his impression of how his parents regard him. If he sees them as full of shame and anger about his condition, he will, in turn, feel intensely negative toward himself. Feelings of inadequacy will pervade everything he does. It may be surprising to learn that the seriousness of the defect is not the key determinant of how uncomfortable the child feels. Many children with relatively minor body defects are more disturbed about their condition than are those with gross deficiencies. It is also important to note that children who have had a defect from birth and who have had a long time to live with it are often less anxious about their appearance than are those whose defect is of more recent origin. Both children and adults can adapt to even the most radical body damage if they have enough time and enough support from the important people in their world. The most extreme example of this point is provided by studies of children who are born with sex organs that are not clearly masculine or feminine. It has been discovered that if parents make a clear decision to raise a child with defective sexual anatomy as belonging to one specific sex, the child has a good chance of growing up with a reasonable sense of identification as a member of that sex. It does not seem to matter whether the parents decide to label the child as male or female. What is important is that they make the decision early and decisively. If they cannot manage their own disturbed and confused feelings about their genitally deficient child, he will probably make a poor adjustment to his state.

It has also been noticed that many mothers of defective children devote themselves with unusual energy to their care. They take refuge in activity and doing. One writer speculated that the intense devotion displayed by some of these mothers is prompted by magical thinking. It is as if they believed that if they only gave enough of themselves, they would be able to undo their children's defects. There is no magical way for parents to resolve their anger and sense of inferiority about having a child who is flawed. But once again, we would underscore that a first step in the resolution is for them to become aware of how they genuinely feel. Until they take stock of their negative attitudes and confusion, they are in no position to do anything about them. It is our impression that most of the "doing" occurs in the exchanges that go on between the mother and father of the child with the defect. They gradually express their bitterness to each other, they vent their frustration, they support each other, they resolve as a team to accept the child, and they mutually become aware of other qualities he possesses that compensate for his deficiencies. Where parents do not talk truthfully to each other about the problem and do not support each other in assigning a meaningful, relatively positive role to the flawed child in their family life, they increase the possibility that they will end up with a "put-down" product.

People are only beginning to recognize the importance of the individual's feelings about his own body in his ability to cope with the world. But there is now an impressive file of scientific reports indicating that how you experience your body is not only a core part of your selfhood but also a key element in how you deal with a number of major life problems (8, 9, 10). The person who feels insecure about his body, as if it were vulnerable and imperfectly protected, will behave timidly and be wary of close involvement with other people. The person who has developed a secure image of his body deals unusually well with trouble. He is also able to adapt particularly successfully to being sick and to serious crippling of his body. It is the person with a sense of body weakness who is most likely to give up or go to pieces when fate visits a serious health problem upon him. Many other illustrations of this sort could be listed. Although the final proof is not yet in, there is good reason to say that parents play a major role in their children's body feelings and fantasies. They are probably the prime shapers in this realm.

CHAPTER 4

Sex: Genital Arousal,
Sex Education,
Learning to Love

Why Do Parents and Children Have So Much Trouble Communicating About Sex?

AS EVERYONE KNOWS, mothers and fathers feel awkward when they try to inform their children about the world of sex. They feel embarrassed and inept. This applies even in the case of "liberated parents" who assume they have no sexual inhibitions and who are determined their children will get an adequate sex education. The reluctance of parents to tell their kids about sex is witnessed by the fact that relatively few people recall their own mothers and fathers as having been the major source of their sexual information. In most scientific surveys it turns out that children get their "facts of life" largely from friends their own age and from reading materials. They also get information from "sex education" courses in school, relatives, and so forth.* Of course,

---

* One study found that children learn about pregnancy first (69 percent by age 10), intercourse next (57 percent by age 10), and masturbation third (43 percent by age 10).

the most practical information comes from early dating and sexual contacts.

It is puzzling that although parents consider themselves more and more liberated sexually, there has been no increase in how often they are the main sources of sexual information for their kids. A strange membrane separates parents and children when sex is in the air. No one really knows why this is true. It is difficult to explain why sexually experienced and sophisticated adults who seem comfortable with their own sexual drives get so uptight when they are called upon to tell their kids what sex is all about. We were unable to find any scientific studies bearing directly on this matter. However, we do have a few hypotheses that we would like to voice, based on our general knowledge of the field. It is our impression that what parents find so embarrassing about explaining the nature of sexual relationships is the idea, implicit in the subject, that they themselves engage in sexual intercourse. That is, if they spell out the copulatory act, this leads the child to the inevitable conclusion, "Mom and Dad must do this very thing." They find themselves confronted with their child's awareness of a part of their life they have kept secret from him. So often, as we have discussed with parents their problems in communicating with their children about sex, we have seen how sensitive they are to keeping their sexual intimacy shielded from their children's eyes and ears. Interestingly, during intercourse, they frequently wonder whether their kids can overhear them. In a sense, a game focused on this issue develops in most households. While parents are trying to be as quiet and private as possible, their children are straining to see and hear as much as possible. Many adults remember that as children they were intensely curious about their parents' sexual activities and would listen excitedly at night to detect sexual sounds. But why do parents, who fluently discuss sex with others, find they are blocked and reluctant with their children? It seems to us that what is special in this context is that the parents identify with how they imagine their children will view them when they find out about their sexual intimacy. They identify with the embarrassment they expect the children to experience. We presume they do so because they recall their own embarrassment about their parents' sexuality when they were kids.

As for the children's point of view, we would suggest that what is so disconcerting to them, when they discover that their parents do sexual things, is the sharp contrast between such sexuality and the more customary role parents play of advocating control and inhibition of body functions. From the very beginning, parents embark on a program of "civilizing" the child's body. No matter how free and liberated they themselves are, they try to get him to eat "properly," to put his body sphincters under formal control, to cover his nakedness with clothes, to keep his body functions private, and to master body feelings that might lead to impulsive looseness. They align themselves with the position that the body is a private thing that needs to be restrained and disciplined. Parents almost universally strive to get their kids to master the "animal" side of the body. So it is no wonder that the kids are disconcerted when they discover their parents use their own bodies for sexual purposes that seem to be grossly animal-like. Children are shocked at the difference between the image their parents have given them that the body is something to be tamed and groomed, and the image of abandon conveyed by the body in sexual action.

While we attach importance to the view just expressed, we are aware that other factors may be just as (or even more) important in instigating negative vibrations between parents and children in the sexual realm. Certainly the puritanical attitudes of many of our major religions toward sexual expression play a part. Furthermore, Freud, the originator of psychoanalysis, considered the so-called Oedipus complex to be a powerful source of trouble for the average family in its attempts to cope with the sexual side of life. He asserted that the child is sexually responsive from the day that it is born, but that the responsiveness is not like that in the adult. He described a pattern of shifting sexual sensitivity focused initially around the mouth, then the anal area, and finally the genitals. He said there were distinct erogenous elements in the child's shifting responses to stimulation of the mouth, anus, and genitals. It was originally a great shock to people to be told there were sexual-like drives in young children. Freud specified that the sexual drives of the child normally culminate, in the age range of four through five, in an intense desire to sexually possess the parent of the opposite sex and to eliminate the parent of the same sex, who is cast in the role of a love rival. He also stated that the tense rivalry produced by this Oedipal situation is so frightening to the child that it is forced to renounce its sexual wishes and to retreat into a period of minimum sexual activity (latency). This period is then finally succeeded at adolescence by a reawakening of sexual drives and fantasies that normally progress to so-called mature heterosexual love relationships.

Freud's view that the child experiences sexual sensations and actually has sexual fantasies about the parent of the opposite sex makes people uncomfortable emotionally, even though there is apparent widespread acceptance of the notion intellectually. It is one thing to joke about the Oedipus complex and quite another thing to see it as influencing your relationships with your own children. Really, it is a bit amusing to trace the fortunes of the Oedipal theory in popular circles. When Freud first proposed the theory, people widely rejected and ridiculed it. This rejection occurred on purely emotional grounds; there was little interest in whether there was any confirmatory scientific evidence. But just as irrationally, the idea of the Oedipus complex has now been embraced by the intellectual communities of most Western cultures without any knowledge of whether it is scientifically sound.

Several major attempts have recently been made to weigh all of the objective information bearing on it (11). The results seem fairly supportive. There is evidence that even babies may respond with genital arousal to certain kinds of excitement and that children may consciously and unconsciously entertain sexual fantasies. Also, studies of different cultures indicate that certain patterns of intimacy between the child and the parent of the opposite sex seem to influence sexual attitudes in the child in a way that Freud predicted. The evidence on this last point is more solid with regard to the relation between mother and son than that between father and daughter. In general, it does seem reasonable for parents to assume that their very young children are not asexual and that they do have erotic sensations and feelings. It does seem reasonable to expect that children will develop sexually tinged feelings about the parent of the opposite sex and will, to some extent, see the same-sex parent as a potential rival. However, we would add that Freud's insistence that Oedipal feelings are inevitable and decisive in every individual's development remains unproven. It is more likely that Oedipal feelings vary in their intensity and importance from family to family. They may be very powerful in some children and of low significance in others.

The idea that children may have sexual feelings toward a parent comes alive only after you have a chance to witness it in a real child. This is difficult to do, because such feelings are rarely observable on the surface. But they do become visible when you have methods for looking beneath the surface. Many professional child watchers, such as psychologists and psychiatrists, have glimpsed children's Oedipal fantasies as revealed in their play, their drawings, their story telling, and their conduct with their parents. We have seen numerous young children create imaginative play situations in which the child doll bumps off the parent doll of the same sex and marries the parent doll of the opposite sex. During such play the child and the parent doll of the opposite sex may be placed together in ways that have obvious sexual meaning. We have talked with mothers who were embarrassed by the sexual overtones of their sons' attempts to come into intimate contact with them in bed or in the bathroom. We have spent hours talking with young boys who were filled with jealous fury toward their fathers, whom they perceived as rivals for mother's love. We have also found, in some of these instances, that the fathers regarded their sons as rivals; we even know a few instances where fathers developed uneasy transient fantasies that something sexual was going on between their wives and young sons. The incest taboo in our culture is extremely strict, and it is considered disgusting that there should be any form of sexual attraction between a parent and a child. So there is great pressure to keep such attraction hidden and unlabeled. However, it is interesting that, despite this fact, parents and children do get involved in overt sexual relations with each other much more frequently than is realized. In any case, Oedipal tensions within a family can transform the whole area of sex into a dangerous one that is too potentially upsetting to be discussed freely. If mothers and fathers are aware of the reality of sexual tensions and Oedipal wishes in children, they may be more prepared to deal with the sexual expressions of their own kids and their own reactions to these expressions. Parents grow frightened when they come upon sex in their own family in places where it is not supposed to exist. Their fright is contagious and it can painfully complicate a child's efforts to make sense out of his own sexual impulses.

What Is Normal, Acceptable, Sensible Sexual Behavior?

We know that a great many parents are uncertain and adrift about the standards they should set sexually for their children. Every month a new survey appears announcing further liberalization of what is acceptable sexual behavior. We are told that premarital intercourse has increased by some huge percent, that girls are now rarely virgins when they get married, that the American Psychiatric Association no longer considers homosexuality a sign of psychological deviance, and so forth. The entertainment media briskly advertise the joys of sex and the fact that new sexual styles are on the scene. Parents find that what they have assumed to be proper sexual standards are labeled as old-fashioned and prudish. Any parent who hears what is going on in the world cannot help but feel confused by the rapid shifts in sex codes. This interferes with confident decision making. Every day parents have to act on matters that reflect their sexual values. Consider the following common problems that arise:

Should you allow your four-year-old to walk out nude into the living room when someone is visiting?

At what age should brothers and sisters stop seeing each other in a state of undress?

Should young children be permitted to watch television programs that have explicit sexual content?

Should children be discouraged from referring to copulation and using four letter words?

Should you get angry and punitive if you find your six-year-old engaging in sex play with one of the kids from the neighborhood?

At what age should you allow your sons and daughters to have formal dates?

Should you object if your daughter wears sexually provocative clothes?

Should your adolescent children be allowed to entertain their friends of the opposite sex in their rooms with the door closed?

Many more tough questions could be cited with reference to providing sex education, contraceptive information, permitting necking with dates in the house, and so forth.

We will not pretend we can give parents a simple formula for coping with their confusion. But we think it may be helpful to dissect several of the criss-crossing issues involved. The first point we would make is that there is a difference between what is statistically "normal" and what may be considered sensible. The fact that homosexuality is increasingly accepted does not mean it is necessarily a sensible mode of sexual adaptation. Many forms of disturbed behavior and pathology occur with high frequency, yet no one argues that they are therefore good things. The frequency argument has been used to convince parents that they should accept any new, widely occurring forms of sexual behavior. Obviously, they have the right to contemplate whether the adoption of a new sexual standard will damage their children who, of course, have their own unique traits and attitudes. It is important to realize that normality can be spelled out in lots of ways other than how common something is. It may be stated in terms of moral concepts, an ideal, or a definition based on scientific information. The teacher in a classroom may choose not to define a passing grade by the average, most frequently occurring test score in her class, but rather by a more general standard she or he has built up over the years from working with many classes.

A second issue worth considering is that a distinction has to be made between the effect a new sexual standard will have upon the parents, as compared to the children. While parents may see no direct harm in permitting their kids to experiment with new forms of sexual freedom, they need to ponder how they themselves would be affected. It may be a wrenching experience for a father to accept some new idea such as it being all right for unmarried seventeen-year-old daughters to engage in sexual intercourse. To accept this sort of idea may mean that he has to revise his system of morality so radically that his core sense of identity is threatened. Parents have the right to weigh the damage to themselves that will ensue from a sharp change in moral perspective. If they are too seriously threatened, it may impair their general ability to function as a model for their children. If they lose too much self-confidence or feel too alienated, this may, in the long run, do more harm to their children than refusing to let them keep up with the latest alteration in sex norms. It is pertinent to this same matter that the equilibrium of a family depends to some extent on whether mother and father agree or disagree. In adopting new sexual norms, it becomes important to ask whether what is acceptable to one parent is also acceptable to the other. If father thinks open masturbation is all right but mother is repelled by it, the tension resulting from their divergence can shake up the family. Thus, the question of whether new sexual ideas should be incorporated into a family has to be judged partially on the issue of how much conflict these ideas may create between the two parents.

A third issue we would like to mention relates to the fact that some of the most drastic changes in sexual morality have involved the behavior of the female in particular. Many of the revolutionary alterations being reported have to do with the fact that young women are adopting the same standards of sexual conduct that have applied to men (2, 4). This is especially true with regard to such things as frequency of masturbation, premarital intercourse, and ability to enjoy sexual encounters without guilt. Therefore, parents should try to disentangle how much of their feeling about new sexual norms pertains to sexuality as such, and how much represents a special reaction to the shifting role of women in our world. We are not saying that people do not have a right to adhere to a value system that declares girls should be more sexually controlled than boys, but we do think that they will make more rational decisions if they honestly face up to what is shaping their attitudes.

In short, we are proposing that parents not let themselves be intimidated by the sheer pressure and complexity of what is happening on the sexual scene. They need to disentangle the diverse issues involved. They also need to realize that their decisions about sexual norms impinge not only on their children but also on their own security and identity.

Masturbation, Questions About Sex, and So Forth

One of the first signs of sexuality that parents come upon in their children is masturbation. Very early in their contacts with them they will observe that the children enjoy touching their genitals and that they do, at times, stroke themselves into flushed excitement. Careful observation of babies has revealed that boys usually begin genital play at about six to seven months of age (19). Girls seem to begin at about 10 or 11 months. The genital play in boys typically continues sporadically until the onset of active masturbation at about 15 or 16 months. This active masturbation is accompanied by clear signs of pleasure (for example, smiling) and also focusing of attention on the genital area. The initial genital play observed in girls tends to disappear in a few weeks, and active masturbation reappears at around 15 months. It seems to continue for about two months, but then manual masturbation is often given up in favor of indirect forms of self-stimulation, such as rocking and thigh pressure. This information was derived from a systematic analysis of genital play in babies in a nursery.

Studies have shown that the great majority of parents are embarrassed by the masturbatory behavior of their children (8, 10, 19). It seems alien to them that their own tiny human being should be publicly caressing and enjoying its genitals. All sorts of defensive reactions are stirred up. Some parents (about 25 percent according to one study) immediately restrain the child. They push his hand away from his genitals and put him into a position where he cannot easily continue his genital manipulation. A fairly large number of parents resort to indirect techniques for discouraging masturbation. For example, they will do something (like shaking a toy or making loud sounds) to distract the child and get him to turn his attention away from his body. Or they will keep the child's genital area covered as much as possible so that it is rarely accessible for touching. As the child gets older and can understand language, they will give him messages implying that he can "hurt himself" if he is not "careful" about how he manipulates his genitals. Or he might "catch cold" if he leaves his body naked and exposed very long. Some parents tell their kids things like it's "not nice" and "we don't do things like that." It is well known that just a few decades ago children were commonly informed that masturbation would make them sick or crazy or perverted. Also, there were a fair number of parents who would spank their kids for touching their genitals and threaten punishments with castrating implications. It is sadly amusing to look back and see that various medical and psychological authorities wrote books at that time in which they unequivocally said that masturbation was bad for your physical and mental health. While the average mother and father in Western cultures have given up such outlandish notions, there is no question but that they are still quite uncomfortable about seeing their own children playing sensuously with their genitals. Occasionally, parents who have strong negative feelings about masturbation tell themselves that their kids will "outgrow" it. But masturbation is not something the child "outgrows." Surveys indicate that not only do most kids masturbate but that this form of enjoyment becomes more frequent as they get older, especially as they enter adolescence. Masturbation is just about universal in both boys and girls, although girls until recently reported that they engaged in it less often than boys.*

The primarily negative feelings that most parents have about masturbation get across to their kids. The kids learn to conceal this activity and to feel ashamed about it. They experience masturbation as something

* Studies at the Institute for Sex Research also suggest that somewhere between 50 to 70 percent of children probably engage in sexual play with other children before puberty, most of it occuring between ages 8 and 13.

their parents reject. No wonder, then, that one study discovered that in adult women, masturbation represents not only a sensual satisfaction but also, partially, an act of defiance (10). For a woman it may be an unconscious way of declaring to the disapproving image of her mother, ''I know you don't like me to play with my genitals, but they are mine. I will do with them as I please. You can't stop me.'' Since masturbation is one of the earliest genital sexual experiences of the child, it may be that parents' responses to it are especially important. No one really knows, because the issue has yet to be probed scientifically. But let us, on logical grounds, assume for the moment that the reactions the child stirs in his parents with his genital play do affect his sexual development. Perhaps if their reactions are too scared or too hostile or too irrational, this will distort the child's view of sexuality. If so, what are the implications for the way parents should conduct themselves when they learn that their children enjoy genital stimulation and intend supplying it to themselves?

In the spirit of what we have said in a number of other contexts, we would urge that it is better to make a conscious thought-out decision about this matter than to respond repeatedly on the spur of the moment. First of all, you should decide whether you are opposed to masturbation. If your own values or religious beliefs make you feel you cannot tolerate it, face up to the fact squarely. It will probably be less confusing and ultimately less disturbing to the child if you openly and directly prevent him from masturbating than if you resort to sneaky strategies to stop him, particularly since they often involve stirring up a sense of guilt and unworthiness. If intellectually you see no reason why you should disapprove of masturbation, but find that when your children play with their genitals it upsets you and results in your ''indirectly'' stopping them (for example, by trying to distract them), face up to the fact that a part of you is opposed to masturbation. It then makes sense for you to keep an eye on yourself and to screen out all of the sneaky disapproving acts that you can. When you are tempted to communicate that masturbation is potentially injurious, restrain yourself. When you are about to launch into an elaborate stratagem for distracting your child from his genitals, stop yourself. Your resolve will probably not prevent him from sensing some of your disapproval, but it may help by decreasing the number of irrational messages about sex with which he has to cope. It is almost impossible to conceal from your kids how you feel emotionally about any particular issue.

As soon as children can talk fairly fluently, they have the potential for blurting out sexual ideas and asking questions about sex. They may un-inhibitedly refer to their sex organs or to sexual things they have wit-nessed. They ask questions about what sex organs are used for, where babies come from, what mothers and fathers do in bed, and so forth. Parents, with few exceptions, find such talk embarrassing.* Even when they respond in an outwardly cool and collected manner, they actually feel uncomfortable inwardly. One study, which conducted detailed in-terviews with mothers, definitely found a majority got tense and felt defensive when their kids probed for sexual information. Some mothers were openly indignant about the sorts of things kids ask. They were also hostile about the "modern" idea that all questions about sex should be answered openly and fully. They were irritated with "experts" who said that complete openness was the only proper attitude. Anyone who reads the newspapers knows there are still many, many people who are opposed to uncensored transmission of sexual information to kids. There have been repeated organized protests against sex education courses in school. The embarrassment of parents about releasing sexual information gives their kids the impression that there is a secret stock of knowledge in this area. It is like classified government information. As they begin to build up their own knowledge about various aspects of sexuality, kids feel as though they are piecing together the intricate fragments of a puzzle. They often feel as though they are storing up illicit stuff. When they share sexual data with each other, it is almost as if they were members of a secret society, having the common goal of hiding what they have found out from the prying eyes of the adult world.

What is the proper way for parents to behave when their kids ask for sexual information? Typically, the answer to this question is phrased in terms of detailed instructions about being open and honest. Elaborate advice is offered about being straightforward and using language that children can understand. Other things may be specified, such as not telling the child more than he is really asking for, giving truly accurate material, and so forth. We were unable to locate any systematic inves-tigations that would permit one to declare with authority that one spe-cific approach to answering children's questions about sexuality is bet-

---

* Fathers are even more reluctant than mothers to impart sexual information. Several investigators have found that fathers rarely engage in the "man-to-man" talks about sex with their sons that are touted in movies and novels.

ter than others. But we would like to raise some questions about this entire matter.

The first thing that strikes us is that for most people sexual behavior represents something uniquely intimate and private. We do not, except in certain very special situations, go around telling others about our personal sexual practices. It is therefore not surprising that the average person feels defensive when his child asks him questions that frequently imply that he is curious about what goes on sexually between his parents. *The fact that the child is curious does not mean that he has a right to invade his parents' most intimate privacy.* If a child were to approach a parent with the request that he reveal his innermost thoughts and fantasies, the parent would probably consider this unreasonable and not feel guilty about delivering only a partial, not very revealing reply. By analogy, one might ask: what is wrong with parents giving their children the message that they consider their own sexual behavior to be a private thing and that they are willing to communicate about sex only at a certain level of reserve and objective fact? If parents feel justified in clearly setting a limit as to how far they want to go in communicating about sexual themes, they might feel less generally embarrassed by children's questions and therefore able to communicate more rationally about objective facts such as sexual anatomy and the mechanics of copulation. But perhaps more importantly, they would feel less threatened and therefore less anxious. By clearly and comfortably setting a limit on how personally intrusive the child can be in his probings about sex, the parent could approach his child with more composure.

Along with others who have speculated about the problems of giving children sexual information, we would guess that what is of prime weight in this process is not what parents say, but the amount of anxiety they convey. A parent who gives highly accurate data to his child about how the penis and vagina fit together, but who is very uneasy and threatened by what he is doing, may be doing more harm than good. If kids find that every time they ask a question about sex they evoke alarm and irritability in their parents, they get the idea that danger is attached to the entire domain. In other words, it may be more important that parents be psychologically comfortable in their discussions of sex with their kids than that they give specific types of information. Finally, we would emphatically raise the issue of whether experts and "sex educators" have not exaggerated the importance of parents personally providing sexual information to their kids. Studies do not indicate that children who receive detailed sexual instruction from their parents arrive at any better long-term sexual adaptation than children who receive their instruction from other sources.

Upsetting complications can develop between parents and children when parents feel so anxious about sexual communication that they resort to unreasonable, extreme defensiveness. A fair number of cases have been described in the literature that illustrate complications that develop when parents absolutely refuse to engage in any formal exchange of sexual information and act as if sex were an entirely taboo topic. It is less well known that trouble can stem from parents trying to master their anxiety about sexuality by forcefully exposing their children to high inputs of sexual information. They sometimes adopt an approach based on the adage that the best defense is a good offense. They answer their kids' questions about sex by flooding them with detailed information, vivid sexual images, and intimate details. They do this so aggressively and intrusively that it overwhelms the child. In one family we know, the kids adapted to such an approach by becoming very loud purveryors of sexual material on their own. They learned to embarrass people by persisting in focusing on sexual topics, usually in settings where it was quite inappropriate. We have also seen a family in which the aggressive sexual stance of the parents resulted in their kids acting very shy and blocked about sexuality. They guarded themselves by retreating as far as possible from further possible inputs of sexual imagery.

How Do Parents Shape Their Children Sexually?

Scientific information has accumulated suggesting that the child's ability to identify, eventually, with a meaningful sex role and to achieve satisfying sexuality is determined not so much by what his parents say intellectually about sex as by the way they feel about people, love, and intimacy (8, 10). As just mentioned, the small impact that mothers and fathers make with what they formally tell their children about sex is evidenced by the fact that there is no relationship between how much information parents give their children about sex and how well these children adjust sexually. More specifically, one large-scale investigation reported that no correlation existed between the kind of sex education women received from their parents and their ability to enjoy sexual stimulation as adults (10). A woman's capacity for attaining orgasm proved to be unrelated to how she had acquired her knowledge about sex.

This does not mean we are opposed to giving children correct and abundant sexual information. We are for it, simply because we favor supplying kids with as many realistic facts as possible about their world. Formal sex education may prevent a certain amount of confusion and aimless nosing around for information, but it will probably be of secondary importance in shaping basic sexual attitudes. Incidentally, it is obviously becoming quite easy for children to acquire accurate data about their sexual anatomy and the nature of copulation and reproduction. Even highly sophisticated information about contraception is readily available. Books, films, and magazines are transmitting knowledge about sexual functioning. It looks as if sex education, as a purely informational thing, will become increasingly easy and routine. But it is doubtful that parents will get any more involved in the sex education process than they have in the past. The influence of parents in the sexual development of their children seems to be tied mainly to how they conduct themselves as human beings. We say this with conviction, but we have to caution that the proof is just coming in. The most definite evidence bears on the role parents play in the sexual behavior of their daughters. A series of recent studies has shown that a woman's ability to enjoy sexual stimulation in her contacts with a man is related to how she remembers her father treating her (10). The studies found that the woman most capable of reaching orgasm remembers her father as someone who focused a lot of attention on her, kept track of what she did, and made it clear he had definite expectations of her. The non-orgasmic woman remembers her father as "casual" and indifferently permissive. Indeed, she experiences him as psychologically absent and not as being dependably her friend. In other words, a woman's sexual adaptation seems to be related to how much interest and energy her father invests in her. It is not related to his attitudes about sex or how open he was in talking about sex. Surprisingly, the studies did not detect a link between a woman's sexual adaptation and her recall of how her mother treated her. It remains to be seen whether future studies will come up with the same result on this last point.

Turning back to the role of the father, several different investigators have confirmed that the woman with sexual adaptation problems is likely to have had a father who either was literally not there or who acted as if his daughter were such an unimportant part of his life that he might, without notice, drop her. The father of such a woman had, with unusual frequency, died when she was young, or he was psychologically unavailable because he was an alcoholic, or he had a job that kept him away from home for long periods. Such findings add up to the fact that a father's conduct plays a special, vital part in his daughter's feelings about sex. This is perhaps not surprising, if one considers that a woman's sexual adjustment involves her learning to relate intimately to men. Her original pattern of experience with her father apparently becomes a prototype for her ability to have intimacy with other men. Incidentally, it was such material that led one of the authors to construct a theory, described in detail in another book, concerning the source of orgasm problems in women (10). This theory ties a woman's orgasm difficulties to her fears that men are not dependable and may unpredictably leave her in the lurch. It proposes that women with such fears find the blurring of consciousness—a well-known phenomenon that accompanies the build-up of sexual excitement and orgasm—too much of a threat, because they react to it as a loss experience. They are so sensitive to loss that any sensation of losing contact with things really upsets them. It is this upset feeling that presumably interferes with their ability to reach orgasm.

On the basis of what we have just outlined, we think it is reasonable to suggest that fathers should be alert to the fact that their behavior may affect the sexual lives of their daughters. The father who keeps himself aloof from his daughter, and who gives her the impression he is not firmly and interestedly committed to her, increases the chance that she will be uncomfortable with sexual intimacy. The father who takes a job that keeps him away from home for long periods of time may eventually have the same impact on his daughter. This is similarly true of the father who is so steeped in alcohol that he is psychologically detached from his family. The mother who loses her husband when her daughter is still small should consider that the absence of a father may negatively influence her daughter's sexual future. How does a father know whether he is acting in a way that tells his daughter he is not dependably invested in her? We would like to offer a brief checklist of warning signs:

1. Has it been quite a while since you spent as much as an hour with your daughter discussing in detail what she is doing and thinking?

2. Have you been chronically away from home as much as three or four days a week?

3. Do you find that it is easier to let your daughter "get away" with things than to invest the energy in disciplining her for breaking the rules?

4. Do you not bother to let her know clearly what you think is right or sensible?

5. Are there large chunks of time when you don't think about her or consider what problems may be challenging her?

While we do have some scientific clues about how a father influences his daughter's ability to enjoy sexuality, we know just about zero about how he affects his son in this respect, or how a mother influences the sexuality of her son and daughter. All we can suggest at this point is that the influences probably relate more to how the parents express feeling and how they set up relationships than to the formal things they say about sex.

There are a number of false beliefs in circulation about conditions in childhood that are supposed to lead to poor future sexual adjustment. One of these beliefs is that a child raised in a family with strong religious values emphasizing restraint in sex behavior will end up with damaged sexual capabilities. No one has shown this to be true (10). Neither the Kinsey report nor other studies of sexual behavior have found any consistent or really significant correlations between religiosity or religious background and ability to perform sexually. One recent survey even found a small advantage in sexual responsiveness for religious as compared to nonreligious women. This is not to deny that a few relgous sects have been observed that were so fanatically devoted to strangling sexual feelings that they did produce sexual impairment in those growing up under their influence. But the atmosphere typically associated with the major religions of the Western world does not create such extreme inhibitions. There are no indications that parents who conscientiously practice their religious beliefs are damaging their children's sexual futures. Still another common assumption that is probably not true is that sexual difficulties in adults reflect exposure to some shocking sexual experience in childhood. Many parents are haunted by the fear that their children will witness an outlandish sexual event that will scar them for life. A survey of the scientific literature does not support this perspective. For example, women who have orgasm difficulties do not seem to have been exposed to an unusual number of shocking sexual experiences in childhood. They are not especially likely to have been raped or to have encountered an exhibitionist. Sexual difficulties seem to stem from persistent, long-term family conditions rather than isolated incidents (10).

Parents may also believe that unless their kids begin to date members of the opposite sex fairly early and regularly, they are sexually retarded. This has not been demonstrated at all for girls. There is no relationship between how often girls date in early adolescence and their ability to get involved erotically as adults (10). Studies have been unable to establish this link. The fact that a girl began to date rather late in her development was not found to indicate that she would turn out to be any less sexually capable than a girl who began to date frequently in her early teens. Of course, we do not mean to suggest that parents should not become concerned if they observe that one of their daughters is unusually inhibited about making contact with boys and refrains from dating well into late adolescence. We have seen many girls with such a history, however, who went on to happy, sexually satisfying marriages. As a matter of fact, unusual inhibitions in relating to persons of the opposite sex may be more a sign of difficulty in relating to people in general rather than something specific to sexuality, as such. This could be an indicator of generalized maladjustment.

The findings with regard to boys are a bit different. One careful longitudinal study did show that boys who refrain from interacting with girls in early adolescence (ages 10–14) are likely to be relatively inhibited sexually as adults (13). But it should be emphasized that while the correlation found was statistically significant, it was not of large magnitude. Plenty of boys who have nothing to do with girls in early adolescence go on to be very sexually active adults. Also, many boys who relate easily to girls in early adolescence turn out in later years to be sexually inhibited. The moral to be drawn from our existing knowledge is that it is very difficult to predict, from childhood or even adolescent behavior, how well an individual eventually will adapt sexually.

We would like to say a few words at this point about the connection between mental health and sexual capability. To many people's surprise, the objective evidence indicates that people with neurotic and even schizophrenic symptoms are quite as capable sexually as people without such symptoms (10). It is true that a schizophrenic woman might have special difficulties in establishing a relationship with a man; if and when she does establish one, however, she is quite as able to respond to sexual stimulation and to achieve orgasm as any normal woman. We think this is important for parents to understand, so that they will not unthinkingly assume that a child who is slow in becoming sexually active is necessarily psychologically disturbed—or that, vice versa, one who is interested in, and involved with, sexual liaisons is therefore psychologically sound. The surface aspects of adolescent sexual behavior can be quite deceiving. We have seen seriously disturbed adolescents who·tried to maintain a facade of normality by a heavy round of dating and sexual interaction. It should be remembered that the speed with which your child becomes invested in dating and sexual intimacy depends upon numerous things, such as his rate of physiological maturation, the dating patterns of his peers and friends, his attractiveness, and so forth. One study definitely found that the more good-looking a boy is, the more quickly he gets involved in heterosexual experiences. The same pattern was found for girls, but the correlation was less strong. Practical circumstances are important in determining at what age an adolescent will acquire sexual experience. This was pointed up by a survey showing that frequency of sexual activity is positively correlated with the availability of facilities that provide privacy for sexual contact. Incidentally, the availability of formal sex education seems to have no influence on how early or late adolescents have sexual experiences.

Menstruation

A great deal has been written about the role of menstruation in a girl's life and the problems she has in coping with her first menstruation. Detailed advice has been offered concerning what girls need to know to be prepared for their first menstruation and so forth. We will not repeat such advice. Frequently there has been an emphasis on what a tough time the average girl has in her encounters with menstruation. But we do not think the available information supports such a negative perspective. In most cultures the onset of menstruation means that a girl has become sexually mature. It means she has shifted from being a "little girl" to a young woman with the potential to produce a child of her own. A girl's first menstruation is a signal event and it has considerable significance to both her and her parents. Until fairly recently there were still a fair number of young women who received no preparation for menstruation and who therefore reacted to the sudden flow of blood as a traumatic emergency. But there has been an increasing trend for some form of preparation to occur—often from mother but also from sister, peers, books, magazines, and advertisements.

Interestingly, several surveys have shown that most girls do not get more than mildly anxious at the onset of their first menstruation. One study that asked women to recall how they felt when they initially menstruated reported that the average response was more in the direction of feeling happy than disturbed (10). Of course, each girl's level of anxiety varies not only in terms of whether she was briefed in advance about what is going to happen, but also of such things as the amount of pain and discomfort she experiences. Parents' attitudes obviously play a significant part, too. If parents respond negatively or anxiously, this can set off disturbance in their daughters. However, one study found that women quite consistently recalled both their mothers and fathers as reacting more positively than negatively when their first menstruation occurred. It has been particularly fashionable for psychoanalytic writers to highlight the negative symbolic meaning of the first menstruation and to cite cases they have known in which it resulted in panicky reactions. Early psychoanalysts have talked about the possible troubles that could ensue from the onset of menstruation because it might stir up Oedipal conflicts, fear and guilt about pregnancy fantasies, and so forth. The actuality is that most girls cope with it quite adequately and with reasonable composure.

What has increasingly become evident is that women equate menstruation with being feminine and capable of normal sexuality. Despite the discomforts many experience with each menstrual period, they value their ability to menstruate. In a study in which women were interviewed who had ceased to menstruate because conditions required the surgical removal of their uterus, it was found that there was universal mourning for the lost function. Most of the women missed the ability to menstruate. They associated this function not only with femininity but with the capability to be sexually active and responsive, as well. In short, menstruation is not the negative or threatening phenomenon that most previous "experts" (most of whom are male) envisioned.

Our main intent in spelling this out is to make clear to parents that the potential psychological threat of menstruation to the average young adolescent girl has been exaggerated. We do not mean to imply that individual girls may not get fairly upset at the onset of menstruation and also, again and again, in their future cycles. In such cases it is doubtful that any one or two primary causes for the disturbance can be specified. One cannot even say that such disturbance means that a girl is *generally* more maladjusted than other girls. By the way, this also applies to the matter of how much pain and discomfort accompany menstruation. No one has been able to demonstrate convincingly that psychologically disturbed women have more menstrual discomfort than do women who are psychologically stable (10). If your daughter is obviously upset by her menstrual functions, this is something that should be evaluated. There are many possible reasons for her anxiety. She may be alarmed by the implication that she has arrived at a new level of maturity and will be expected to take on grown-up responsibilities. She may be confused and threatened by the suddenly-increased implied closeness of sexuality in her life. She may find the bleeding from one of her body openings a threat to the integrity of her body, and so forth. Should your daughter continue to exhibit alarm with each cycle, it would probably make sense for you to consult a psychological expert and try to map out the source of her alarm. Having done this, you will be in a more rational position to decide what remedial steps you might want to take.

Myths About Female Sexuality

Parents can scarcely help taking different attitudes toward the sexual behavior of sons as compared to daughters. The sexual "double standard" is met up with everywhere. Generally, mothers and fathers are fairly positive about their adolescent sons acting sexually aggressive. They are more likely to feel that a girl should be restrained and passive in the way she expresses herself sexually. It is widely assumed that girls are less in need of sexual expression than boys, and that their sexual drives are more muted. However, as scientific information accumulates about this matter, the old assumptions do not seem to hold up. Let us consider the idea that the female gets less excited by sexual stimulation than does the male. The work of Masters and Johnson demonstrated that, physiologically, this was not true. During sexual arousal the female body registers a series of physiological changes as definite and intense as those found in the excited male. Further, Masters and Johnson observed that the female can, after one orgasm, go on more easily than the male to another round of arousal and orgasm. The female orgasm is a clear-cut phenomenon that is reflected in muscle tension build-up, accumulation of blood in the pelvic vessels, and contractions of the uterus.

Closely related to this myth that the female has less intense sexual arousal than the male is the idea that she does not respond with sexual excitement to the same range of things that the male does. For example, it was believed for some time that females do not find pictures of nudity or of explicit sexual acts at all arousing The Kinsey researchers perpetuated this myth on the basis of the answers they got from women who were straightforwardly asked if pictures with sexual themes excited them. Most of the women said no. We know now that their answers were shaped by their assumption that women are not supposed to get excited by such pictures. But interestingly, when one looks back on the Kinsey reports, one finds that, even so, *some* women did report that pictures with sexual themes were highly exciting to them (in fact, more so than to most of the men interviewed). A number of studies have since shown that women do, indeed, find visually-presented sexual themes arousing (10). The difference between males and females in the level of excitement experienced is of insignificant proportions.

Another myth concerning the sexuality of females that should be dispelled relates to the so-called superiority of the vaginal as compared to clitoral orgasm. We think it is important to discuss this issue, because it illustrates the general falsity of existing theories that presume to dictate to women (or anyone else) the "right" or "mature" way to experience sexual gratification. If parents are convinced that certain things are true concerning the nature of sexuality that actually are not so, they may allow their false premises to influence how they deal with their children. Freud and other psychoanalysts theorized that if a woman required stimulation of the clitoris to attain orgasm, she was not as mature as the woman who could reach orgasm from penile stimulation of the vagina. This theory was widely publicized and widely accepted, particularly in intellectual circles. There was never any scientific support for it. New studies have discovered that clitoral stimulation is highly important to the majority of women (10). Also, they have shown that those women who do prefer vaginal stimulation are not psychologically more mature than those preferring clitoral arousal. The real picture is quite different from the psychoanalytic image of how women function sexually.

What significance can this possibly have for parents? As we mentioned, it simply seems sensible to assume that the more inaccurate that parental understanding is of any important area of human functioning, the greater the likelihood is that parents will make unreasonable decisions about how to deal with their children's behavior in these areas. For example, a mother who is convinced that clitoral arousal is linked with immaturity may get quite upset and rigidly forbidding when she sees her daughter stroking her clitoris, but a mother who has a realistic understanding of the facts will see the situation differently. Or a parent who accepts Freud's clitoral-vaginal theory, with its assumptions that girls can become sexually mature only if they go through certain fixed stages from clitoral activity to vaginal passivity, may mistakenly worry just because his own daughter's developmental path does not seem to fit the narrow frame of reference he believes to hold true.

Becoming Feminine or Masculine

Parents usually want their daughters to be feminine and their sons to be masculine. We have found a good deal of anxiety in American parents about whether their kids will stray into deviant sex roles. Although homosexuality is becoming more accepted in our culture, it is a rare parent who does not become alarmed at the prospect that his or her child might end up as a homosexual. Parents watch their kids develop and wonder whether they are conforming to sex-role norms. Studies show that mothers are not as concerned about this issue as fathers (18). It is Dad who is especially sensitive about sexual differentiation. He is the first to complain that his son is behaving too much like a sissy or that his daughter is not acting the way a girl "should." Mothers are more likely to see their sons or daughters as "just children." We have found great differences from family to family in the degree to which they are sensitive about how masculine or feminine their kids are. Middle-class families are somewhat more tolerant of sex-role deviance than are lower-class families. A middle-class father will usually get less uptight about his son playing with a doll than will a lower-class father. Also, we have observed that in families where the father or mother had special difficulties in resolving sex-role conflicts as they were growing up, there is likely to be an extra amount of anxiety about whether the kids are acting normally in a masculine or feminine sense. Their kids sense their sensitivity and develop heightened anxiety of their own in this area.

Let us consider how children evolve a concept of their sex identity, and the factors that determine how smoothly they learn to take on either the masculinity or femininity of the parent of the same sex. One of the first steps in learning sexual identity is the simple realization "I am a girl" or "I am a boy." This understanding usually crystallizes clearly by the age of three or four (17). Interestingly, it is not accompanied by a clear understanding of the differences between female and male genitals. One study reported that in the four-through-six age range, only 50 percent of a sample of children accurately recognized genital differences. At ages seven through eight accurate recognition was 72 percent, and at ages 11 through 12 it was 86 percent. It should be added that another study discovered that girls in the younger age groups were more accurate than boys in discriminating genital differences. This was attributed to the fact that girls spend a lot of time with their mothers, are allowed to see them dress and bathe, and thus acquire a good knowledge of female genital attributes. With this knowledge they can distinguish female from male genitals (even without an accurate idea of what male genitals look like). Boys, on the other hand, are not only less likely to see their mothers nude but have few opportunities to observe the bodies of their fathers, who are usually away from home for long periods (6, 7, 10). The fact that children can see their own genitals does not meaningfully give them the information they need to distinguish male and female genitals in general. This is true because they do not, for quite some time, clearly understand their own sexual classification and the fact that it represents a general class. Apropos of this topic, we would like to mention that parents do get troubled from time to time by the fact that their young children express strong curiosity about genitals. The children may try to look at and touch their parents' genitals. They explore genital differences in their brothers and sisters and friends. They may ask a lot of questions about the whole topic. While such behavior obviously has sexual and sensuous motivations, it may also be intended by children to define themselves—to figure out what characterizes male versus female and where they themselves fit into the male-female scheme.

The shaping of the child's sexual role goes on night and day after his birth, in terms of the fact that his parents see him as either a boy or a girl. They dress him as one or the other. They express their boy-versus-girl identification by the tone of voice they use, how vigorously they handle his body, how they interpret his emotional expressions, and so forth. A beautiful example of how parents make these biased responses was provided by an experiment in which a psychologist played a tape recording of a child's voice that was ambiguous as to sex to two different groups of parents (10). One group was told that they were listening to a boy and another that the voice was a girl's. The child's voice made a series of remarks (for example, "Daddy help me" and "Mommy come look at my puzzle"). The parents were requested to imagine that they were at home with the child and to write the response they would make to each of the statements. It turned out that both fathers and mothers responded differently to the fictitious child according to which sex they had been told it was. For example, fathers were more permissive of dependency and anger when they thought the child was a girl rather than a boy. Mothers were more permissive to the child when they thought it was a boy. Just putting a sex label on the voice made all the difference. In the same vein, the sex-role shaping process is reinforced by biases in the kinds of toys parents give kids, the differences in the ways they punish boys versus girls, and even in the relative amounts of spatial mobility they allow them. Little girls learn to act "like Mama" and little boys are encouraged to be "like Daddy." But each child has his problems cut out for him as he tries to integrate all the things he experiences into a clear sense of being either masculine or feminine.

There are conflicting values in many families about what masculine and feminine mean. For example, mother may not agree with father's view that girls should be passive. Father may expect his son's masculinity to express itself in aggressiveness, whereas mother may encourage its expression in scholastic excellence. The average boy's sex-role problems are complicated by the fact that he is with his mother much more than he is with his father. He is also psychologically closer to her for a good part of his early years. This encourages him to accept her values and to be like her. But in some amazing way, not really understood, he usually manages to keep her femininity out of his personality. That is, he does so on the average. There are many cases in which his intimacy with mother is so great that he does mix up his identity with hers; he then has to struggle to deal with the femininity that has become a part of him. Our general cultural values are such that males find it alarming to have more than a trace of femininity in themselves. If they detect more, they get upset and resort to special defense strategies. For example, it is not uncommon for the male who is fighting feminine elements within himself to adopt a super-masculine, super-tough facade to prove beyond a doubt that he is an undiluted male.

There seem to be two ingredients that are most potent in deciding how clearly and smoothly a child identifies with the sex role of the parent of the same sex. They have to do with friendliness and competent power. Numerous scientific results indicate that, other things being equal, a child is more likely to identify with his same-sex parent if that parent is friendly, nurturant, and warm (9, 10, 11). The parent who is unpleasant and hostile discourages his child from wanting to be like him. So, once again, parental warmth turns up as a factor that plays a vital positive part in the child's adjustment. The second major ingredient in successful sex-role identification has to do with parental competence or power. That is, a boy is more likely to want to be like his father, or a girl to be like her mother, if the parents demonstrate that they are good at what they are supposed to be good at and capable of exerting significant influence. We have consulted with families in which children were painfully slow in working out a sex identity because the parent of the same sex was such a weak, unpleasant person. The weakness can take different forms. In one family it may be incompetence. In another it may be weakness associated with chronic illness.

We recall an instance in which a boy could not tolerate the idea of being like his father because father permitted himself to be endlessly depreciated by his wife. He could not see the point of being like his father if it meant ending up in such an exploited position. This left him confused about who should be his model. What added even further to his confusion was the fact that his mother's obvious power superiority over his father made her an attractive model. He was attracted to the idea of being like her, but this was not palatable in view of the fact that she was a woman. When we examined his responses to the Rorschach inkblot test, we could see his intense sex-role confusion expressed in such images as "woman with a man's head" and "man wearing a girl's bracelet.'' There was also serious pathology present in his Rorschach record. This was not surprising. After all, sex-role identification is such an important part of deciding who you are that difficulty in this area leaves you confused and unintegrated. In a related vein, we worked with one family in which a young girl was deeply confused about her sexual identity because her mother was chronically scared about the implications of having a female body. She was frightened by menstruation, intimidated by the idea of being vaginally penetrated, and doubtful that she could endure living through a pregnancy. Her daughter picked up her feeling that to be a woman is to get your body into a dangerous, vulnerable position.

It is an unfortunate truth that a great many people in our culture do entertain feelings of incompetence about fufilling their sex role as they define it for themselves. Very many families are populated with fathers and mothers who provide weak or uncertain sex-role models for their children. We have observed this fact in our clinical work, and similar reports have come from other sources such as sociologists and psychoanalysts. One of the difficulties in helping people with this type of problem is that they are rarely aware of their inner sense of weakness. Futhermore, the whole matter of sex identity is such a sensitive issue that people become sharply defensive when you raise questions in that area. They deny their doubts and fears. They become angry and negativistic. They turn things upside down and insist that if there is any sex-role anxiety, it is centered in their spouses and not in themselves. We have found it very difficult to resolve the brand of disturbance in families that is tied primarily to feelings of sex-role incompetence in one or both of the parents.

Homosexuality

As we commented earlier, even with the shift toward greater tolerance of homosexuality that has occurred, parents still are usually greatly shocked when their offspring choose to ally themselves sexually with persons of the same rather than the opposite sex. It is common for parents to request psychological consultation when they become concerned that a son is too feminine or a daughter too masculine (although this second instance is less frequent).

Parents and psychologists have wondered whether there are particular things parents do that turn children toward homosexuality. Freud was one of the first to construct a fairly complicated theory about the dynamics of the homosexual stance in life. We will not go into the fine details of the theory. But essentially, Freud proposed that the male child who later becomes homosexual has a pattern of early relationships with his parents such that his mother is overly close to him and his father overly hostile and distant. Freud said this pattern mirrors an unusually disturbed Oedipal entanglement between the parents and the child. It presumably results in great fear and guilt in the boy about forming a sexual relationship with a woman. The boy perceives the hostile, distant father as resenting his closeness to mother and, by implication, to any woman. He is left with the underlying conviction that if he dares to relate to a woman sexually, he will bring down the overwhelming wrath of his father upon himself. Freud indicated that this eventuates in the male child identifying with his mother instead of his father and choosing males rather than females for sexual intimacy. Freud also outlined a theory having to do with how females become homosexuals, but it was less completely spelled out than the one dealing with males. He said that the girl who eventually becomes homosexual is, like the male, caught in an unusually intense Oedipal triangle with her parents. He indicated that unlike a normal girl, she cannot resolve the Oedipal struggle by identifying with her mother and taking men as love "objects." Presumably this occurs because of certain of her mother's attitudes and also because of the fact that she finds father too frustrating and disappointing as an object of love. So, said Freud, she identifies with her father and turns to women as her source of sexual intimacy. Over the years, many studies have tried to test the validity of Freud's theories about homosexuality. Those having to do with the male have supported what he said, by and large, but those concerning the female have either been inconclusive or contradictory. At this point it would seem logical to take the position that Freud's theory, only as it deals with males, is reasonably sound. We should add that we have not been able to find any other theories of homosexuality that have been even moderately verified scientifically.

There is sufficient support for Freud's concept of how males become homosexual to discuss what implications it has for parents (1, 11). The two major elements Freud attributed to the family that creates a homosexual son are a mother who is overly close and possessive and a father who is too cold and hostile. It is perfectly logical, then, for parents who want to avoid pushing their sons in a homosexual direction to ask themselves if they are providing these two elements.Let us consider in more detail what each involves. The mother who is too close and possessive does the following sorts of things:

She makes her son feel that she is closer to him than she is to her husband.

She gives her son the concealed message that he is replacing his father as the center of affection in her life.

She tries to get involved in too many of the things her son does and thinks about.

She encourages physical intimacy with her son (for example, in terms of body exposure, sleeping together) that would normally be considered inappropriate.

She resents any show of independence on her son's part.

She encourages feelings of weakness and "I need you, Mom" in her son.

She is generally controlling and prying in her attitude toward her son.

The father of the potential homosexual boy is likely to act as follows:

He is cool, distant, and irritable when his son is in the vicinity.

He spends an unusual amount of time away from his son.

He acts jealous and competitive with his son.

He displays streaks of cruelty in his contacts with his son.

Can parents detect if they are showing such patterns of behavior? We must frankly admit that the experts will disagree in answering this question. Some would argue that the motivations and feelings involved are unconscious and that parents' needs to hide their true motives from themselves would blind them to how they are acting. We certainly agree that strong unconscious attitudes are involved. But, on the other hand, we would not discount the potential power contained in the determination of two parents of at least average intelligence who, in the name of their son's long-term future, decide to cooperate in taking stock of their own behavior. We have seen many instances in which spouses, after intense and sometimes stormy discussions with each other, have discovered irrational things they were inflicting on their kids and decided to do something about them. Sometimes this decision leads to their consulting an expert on child behavior who may be able to help them analyze the irrational pattern to which they have been committed. We have seen instances in which just a few hours of consultation were enough to produce a significant shift in parents' behaviors. More often it takes considerably longer. Unfortunately, it is true that a sizeable minority of parents do not alter their behavior even after they are shown what they are doing that is causing trouble. No specific statistics are available as to how frequently therapeutic experts have been able to get parents who encourage homosexuality in their son to change their style of responding to him. But our view is that it still makes sense for parents to find out if they are encouraging a homosexual orientation. This will provide them with a more rational basis for decisions and action.

The Tension of Not Knowing

When your kids move into adolescence and begin to establish close relationships with members of the opposite sex, a state of unusual ambiguity arises that is difficult for you and them. It is almost unheard of for adolescents to communicate with their parents openly and accurately about their evolving sexual experiences. Parents observe that their children are dating more and more frequently. They observe that they are staying out later. They observe their zest and commitment to someone with whom they seem to be on intimate terms. But they really have no idea about what kinds of sexual experiences the children are accumulating. They usually are pleased that their children are moving in the direction of mature heterosexuality, but at the same time they are concerned that they may be learning "too much" about sex and becoming sexually corrupted. This is especially true with reference to the way many parents feel about their daughters.

Parents find themselves living in a state of ambiguity about what is happening in an area of behavior that has great importance. But the rules of the game are such in our culture that they can rarely ask for information or details. They cannot directly ask what kinds of sexual experiences their kids are having. They typically confine themselves to indirect hints about the need for prudence and caution, or they utter warnings about the dangers of getting pregnant or picking up a venereal disease. Communication in this area remains stilted and fragmentary. At the same time, sons and daughters find they cannot talk openly about what is happening sexually to them. They sense their parents have great curiosity and anxiety about their sexual experiences, but they cannot respond to them. They feel they are hiding or concealing something. Obviously, this set of conditions is conducive to creating guilt. The adolescent experimenting with sexuality is inclined, without the opportunity for communication, to feel that he is acting illicitly. The daughter who has had her first experience of being touched on the genitals the night before may—especially in the face of her parents' obvious chronic expectations that she will do something too extreme sexually—feel guilty at the breakfast table the next morning. Her parents may sense her guilt and reinforce it by giving her indirect signals that they are aware she is uncomfortable.

The distrust parents feel about whether their kids are doing bad things in their heterosexual contacts creeps into their communcations in many guises. They have many different ways of telling the children that they are suspect and that they should feel guilty. Presumably the hope is that such guilt will serve as a brake to stop them from doing really bad things. We would like to convey the flavor of the guilt-provoking scripts and code references parents compose. There follows a series of the variations we have heard most often as we have listened to families.

Variation 1

MOTHER: Where did you and your friend go last night?
DAUGHTER: To a movie.
MOTHER: What time did you come home? [Mother's question immediately raises the issue whether the daughter and her boyfriend dallied somewhere and did something bad.]

Variation 2

FATHER: Where did you go last night with your friend?
DAUGHTER: To a movie.
FATHER: What kind of a family does your friend come from? [Father's inquiry implies that the daughter's date may have questionable origins and therefore that he might not be properly virtuous.]

Variation 3

FATHER: Where did you go last night with your friend?

DAUGHTER: To a movie.

FATHER: Was it one of those new sexy ones? [Father, by focusing on a sexual theme, is sidling up to the issue of whether anything sexual happened between his daughter and her friend.]

Variation 4

MOTHER: Where did you go last night with your friend?

DAUGHTER: To a movie.

MOTHER: Was anyone else with you? [Mother's remark implies that her daughter should not have been alone with her boyfriend, because of the illicit possibilities of such aloneness.]

Variation 5

FATHER: Where did you go last night with your friend?

DAUGHTER: To a movie.

FATHER: Did you do anything special after the movie? [Father's question hints that his daughter and her boyfriend did something "special" (perhaps sexually).]

Of course, the impact of any of the parental comments and questions just considered will depend partially on the amount of distrust existing between parents and their adolescent offspring, especially in the area of sexuality. It is possible that a parent could make such comments and be innocent of any intent to arouse guilt, but we have so often seen the opposite to be true. In any case, most parents can determine their own true intent with a little bit of frank introspection. What we are suggesting is that if parents observe themselves often making comments of the type we have described on the morning after their kids have been in situations with sexual potential, they should not deceive themselves about the suspicious impression they are probably creating. Teasing games develop between parents and their children when they maneuver in an atmosphere of distrust. The adolescent gets to be quite expert in detecting the concealed messages his parents direct at him. He may play their game and provocatively make remarks that magnify his potential sexual looseness. Actually, one of the best strategies for doing so is to be noncommittal and obviously vague about what he does when he is in heterosexual situations. The young girl who is very vague about what she and her boyfriend did for an entire evening can stir up a good deal of concern in her mother and father. Such teasing conjures up extreme visions of illicit sex in parents. They then probe even more clumsily, their kids feel more guilty and more hostile, and the cycle mounts. Such cycles can build up intense tension and seriously disturb a family. They not infrequently fuel differences in other areas. They intensify all of the differences in values between the one generation and the next. One study found that young adolescent girls who begin to get intensively involved in sexual activity unusually early often see themselves as having values sharply different from their parents. They feel their families are too restrictive and that they have to break away from them.

A general state of anxious vagueness about what is happening in the sexual realm may prevail for years between parents and their maturing offspring. It often places considerable strain on their relationship. It is obviously a clumsy state of affairs and mirrors the dumb, inept sexual socialization ceremonies we have adopted. Such an irrational system produces a lot of casualties. We would like to cite a few examples for which we have been consulted and which illustrate the sometimes desperate length to which parents and children go in the course of their alienation from each other. One set of parents we know became highly upset when they found letters lying around the house in which their adolescent daughter described to a friend a number of sexual "orgies" in which she had participated. The parents came for advice on what to do about their "discovery." They did not see how they could directly confront their daughter with what they "knew," and yet they felt an overwhelming need to save her. As we explored the problem, first with the parents and later with the daughter, we discovered that for years they had given her contradictory messages about sexuality. Although they had verbally emphasized rather strict puritanical moral standards, within the family they had been unusually exhibitionistic about nudity and toilet functions, creating an atmosphere charged with intimacy that had sexual connotations. The daughter had explored sexuality with boys eagerly and adventurously. But she developed a press of anxiety and guilt about it that she did not know how to handle. She did not know how to communicate to her parents her confusion about the double sexual messages they had given her and which she was acting out in her own life. It was her need to get through to them and to institute a dialogue in this area that probably resulted in her "accidentally" leaving letters around the house which they might find that described her sexual escapades.

Another example of the trouble set off by vacuous noncommunication between parents and their sexually maturing adolescent kids is that of a mother and father who asked for help with their fifteen-year-old daughter because she often demanded the right to be alone with boys in a sexually provocative situation and interpreted parental refusal to mean she was not trusted and, by implication, not loved. She would assert her right to spend hours in her bedroom with boys, with the door closed. She expected to be free to go camping with several boys and girls in the woods for a weekend without any parental supervision. When we explored the problem we discovered that she felt her parents considered her to be inferior, a failure, someone bad. As she matured sexually and began to relate to boys, she translated her feeling of being bad into the conviction that her parents would interpret her heterosexual contacts in the worst possible light—that they would perceive her as sexually bad. She became deeply concerned with their possible view of her as someone besmirched. She had no direct way of discussing this with them or clarifying the whole matter of what should be considered sexually good or evil, so she was driven to create situations which put the inescapable questions to them: "Do you think I am sexually bad? Do you disapprove of me? Do you expect me to besmirch myself?" A good part of her provocative behavior represented a paradoxical effort to break through a wall between them.

We do not have any worthwhile practical advice to give parents as to how to master the alienation between them and their adolescent children with reference to sexuality. This represents a deep division that has endured for a long, long time. It grows out of fundamental irrational images about sex in our culture. We realize that the fact that the problem is pervasive is little comfort to individual mothers and fathers, each of whom is struggling with an individual version of it.

CHAPTER 5

School: Grades, Success, Sitting Still

UP UNTIL the time they start school, children live largely inside the family cocoon. Mother and father and brothers and sisters are the prime people in their lives. The ideas and demands to which they are exposed are usually home products. It is true they may have a good deal of contact with playmates, relatives, and the assorted personages featured on their TV screens, but they can pretty well break off such contacts whenever they please. They know they can always step back over the line into the forcefield maintained by Mom and Dad.

Once a child has to attend school regularly, though, life begins to look quite different. For the first time he is required to leave home, without parental convoy, for long periods of time—whether he wants to or not. Also, he comes under the influence of people (teachers) who have a lot of power over him even though they are not members of his family. These people expose him to new ideas that may or may not agree with what his parents have said. They confine him to a fairly small amount of space and decree that he can't move around much (or at all) unless they give special permission. They watch him and keep judging how well or poorly he is doing as measured by their standards. They send home reports (grades) to his parents about his behavior and can inflict punishment if he violates their rules. Success and failure take on major importance in his life. Every known kind of test is administered to him, and the school constantly lets him know how good or bad his standing is.

Parents are usually just as upset and put under stress by these happenings as are their children. They are faced with a series of new problems and emergencies. They have to cope with the child's increased tension and anxiety. They have to help him get used to his new way of life. They are confronted with outside evaluations of their "flesh and blood" that may be disconcertingly negative. They may suddenly get messages that their children do not stack up too well against other kids. Their offspring may be described as too shy or too rambunctious or too immature. They may be labeled as limited in intelligence or as "underachievers." They may bring home ideas and attitudes that have a foreign ring. They may communicate that their teachers feel you, their parents, have not done a good job in preparing them intellectually. They try out in the school world what you have taught them and bring home repeated feedback about whether they have succeeded or failed. In so many ways, parents feel that the school is indirectly testing them through their children.

The dilemmas created by your schoolchild can seem endless. What do you do when your daughter tearfully declares she doesn't want to go to school any more? How do you persuade your son to get up fast enough in the morning so that he will not miss the school bus? How much should you directly supervise your child's studying after he has brought home several "bad" report cards? What should you do if your child bitterly complains that one of his teachers is "unfair" and the cause of his school difficulties? How do you cope with the loss of self-confidence in a child who keeps falling short in school? Is there any way to inspire a zest for success in a child who seems unmoved by the school's exhortations to achieve? In the most general sense, your child's entry into school creates difficulties for you because it signals his entry as a citizen into the outside world. Suddenly he has to deal with all those people "out there," and you are the witness of his twistings and turnings as he learns to adapt. Furthermore, not only do you have to cope with his bruised emotions but also with an upsurge in yourself of childhood memories and images concerned with what you experienced when you first plunged into the school world.

Background Ideas

It will be helpful to browse through some preliminary facts having to do with the intellectual prowess of your children and how well or poorly they will do in school.

Considerable energy has gone into tracing the intellectual development of the growing child. Strong controversy has existed for years as to whether children inherit their intelligence or build it up out of life conditions. Probably inheritance is an important component. However, there is little question that the way a child is brought up also plays a powerful part. The manner in which you relate to a child and the things you do to him will actually affect his intelligence. Also, it will influence how interested he is in the intellectual sphere and how well he can cope with different types of intellectual problems. One finds hints in the scientific literature that parents' attitudes may even play a part in whether their children prove to be more proficient in dealing with numbers as compared with words, how well they grasp spatial relationships, or how much imagination and fantasy they can bring to bear in looking for solutions. A surprising number of studies have reported correlations between parents' attitudes and the Intelligence Quotients (IQ) of their children. For example, one project that investigated four-year-old children discovered that the greater the "warmth" displayed by mothers, the greater the IQ levels of their children, and also the greater the gains in IQ over the course of a subsequent year. Another study found that the IQ levels of young boys were positively correlated with how warm and friendly their fathers were. In still another instance, it was reported that in a large group of third-grade students, the greater the "malevolence" (hostility, rejection) shown by their parents, the lower the students' IQ scores. This was especially true in the case of girls and their mothers. Incidentally, there are hints that mother's behavior may be a bit more important than father's in the child's early years in shaping his intellectual behavior (2, 22, 29, 36, 39, 43, 48, 76, 78, 95, 98).

The intellectual capability of your children is not a fixed quantity. Studies of young children over time reveal that their intellectual capabilities keep shifting and changing. This applies even to the IQ derived from standard intelligence tests. A child may show huge decreases or increases in IQ from year to year. The very early behavior of the child (for example, from birth to age three) gives you few clues as to how clever he will be in later years. Even the best "infant" intelligence tests have negligible correlations with test scores obtained with standard tests in later years. It is also interesting that the proficiency a very young child shows in dealing with simple and repetitive motor tasks has zero relationship to his later intellectual ability. His agility in putting blocks together or stringing beads does not foretell his later intellectual power. Of course, if he is seriously delayed in mastering basic life skills such as walking or talking or understanding language, this may be an early sign of mental retardation. By the age of nine or ten the child's behavior begins to be fairly predictive of how intellectually inclined he will be in high school and early adulthood. If he involves himself with intellectual things and achieves intellectual successes (good school grades, or proficiency in a "scholarly" hobby), this suggests that he will make out well in future school ventures. We would emphasize, though, that we are talking about what happens *on the average*. There are many exceptions. Some kids who perform terribly in school at age ten later become outstanding scholars. The reverse is true also. Some kids who earn high grades at age ten have little future scholastic success. In any case, there is a definite trend for kids who have a lot of achievement drive and intellectual energy to show progressive improvement in this area. They are the ones, for example, most likely to increase their IQ levels. They seem to thrive best in middle-class families where the parents are well educated and demonstrate their support for intellectuality in terms of reading, the topics they talk about, and the kinds of people they admire (78).

The boy or girl drawn to intellectual things discovers there are contradictions in moving in that direction. The American images of ideal masculinity and femininity do not headline brain power. The male hero who is romanticized in story and legend is brave and strong. The aggressive strength of his body is his most celebrated trait. Relatedly, the ideal feminine person is beautiful, physically attractive, and cutely dependent. In neither case is real value placed on the ability to think or be intellectually creative. So the boy or girl with intellectual aspirations has to come to grips with the fact that he or she does not fit the popular ideal. This is especially true in the younger years, but several studies have found that even in high school and college many girls find intellectual goals to be seriously in conflict with what the culture apparently expects of them within the framework of conventional femininity. For boys, the contradiction between the masculine ideal and intellectuality is underscored by scientific data indicating that those who are attracted to intellectual activities are often timid about using their bodies aggressively and also quite concerned about getting hurt. One study followed the development of boys from birth on to adulthood. It was repeatedly observed that those who later distinguished themselves intellectually were in their early years reluctant to enter into body-contact games (for example, football) and potentially dangerous activities (like climbing). Boys heavily involved in athletics during the age period of 10–14 years seemed to withdraw in the subsequent years from tasks that involved intellectual mastery. They did not do well academically. Once again we would like to repeat that these observations refer to averages. Many exceptions are possible. Obviously, some athletes are first rate in their schoolwork (45).

Parents need to be alert to the potential role conflicts of their intellectually inclined offspring. Their intellectual success will be tempered by their uncertainty about whether they are "real" boys or girls. Since parents often harbor the same biases about what real masculinity or femininity is, they may unknowingly contribute to the confusion. A father may, at one level, feel proud of his son's intellectual achievements, but at the same time be ashamed of his timidity in using his body aggressively. A mother may feel good about the high-level report cards her daughter brings home but cringe at the nonfeminine overtones of the forceful way she plunges into the solution of puzzles and problems. Anxiety about sex role is so deep and powerful in our culture that it is scary to parents to see "deviation" from the sexual ideal in their children. To add further to the confusion, parents also know that intellectual prowess is more and more a prime ingredient for success and getting ahead. They are caught between these conflicting standards, and so are their children. By the same token, parents who have a son who is successful athletically but who does poorly scholastically are in a similar dilemma. Probably their disappointment will increase as he grows older and the payoff for intellectual superiority increases, while that for body prowess decreases (unless he becomes a professional athlete).

We would suggest that parents will not be in a position to help their children with role conflicts tied to the potential opposition between the body and the intellect unless they are explicitly aware of the importance of these conflicts and are therefore ready to face up to them. Let us illustrate what we mean. Imagine the following conversation between a father and his son:

131

INTELLECTUAL SON: I've been doing a lot of reading about astronomy. It's really exciting. I am going to give a report in my science class. But I've had a hard time concentrating on this new book I just got from the library. There are a bunch of guys out back playing baseball and they're making so much noise I can't think straight.

FATHER: They are noisy. They probably don't have much else to do.

INTELLECTUAL SON: I've been thinking of fixing up my bicycle and taking some long rides out into the country.

FATHER: Tell me about that new book you're reading.

During this interchange the son strongly hints at his sense of conflict about being so intellectually invested rather than doing the sorts of things boys are supposed to do like playing baseball and riding bicycles. His father does not face up to the issue. He simplistically acts as if there were no conflict by downgrading what is distressing his son.

Let us rewrite the interchange so that it takes a different direction.

INTELLECTUAL SON: I've been doing a lot of reading about astronomy. It's really exciting. I am going to give a report in my science class. But I've had a hard time concentrating on this new book I just got from the library. There are a bunch of guys out back playing baseball and they're making so much noise I can't think straight.

FATHER: When you concentrate on one thing too long it can get tiring. Do you know any of the fellows playing baseball?

INTELLECTUAL SON: Sort of. But we aren't interested in the same things. You can't talk to them about science and stuff like that.

FATHER: Everyone has different interests. I guess that's one of the things that gets people mad at each other.

Here the father encourages his son to talk about his dissatisfactions and his feelings about his own orientation as compared with that of the "other fellows" who are interested in things like baseball. Father, with his comments, invites his son to explore the whole matter of conflicting perspectives and roles. His task is to make sure he encourages his son to explore the topic, but at the same time to avoid going too far and jarring him with an overly vivid confrontation with the disturbing issue.

We think this is a much more common problem in middle-class families than is usually realized. It is also a particularly important one, because it is especially likely to involve children who in later life will become the intellectual and scientific leaders of the community.

Achievement

The message every child gets loud and clear as he enters the school system is that achievement is one of the biggest ingredients of life. He is endlessly exhorted to learn, to master, to show that he is as good as or better than his student colleagues. There are few situations as competitively focused on achievement as is the typical school. But children differ radically in how prepared they are for such competition. Some are already highly revved up for achievement; others are limply passive. It is doubtful that any child can make his way successfully through the educational maze unless he can be aroused to a certain pitch of competitiveness. He has to have a fair amount of lust for achievement or he will not do well. Achievement drive is especially important if he intends to go to college and bid for the limited spaces in medical schools and other graduate specialities.

Psychologists have been fascinated with what makes people want to achieve. They have invented various ways to measure how interested an individual is in winning and getting ahead. One of the most widely used achievement measures is based on asking people to compose imaginative stories about pictures and then to ascertain how much of the story imagery refers to themes of success and coming out on top (61). Such achievement scores have often been found to predict school grades and different areas of school performance. They also predict success in other competitive situations. One well-known psychologist has even presented evidence that the productivity and output of entire nations may depend on the achievement drives of their respective citizens.

All sorts of interesting details have been uncovered by investigators that highlight the ways in which achievement motives permeate a person's life. For example, it has been reported that high-achieving persons are so concerned with using their time profitably that they fall into the habit of setting their watches "ahead." In this way they can be sure not only that they won't be "late" but also that they will have a time edge on others. Those with high versus low-achievement motivation also differ with respect to such diverse things as how they play games, the kinds of people they like, their favorite colors, how long they will stick it out in a tough situation, and their attitudes toward themselves. There is little question but that a child's feelings about achievement will color not only his school career but also various other features of his life.

Tension between parents and children is expressed very often in the achievement arena. So many wrangles have to do with the fact that kids do not live up to their parents' expectations of success. There is a dramatic upsurge of tension in families when kids go back to school in the fall and fail to achieve what the school expects. This is often what triggers parents into seeking help with their child-rearing dilemmas from outside experts. The typical dilemma involves a child who seems to be of adequate intelligence but who is doing poorly in school because he does not put more than minimal effort into his school assignments. Sometimes the situation is even more extreme and the child has stopped doing his schoolwork altogether—or may be openly refusing to go to school. The parents are alarmed because their child is failing and is displaying a brand of passivity that does not bode well for the future. They want to know what they can do to get him ''motivated'' and competitively invested. We have encountered many tricky family patterns that can stir up such achievement crises in children. They range widely. Quite commonly, one simply finds that the parents are, for their own reasons, so frightened of failure that they have pushed their kids too hard to be big achievers and as a result have stirred up so much resentment in them that they are in a state of revolt, balking at doing anything that even faintly smacks of success. We have also seen instances in which the failing child is the family scapegoat and labeled as the nonentity who messes up anything he undertakes. He is expected to display no achievement interests, and he obliges. We have seen even more esoteric patterns. In one family the child's passivity was a technique for reassuring his jealous father that he had no intention of competing with him. In another case a child's passivity in school was a reflection of depression and discouragement, related to the fear that his parents were about to separate and leave him without a real home base in the world.

Psychologists have tried to find out the parental attitudes that normally encourage or discourage achievement in their children (6, 12, 20, 27, 34, 41, 46, 61, 62, 63, 64, 68). Several points have been verified. (However, most of the scientific findings in this area have been based on the study of boys. While some aspects have been confirmed for girls, it should be kept in mind that there is a difference with respect to the two sexes.) One general finding offered by psychologists is that high achievement seems to be encouraged by mothers who begin early to expect their children to take responsibility and to master tasks. They expect their children to try new things without asking for much help, to make decisions for themselves, to have interests and hobbies of their own, to be able to undress and go to bed by themselves, to do regular tasks around the house, and so forth. Secondly, such achievement-encouraging mothers are not *overly* restrictive or authoritarian. They do not restrict just to show they are in command. They expect early mastery of tasks, but the training they give is not designed to "put down" or prove their dominance. Their expectations of mastery do not reflect a concealed unfriendliness or intent to reject. They do not represent an effort to get rid of burdens imposed by having children.

One investigator carried out a study in which he compared the ways parents of high versus low-achievement-oriented sons (ages 9 through 11) interact with their children. A situation was set up in which each son was blindfolded and told to build a tower with blocks. But he was also told he could only use one hand. This was done to make him rather dependent on his parents, who were in the room with him. The parents were told their son was being tested to see how well he could build things and that they could say anything they wanted to him, but that they could not touch the blocks. An analysis of parental behavior in this situation (and also others of a related kind) indicated that the parents of the high achievers gave all sorts of messages that they expected higher levels of performance than did parents of low achievers. Further, they displayed more warmth (happy, anxiety-relieving, laughing-joking behavior). This was especially true in comparing the *mothers* of high and low achievers. Such behavior fits the observation of another study, that mothers of high-achieving sons are especially likely to hug and kiss them when they succeed at something. It should be added, however, that the mothers of the high achievers in the present study were also more "pushing" than were the mothers of the low achievers. In contrast, this trend was *reversed* for the fathers: the fathers of high-achieving boys were less pushing and dominating.

If a mother starts to expect a lot of high achievement very early (before age four), this does not stimulate long-term interest in achievement. In fact, such behavior has an effect opposite to that intended. It has a squelching impact. The ways in which parents impose high-achievement demands on very young children can be quite varied and also, at times, well concealed. Many overly pushy parents are innocent about what they are doing. They are convinced they are only trying to produce a superior product. We have known parents who used such strategies as the following to urge their "babies" onward and upward:

1. One mother made it clear to her four-year-old son that she expected him to be fully responsible for anything that happened to his baby brother whenever she was not around.
2. A mother expressed frustration and anger to her four-year-old daughter because the child was not able to read well enough.
3. A father communicated irritation to his three-year-old son because he would not stick to the little projects he undertook with certain toys or games, but instead preferred to keep shifting his activities.
4. A father persistently interrupted his four-year-old son when he talked, suggesting "better" words that would presumably improve his vocabulary.

The overly high expectations in such parental behavior are obvious.

We would propose that by their own behavior parents can also put forward high-achievement imagery that makes a strong suggestive impression on their children even at a very early age. The mother who works hard around the house and who does not spare herself a moment for relaxation cannot help but communicate her high-achievement outlook. This would likewise hold true for the father who comes home from his job and then spends most of his time invested in work activities. It is also possible that parents convey achievement goals to quite young children by what they say to each other and the themes that predominate in their conversation. How much do they talk about such things as work, getting ahead, success versus failure, the waste in relaxation, and their admiration for people who are outstanding examples of high achievement? How much do they derogate "taking it easy" and praise big output?

In actual fact, high achievement in children is probably most likely to be encouraged by *moderate* pressures toward goals like responsibility and autonomy. Extremes of parental behavior in these areas more often result in low-achieving offspring. For example, mothers who have unusually intense achievement drives seem to shape low-achieving sons. They push too hard. It has turned out also that very dominating fathers inhibit the growth of achievement behavior in their sons. They seem to make them overly dependent and unsure of themselves. This has been shown to be true not only in the United States but also in other countries (for example, Turkey). Thus it appears that *highly* dominating behavior by either parent interferes with the development of achievement drives in their children. The opposite extreme that also gives rise to low achievement in boys is an attitude of parent indulgence, which tells the child that he does not have to meet any real standards of excellence. He learns that things will be done for him and that he can get along with a minimum of self-exertion.

We would emphatically repeat what we have just said: parents who go too far in one direction or the other in their achievement attitudes discourage "getting ahead" behavior in their children. Those who expect too much and those who expect too little from their kids have a similar effect. Of course, a key question that arises is, how do you know whether you are expecting too much or too little? We would suggest that it is possible to make roughly accurate judgments about this matter. First of all, most parents can draw on a whole lifetime of experience in which they have had the chance to observe the achievement standards of many other people, including their own parents. In fact, the pooled experiences of both husband and wife are available, and this doubles the amount of information they can consult. What is essential is that there be a genuine desire to use such information. If seriously interested, parents of average intelligence are capable of appraising the achievement standards they set and comparing them with the standards applied by various other people they have known. They are quite capable of finding out if they are expecting a good deal more or less than other parents do. We have witnessed this again and again in our clinical work with families. Mothers and fathers who have played dumb about their extreme achievement demands quickly show that they can sensibly evaluate what they are doing once they are persuaded that this will help them to deal with some problem that has been plaguing them.

Another important source of information available to parents about whether they are making reasonable achievement demands is the simple fact of how their kids behave when there are things to do. It does not take long to detect whether they have a zest for accomplishment. If they seem to prefer passively sitting around or if they exhibit a lot of stubborn resistiveness when accomplishment is called for, this should alert you to the possibility that you are too extreme (in one direction or the other) in what you are expecting.

Doing Well in School

Many ingredients go into how well your children fare in school. Their intelligence level plays a part. The intensity of their achievement drive has an effect. Also involved are such things as their reaction to being confined and restricted in classrooms for long periods of time, their amount of interest in intellectual as compared to muscular kinds of activities, their general level of emotional stability, and the adequacy of their teachers. At this point, we would like to focus on what is known about how parents' attitudes and practices affect their children's school success. What typifies parents whose kids get high grades in school? What characterizes parents whose kids get low grades? We were able to locate a number of scientific studies concerned with these questions.

We discovered that the child's academic success is tied to several of the same aspects of parent behavior as hold true for the child's emotional stability. Quite consistently, studies have shown that kids who get high grades in school have warmer and friendlier parents than those who get low grades. Psychologists have demonstrated this by interviewing and evaluating parents of a variety of kids (6, 17, 31, 33, 50, 72, 86, 94, 98). They have also found it to be true when they used techniques to find out how warm and friendly the child himself perceives his parents to be. One such study assessed boys' feelings of closeness to mother by asking them to place miniature figures of an adult woman and a male child on a background in any way they preferred. Previous work had indicated that the closer these figures were put to each other, the closer the child felt to his mother. In this instance it was found in two different groups of boys that the higher their grades and the greater their knowledge of several school subjects, the closer they placed the miniature mother and child figures. Relatedly, it has been demonstrated that kids with good grades feel psychologically more allied with the parent of the same sex than do kids who get low grades. They feel more identified with that parent and find it easier to use that parent as an example or model. The value of parental friendliness in encouraging school achievement has been detected in different social classes and in both black and white populations.

Children who see their parents as largely disapproving and who expect authority figures to specialize in doing negative things to them do not adjust well to the school world. Their teachers describe them as acting "immature" and "inefficient" in the classroom. One particularly well-thought-out study found that mothers of children who earned high grades in school were unusually "warm" toward their children and allowed them "free expression of aggression." It found too that the fathers of such children made sparing use of physical punishment and put energy into encouraging academic success. Interestingly, while the fathers of high-achieving children were noted to offer praise to them for work well done, they did so sparingly rather than "very frequently." They did not go to the extremes of either offering no praise or pouring out great gushes of it. Some of the material uncovered in this study was amazingly pinpointed. For example, children who obtained high grades in English came from homes in which the fathers made low use of discipline and high use of reason, but children who did well in mathematics were noted to have fathers who rarely offered reward and praise. These findings cannot at present be explained. They are, of course, only tentative and await further verification.

In our clinical work we have intimately followed the school career of one child who approached each day of school as a quasi-nightmare. To him school was a place of pain and crisis. His parents were people who believed in tight control. They also believed in fairly severe punishment for violations of their rules. He came to see them largely as dispensers of unpleasantness. Generalizing from such experiences, he assumed that most adults were going to be "hard." When he entered the world of school, staffed by adults who were apparently obsessed with exacting obedience from him, he immediately surrendered. He felt he was in for an inexorable bad time and he turned all of his energies to just surviving. He had very little energy left over for learning and the mastery of school assignments. His school career dwindled into disaster. His experiences with his parents so sensitized him to the negative aspects of his encounters with his teachers that he never had a chance to open himself to the more positive aspects.

Parents who overly sensitize their children to the possibility of being attacked and criticized often do so by creating an image of life as a place where you are always waiting for your next reprimand. Their own frustrations stimulate them to watch for people to do the wrong thing and then to pounce indignantly on them. This "I've caught you in the act" attitude makes the child feel that his life is a string of episodes in which he will end up as the villain. Parents may adopt such a strategy without knowing it. They so skillfully conceal from themselves what they are doing that they do not understand what is happening. One set of parents we know presented their criticisms in the context of "We really love you and while the things we are saying to you sound negative, they aren't. We are only trying to help you." The eternally critical parent can convince himself that he is only trying to make his children aware of their mistakes so that they can correct and perfect themselves.

Another skillful way of concealing persistent criticism is to make it nonverbal. There are parents who rarely express their criticisms in words. If one tape-recorded their interchanges with their children, there would be no evidence of their negative attitudes. But if one had taken pictures, one could see all of the disapproving signals they were sending. Every parent has a rich vocabulary of gestures, eye movements, grimaces, and body postures that can communicate displeasure. A child may, for example, quickly learn that when his mother starts averting her gaze from him, she is angry and disapproving of what he is doing at that moment. Or he may come to understand that when his father stiffens his neck and tightens the muscles around his mouth he is declaring "I don't like what you are doing." This is not mere speculation. There are careful studies in which the transactions of family members have been filmed. When the films were minutely analyzed, it was obvious that each member had fairly consistent unspoken ways of telling the others what he liked and disliked. Anyone who has ever lived in a family knows intuitively that such is the case. It is quite possible for a child to be put down over and over again by his parents without hearing one nasty word from them. What is especially striking is that although the child recognizes he is being attacked, the parents may be quite unaware what they are doing. People have little insight into the ways in which their body postures and gestures convey meaning to others. In any human contact, the verbal interchange is only a part, sometimes a small one, of what each is truly communicating to the other.

A third means that parents not infrequently use to conceal their criticisms involves "displacement." A father may hear his son say a series of things of which he disapproves. But instead of openly revealing his negative opinions about them, he turns thumbs down on numerous unrelated minor things that come up. The son will probably sense what his father is doing; he will feel discomfort and detect that he is somehow under attack, but will have trouble defining the true reason for the attack. The following dialogue illustrates the displacement form of criticism.

SON: We have so much homework! I'm tired of doing homework every day, I'm going to watch television for a while.
FATHER: (Feels angry at son's antagonistic attitude toward school, but determines not to say anything critical. So, he makes a casual, apparently polite comment.) What program are you going to watch?
SON: I think I'll try that new adventure program about policemen.
FATHER: Oh, another one of those shoot-em-up things. Don't you ever get tired of them? (Said in a half laughing, satirical tone.)

Father's jab at the television program is really a jab at his son for being so negative about school. We think that a great many criticisms are launched by parents in this fashion. Of course, children learn quickly to use the same technique on their mothers and fathers. We have also noticed that parents who rely a lot on displacement stubbornly resist examining what they are doing. They vehemently deny that their criticisms of minor issues have anything to do with their negative feelings about other, more important matters. They are indignant that anyone would consider them capable of such deception. We have gone off on this tangent about parental strategies for venting criticism because we want to give substance to the general idea that parents can, with little or no awareness of what they are doing, expose their offspring to persistent criticisms that eventually lead them to expect the worst in most of their encounters with adults (especially those, like teachers, who have controlling power over them).

Since parental friendliness helps children to do well in school, it is not surprising that some evidence has been found that the following kinds of investments by parents facilitate their children's intellectual effectiveness:

1. Being willing to devote time to their children by talking to them and giving them attention when they ask for it.
2. Devoting energy to guiding their children intellectually—for example, by considering toys that are most appropriate or reading books to them regularly.
3. Investing in the idea and the hope that their children will achieve—for example, by giving them the idea that they should do their best or aim for

some definite educational goal like completing high school or going to college.

4. Accepting the view that various outside resources (like nursery school or expert tutors) should be pressed into service to help their children.

Another thing that psychologists have uncovered is that the mothers and fathers of kids successful in school are less divergent from each other in their views than are the mothers and fathers of kids who are unsuccessful. Parents of the successful kids are more likely to have similar values and to agree in their opinions of their children. In other words, they are more tuned in to each other. We would remind you that the same thing holds true for parents of stable as compared to disturbed children. Disturbed kids often come from families in which mother and father are at odds and out of phase with each other. We are tempted to conclude, from these and other findings we have described, that children who do well in school are often those who are least burdened by having to live with unfriendly and inharmonious parents. It is well known that people do not learn or concentrate efficiently when they are uncomfortable. If you leave for school in the morning with the lingering bad taste of your parents' anger and your tense contacts with them, you are not in the right mood for complex and fancy thinking. But if you go off to school feeling good, you have more free energy upon which to draw.

However, at this point we would like to call your attention to a paradoxical contradiction of what we have just said. Observations of children who have shown themselves to be *outstandingly* creative or superior in a special area have revealed that such children do not experience their parents as friendly and harmonious (49, 87). In fact, they seem to come from families in which there is a lot of disagreement and in which there is little emphasis on being nice. One study of college students who had high potential for creativity indicated that they were likely to describe their parents as more rejecting than loving when they were growing up. Students with limited creative ability were more inclined to describe their parents as loving. Another study of the parents of very creative young children demonstrated that they were unusually critical of each other and divergent in their values.

In trying to explain such findings, psychologists have noted that in order to be unusually creative you have to be very independent and even rebellious in your attitudes toward what is conventional and acceptable. They suggest that this brand of rebelliousness is more likely to develop in contacts with antagonistic parents than with those who are nurturantly friendly. It has also been speculated that if you grow up in a household where there is a lot of conflict and tension, and if you survive that ordeal relatively intact, you may emerge with an unusually intricate and strong personality. That is, you are tempered by all the complications you coped with and are therefore well-prepared to advance creatively and independently. By way of contrast, the kid who gets good grades and adapts well in school (but who is not independently creative) can be an extreme conformist. He excels in doing what is expected by teachers. It is interesting, in this respect, that it has been actually shown that highly creative children are not necessarily those who have the highest intelligence quotients or get high school grades. Many highly creative inventors and artists had poor formal school careers. Not a great deal is known about what fosters creativity in children. But we think it is important to call to your attention that high achievement in school and creativity are not synonymous, and that they may possibly be called forth by quite different family conditions.

Finally, even if it is obvious, it should be added that the child's parents affect his school behavior quite directly on the basis of who they are and the values for which they stand. In general, parents of middle income are more supportive of their children's school efforts than are parents in the lower income range. Ethnic, religious, and racial groups may differ radically in how much importance they assign to their children being well educated. A few studies have even shown that children whose fathers are in certain occupations behave differently in school from children whose fathers are in other occupations. For example, sons of office workers have been described as acting unusually shy in class, while sons of dentists have been depicted as acting in a rather aggressive and disruptive way. Daughters of teachers have been judged by teachers as above average in "stable behavior" in school. The very fact that a father is identified with a specific occupation can apparently influence his kids' style of behavior in school.

Sitting Still and Moving Around

Again and again we have encountered children who repudiate school as a way of life because it is too confining. To be forced to sit still all day within four walls is a tough assignment for the average restless kid. He has to lock the excitement in his muscles and keep himself relatively immobile. We have noted that this is especially frustrating to kids who are athletically inclined. There seem to be differences among certain children from the day they are born with reference to how much motoric activity they need. Some quickly reveal themselves to be restless and activated, while others can quite comfortably remain still and placid. So many children get into trouble in school (and elsewhere) because of their need to keep moving and to respond impulsively that the concept of the "hyperactive child" was coined. Many more boys than girls get this label. Typically, the "hyperactive child" is referred for treatment because he upsets people by his restless and pushy behavior. He hurls himself into situations. He often acts like a daredevil. He takes risks (by climbing, jumping) in a way that gives the message "I don't care if I get hurt." He upsets people because he won't stick to the usual limits and boundaries. His pressure toward movement dominates. His teachers complain that he won't stay in his seat, that he is "wriggly," that he won't stop talking. No one really knows what causes such behavior. It has been diversely attributed to "minimal brain damage," genetic factors, and disturbance within the family. It has just as diversely been treated with drugs, behavior therapy, and psychotherapy (8, 9, 90, 96).

So many parents have by now heard about the "hyperactive child" that they get really alarmed when they detect signs of hyperactivity in their own children. They have read all sorts of myths in the popular press about what these signs bode. It is true that there is a tendency for the most extreme hyperactive kids to end up in trouble. But except for this extreme group, most hyperactive children eventually adapt reasonably well. One important study followed children from birth into early adulthood. It discovered that boys who are hyperactive shortly after birth continue to be so during a good part of childhood. Further, it was observed that they displayed a lot of aggression and physical boldness. They (and their mothers) consistently underestimated their intellectual ability. Also, the mothers often reacted to them in a critical, disapproving way and imposed tough penalties for disobedience. What is of special importance, though, is that hyperactive boys eventually got just as good grades in high school and college as did more placid boys. For the girls who participated in this study, a rather different picture emerged. They were not as consistently high or low in hyperactivity as boys. They could be hyperactive in the first few years after birth but then change in the subsequent few years. Also, in contrast to the boys, the hyperactive girls did not seem to evoke unusually negative or critical attitudes from their mothers; further, they did not—as opposed to the hyperactive boys—see themselves as low in intellectual power. This study and others indicate that hyperactivity is a matter of degree, and that only the most extreme cases do poorly in the long run. As time passes the problem is usually mastered. What is called hyperactivity usually gets blended into a forceful, energetic style of personality. One researcher found that hyperactive boys are inclined to end up as particularly strong and masculine individuals.

Many of the problems of hyperactive kids grow out of the fears and mismanagement of their parents. If mothers and fathers consider their "hyperactive" son to have some dread, incurable syndrome, they will treat him as if he were a sure-fire failure without any future. They will communicate their deep disappointment to him, and also their great anxiety. They have a way of going to extremes, either becoming terribly overcontrolling or foolishly overpermissive. The gushing energy of the overactive boy seems to be especially trying to mothers. They apparently get very angry about their inability to exert control and to set limits. In their desperation to "do something" about their whirling-dervish child (often because the school is complaining so loudly about his conduct), many parents allow extreme things to be inflicted on him in the name of treatment. Many children have been put on extended courses of drug treatment that have dubious validity. There are drugs that will quiet some hyperactive children down and help them to behave better in school, but this has to be weighed against the potential harm of raising a child who comes to believe that he can behave acceptably only when he is bolstered by the intake of a drug. For what it is worth, our clinical experiences with hyperactive children who have been given drugs for long periods to control them have been uniformly negative. We have found such children to have serious doubts about their ability to control themselves. They seem to have a hazy notion of their own identity. They wonder what part of themselves is genuine and what part represents the drug effect.

As we mentioned, no one has yet scientifically determined what causes extremes of hyperactivity. It remains for future work to provide more dependable information. But we would like to offer our impression that psychological problems within the family can play a part. In a number of the cases we have treated in which extreme hyperactive behavior was prominent, we have found that the parents had unusually intense conflicts about controlling versus releasing impulses, and that these conflicts predated the arrival of the child. One could see from their histories that the parents had long felt that they could not be their true selves—that they had to bind and inhibit themselves. They were tempted in their daydreams and fantasies to break loose and to blow off steam. But, typically, they had been raised to respect self-control and formal restraint. They could not allow themselves the freedom of real spontaneity. As we interpret it, they communicated their conflicts to their offspring and, at some level, incited them to act out what they were afraid to do. In other words, they unconsciously encouraged them to "let go" and to revolt against restraint. Thus the hyperactivity of children could be traced back to a problem that had long troubled the parents. We have succeeded in reducing extreme hyperactivity in several children by discussing with the parents and the child this theme of restraint versus letting go, and by uncovering how this issue was translated into parental attitudes and behavior. But only systematic future studies, of course, can establish whether such an approach would generally be of therapeutic value to hyperactive children.

Test Anxiety

In the modern school the child finds that he is tested, retested, and retested again, day after day. Most adults have blurred memories of this testing process. They have pretty much forgotten what it was like. The truth is, most schoolchildren are made to feel almost every day that they are potentially on the edge of failure. They are made to feel they are on trial. It is quite natural that they should react with a lot of negative emotion to such stress. Huge numbers of kids go to school every day feeling scared. They have stomach-aches, tense muscles, headaches, and many of the other symptoms that anxiety can generate. Their anxiety also makes them irritable and reluctant to get to school on time, and tempts them to stay home at every opportunity. It has, in most instances, a negative effect on the ability to cope with school tasks, particularly test-taking. A kid who is scared will generally do less well on a test than he should in terms of his actual abilities. (It should be added that anxiety can also act as a spur that facilitates performance. A certain minimum of anxiety about doing well may motivate kids to study thoroughly and to put an extra bit of energy into responding to test questions.)

We would like to focus on the child who is much too anxious when he takes tests. He tends to do poorly. He makes his parents feel frustrated with his poor performance and at the same time worried about his distress. A number of studies have shown that children with high test anxiety are inclined to be anxious about other aspects of the world also (21, 35, 83, 94). They were observed to be especially concerned about getting hurt. They perceive their own bodies as weak and vulnerable. One investigator actually found that boys with high test anxiety exceed those with low anxiety in frequency with which they feel sick. Another characteristic that seems to go along with high test anxiety is an attitude of self-blame and self-derogation. The highly anxious child has little respect for himself. He sees himself as inferior. When things go wrong he is inclined to assume it's all his own fault. He is negative and cruel in his approach to himself. But at the same time he tends to be erratically hostile to others. His frustration results in displays of temper. He may blow up erratically at one parent or the other.

Apparently, one of the things typical of the highly test-anxious child (especially a boy) is his concern with winning the support of adults. He wants to feel that adults approve of him and that they are quickly available to help him if he runs into a harsh problem. In the classroom he does things that will give the teacher the message that he has good intentions and therefore should be liked and supported. In one study, high-anxiety boys were noted to ask their teachers questions in a way that would not only attract their attention but also communicate the sentiment, "See, I am very interested in what you have to say. I want to make contact with you. I want to have a special bond with you." It has also been found that the parents of such children encourage dependence and a sense of not being able to make it on one's own. These parents are depicted as rather nosy. While they are inclined to be "good-intentioned" people who emphasize that they want to help their kids, they have a way of bringing out the children's weaknesses. They seem not to be able to set limits on them or to tolerate their suffering unpleasantness. They have a way of stepping in and trying to patch things up. They offer too much advice and act as if the child cannot solve his problems unless he first consults Dad and Mom. Their need to be protective is reflected in the fact that they infrequently separate from their children. They are loathe to go off on trips that would result in their being out of contact with them for any length of time. It was specifically found in one study that the fathers of high-anxiety boys were less often away overnight than were fathers of low-anxiety boys. At a more general level, there is evidence that parents of high-anxiety children are inclined to be guarded and proper in their demeanor. They are concerned with making a good impression. When interviewed, they are careful to avoid talking about anything that might reflect negatively on them. They evade spontaneity that might give away what is going on inside of them. Their defensiveness results in their hiding even from themselves how they feel. It also prevents them from seeing their own children accurately. They gloss over their children's deficiencies and do not face up to how insecure they are.

Parents who have children who report that they get awfully scared by tests may profit from giving thought to how they may be contributing to the problem. They should do so very early in their children's school careers, because their efforts in this respect are more likely to pay off if instituted before the children get rigidly set in their anxious outlook. We would suggest that such parents may profit by focusing especially on the issue of whether they are treating their kids as if they are fragile and unable to solve problems without help. It may be helpful to allow their kids to wrestle with problems on their own even when they seem distressed. We are obviously not proposing that parents not help their kids, but rather that they permit them to experience what it is like to try mastering difficulty on their own and to discover that the effort does not dissolve them.

Incidentally, we would like to add that teachers could help parents by quickly reporting to them when they detect unusual anxiety in their pupils in test situations. They may be aware of a child's anxiety quite some time before the parents are. Their observations may be especially helpful when a bright child is involved who does well in school despite his anxiety. Parents whose children come home with good report cards may not conceive that the children could feel scared in school.

Homework

School and home contact each other intimately in children's homework assignments. As soon as kids get beyond the elementary grades, teachers begin seriously to extend the schooling process into their home life. Kids are then expected to spend part of the afternoon or evening at home mastering problems that teachers have devised. They experience a lot of frustration over this extension of school control into their hitherto private lives. Parents do too. Suddenly they become live witnesses of how their children deal with school matters and respond to school assignments. They witness just how their children operate. They can see whether they are interested or motivated or conscientious. They get a clear glimpse of how scholastically smart or quick they are. This means they can't avoid passing judgment on their school skills. They start to tell their kids about these judgments and to put pressures on them to do this or that. Of course, they are also given the opportunity to express positive and encouraging sentiments. At the same time, the kids find they are unexpectedly in a position to involve their parents in their school lives in a new, intimate way. Their homework assignments give them a chance to call on their parents for advice and help and even to make them partially responsible for how well the work gets done.

In our experience, the most common form of tension generated between parents and children with regard to homework has to do with who is responsible for it. On the face of it, there is no question but that the child is held responsible by the school for his homework assignments. But in millions of homes, miniature dramas occur each day in which quite a different perspective gets acted out. The truth is that untold numbers of parents get so concerned about whether their children will do well in school that they begin to share anxiously in their homework tasks. They watch their kids to see if they are doing their homework regularly and devoting enough effort to it. They may literally spend a good deal of time doing some of the work. They may insist on checking the homework assignment after their child completes it.

Let us consider some typical statements by parents to their children in which they deliver the message that they have actually taken over responsibility for their homework.

You can't go out and play until you do your homework.
Let me check your work before you put your notebook away.
How can you do your school work while you're watching television?
Get off the telephone and do your homework.
I will increase your allowance next month if you get a B average in your
    homework assignments this month.
Your homework looks sloppy to me.
I am going to talk to your teacher about what we can do to get you to
    take your homework more seriously.

What happens gradually in many cases is that the child correctly perceives that his parents have taken over the responsibility for his homework. He sees that they do not trust him to get the job done on his own. He grasps that they are so anxious about the entire matter that they are moving in on his role. It is our impression that, at one level, many children enjoy this kind of support. It relieves them of the pressure of responsibility. But at another level, they feel pushed around and manipulated. They are somewhat resentful that their parents assume they can't carry their own load. We have been asked to consult with families in which the parent-child homework pattern had spiraled into an aggravating contest. What we have typically found is that the child who feels his parents don't trust him to do well on his own decides that he will let them take over completely. He stops doing his homework or only goes through the motions. He gives his parents the message that the only way the work will get done is if they check on him continuously or if they actually do it for him. They get furious at his behavior and impose an array of exotic penalties. Often they threaten that unless he does his homework he will not be able to go out and play or to watch television. His response is to become even more stubbornly passive. He understands that their anxiety about his homework is greater than his own. In extreme cases the parents or older brothers and sisters finally surrender and faithfully devote a chunk of time each night to getting the problem child's homework assignment completed.

It is our view that one of the root causes of this sort of dilemma lies in the parent's original inability to tolerate weakness or failure in one of their offspring. They are so insecure and so much in need of the sweet smell of success that they cannot stand even momentary failure in someone with whom they are closely identified. They take over a territory that does not belong to them. Of course, it is beyond question that all children get fed up with homework from time to time and may need prodding to ensure that they will do their duty. But there is a difference between prodding and the message "You can't handle this and we are taking over." The child has to learn that if he does not do his work, he, rather than his parents, has the most to lose. Incidentally, it is also true that once parents have annexed the child's homework as their territory, he can no longer derive positive satisfaction from success in that area. If he gets a good homework grade he knows it belongs to his parents. This blocks the possibility of his developing an enthusiasm based on earning praise and honor from his teachers.

Since homework is something that is assigned, that is done regularly, and that requires careful, accurate devotion, it can easily come to stand for all of the demanding, compulsive aspects of life. It can, in essence, represent to the child the whole concept of being controlled. It can symbolize the opposite of freedom and spontaneity. Since it extends into the home the same obligation to sit and be physically inactive that he encounters in school, it is often identified with a sense of being closed in. The average parent probably underestimates the discomfort of such restraint. He may not understand how resentful it makes his kids feel. The chronic complaint of the average student that he "has too much homework" may be justified. We have wondered from time to time whether the educational Establishment has given sufficient thought to the cumulative negative effects of imposing long hours of homework on kids day after day. The negative attitudes induced toward school and learning may outweigh the immediate advantages of being able to cover an extra amount of material each semester. This is an issue that deserves scientific probing. It is a highly important one, because it bears on the possible hidden gripes of entire generations of former students toward brainwork and scholarly effort. Also, it may prematurely discourage attachment to intellectual pursuits in those who, for temperamental reasons, cannot stand being "locked in."

In many cases—since doing homework can easily represent the compulsive, duty side of life—it lends itself well to becoming the focus of disputes between parents and children who have long-standing antagonisms about obedience and control. There are families in which parents have chronically met resistance in their attempts to make their kids obedient. They have not been able to get their kids to eat the way they "should" or to control their sphincters the way they "should" or to sleep on schedule as they "should." Their most decisive battles on this theme may be fought out over homework issues. Such battles usually leave both sides distressed and angrily frustrated. As mentioned earlier, there has been a tendency for child psychologists and psychiatrists to regard the tensions linked to school problems as being of secondary importance. But anyone who has witnessed the abrupt rise in family distress that occurs so frequently when school resumes after the summer vacation cannot easily acquiesce to this view.

Reading

One skill fundamental to a school career is the ability to read well (11, 16). In the first two or three grades, a majority of failures can be traced to poor reading ability. Even by the eighth grade, as many as 25 percent of failures seem to be tied to reading inadequacies. Surveys indicate that eight to 15 percent of the total school population have varying degrees of reading disability. It is also interesting that many more boys have trouble with reading than do girls. The ratio of boys to girls with reading problems may be as great as two to one. No one knows why this dramatic sex difference exists.

The child who has a lot of trouble reading stirs up trouble. He is a burden on his teacher. He does poorly in school and is therefore exposed to repeated experiences of failure. This in turn makes him feel unhappy. There is some fairly good evidence that just being a poor reader in an average school setting is enough to make a child feel tense, irritable, and defensive. Obviously, all of this trouble reflects back on the child's parents, and they grow worried about what can be done to relieve him. There is often a temptation for the parents to put the entire blame on the school. They angrily demand to know why their tax money is being wasted to hire teachers who cannot do something as simple as teach a kid how to read. However, as research results concerning reading difficulties have been disseminated and it has become obvious that the teacher is not necessarily to blame, parents have reached for explanations (and been abetted by glib articles in popular magazines) that will relieve both them and the child of any responsibility for the problem. It has become fashionable for intellectual parents to attribute their children's reading problems to mysterious kinds of "brain dysfunction," "poor right-left differentiation," and vaguely specified defects in the "body scheme." Skilled hucksters have been selling parents on such ideas and offering expensive courses that will presumably produce dramatic cures.

The research dealing with the actual causes of reading problems has shown they are multiple, with some directly traceable to parent behavior and some not. Visual problems, such as difficulty in coordinating both eyes, may play a part. Interestingly, hearing impairment has been noted in some cases to interfere with the process of learning how to read. A number of investigators have reported that to an important degree, emotional disturbance can also lay the foundation for reading difficulties. It has been variously observed that poor readers often come from broken homes, backgrounds of unusual deprivation, and settings in which parents are highly overprotective. There are specific experiments suggesting that some children reject reading because they cannot tolerate taking in a lot of information, at one time, that may have potentially threatening implications. But essentially, no one has been able to pinpoint one specific emotional problem that typifies kids who lag behind in reading.

In our own encounters with families whose children have reading problems, we have seen a variety of interesting patterns. In one instance the reading inhibition seemed to be a response to an overdemanding attitude on the part of the parents. They had put so much extra pressure on their child to excel at scholastic things that he angrily balked and somehow could not master the skills they expected of him. In another case we found that every member of the family was edgy about the stresses and dangers in the world. They did everything they could to retreat and to insulate themselves from outside contact. The child with the reading problem was, in our judgment, trying to duplicate the family's shutting-out attitude by blocking out the input available from reading material. But in a third instance, a child's reading problem proved to derive simply from his poor understanding of certain fundamental operations involved in reading; improvement occurred rapidly with proper instruction. Published surveys suggest that many reading disabilities can be traced to getting stuck in blind alleys of misunderstanding about the reading process. Standardized diagnostic techniques are now available in most schools for analyzing the specific pattern of difficulty of each child who has reading deficiencies. Moderately effective training procedures are also available for compensating for such deficiencies. Careful, intensive tutoring procedures can in many instances produce appreciable improvement. However, they will not solve reading problems growing out of poor motivation or inhibitions based on anxiety and conflict.

Communicating with Teachers

Kids talk about their teachers all the time. The first few days of each semester they bring home their initial impressions of them and verbally vote for or against. Parents rarely see the children's teachers for more than brief periods and are largely dependent on those word pictures to grasp what they are like. In general, they have only superficial relationships with them. But when the child gets into trouble in school, his parents and teachers find they are suddenly psychologically closer to each other. The parents are often told by the child that his trouble is due to the teacher's unfairness or lack of ability. The teacher is presented to the family by the child as a bad person. At the same time, the teacher who is having difficulty with the child considers the possibility of meeting with the child's family personally and acquainting them with what has gone wrong in school.

Parents often have to do a balancing act as they listen to their child's complaints about a teacher. The child declares he is not doing well in a certain subject because his teacher is unfair to him. His parents do not know to what extent he may be telling the truth. They cannot reject his excuse outright and yet they are wary that he may be distorting the truth. They want to show him loyalty and support but they are skeptical that he deserves it. The pressure of this sort of situation can push parents into fairly unreasonable solutions. In some instances they try to resolve the dissonance by going overboard for the child's version. They accept his story without reservation. They express sharp anger toward the bad teacher and relieve the child of all blame. They adopt the child's somewhat strident attitude and promise they will make trouble for the teacher. This can lead to angry confrontation with the teacher when a meeting is finally arranged. Of course, since parents usually get to know their child's blind spots and behavior with a variety of teachers, they have more evidence than provided by the immediate situation to decide if he is telling a one-sided story. But the big difficulty for them is to give the child the sense that they are supporting him in his time of trouble and yet at the same time to communicate that they cannot go along with his effort to put most of the blame on the teacher. No one can adequately describe in words how to do this. It is a matter of attitude, of nonverbal gesture, of facial expression. A parent can express gentle skepticism about the child's assertion that everything is the teacher's fault and simultaneously give the unstated message, "We want to help you. It doesn't matter if this difficulty is your fault or not. You can count on us."

It is our feeling that it can be quite important to enlist the help of teachers when kids are struggling with a severe personal problem. There is some dispute about this matter among the experts. Many psychologists and psychiatrists who take a troubled child into psychotherapy refuse to have anything to do with the child's school. They view the child's problem as something "intrapsychic" and see his school life as peripheral. They also regard any communications on their part to the school about the child as a violation of his right to confidentiality. Our experiences in this area argue against such a strategy of isolation. We have found that the child carries his problem right into the classroom, and he often spends almost as much time with his teacher as he does in direct encounters with his parents. We have seen a fair number of instances in which a teacher who has been briefed about a child's difficulty is able to give him a valuable boost. By way of illustration, we would cite one case involving a child who had learned to regard himself as lowly and inferior and who vengefully did everything possible to provoke people into treating him that way. He had been quite successful in provoking his teacher into putting him down, and this had aggravated his problem seriously. But when the teacher had a chance to meet with the child's therapist and to understand the child's provocative strategy, the teacher's attitude in class changed. He stopped taking the bait and therefore stopped reinforcing the child's sense of being dirty and inferior. Whenever a child's parents agree, and it is appropriate to the child's problem, we try to give the major teachers in his life a perspective concerning what is going on. Our treatment strategy has evolved from clinical observation. We must frankly say we do not as yet have scientific proof that it works better than treatment approaches that do not try to involve the school. We look forward to objective studies that will provide a dependable answer to this issue.

You Are What Your Report Card Says You Are

We would like to go off on another tangent and discuss an issue that is wounding many schoolchildren and distorting their relationships with their parents. This issue has not been systematically studied, but we think it is so important that something should be said about it. We are referring to the fact that once children start school, their worth is more and more measured by test grades and report cards. They find as they advance from kindergarten to the higher grades that they are precisely evaluated; they are assigned numerical values that presumably describe how well they are doing in the school system. Their teachers incessantly tell them their intellectual "worth," and they send home report cards that keep the parents up to date on their educational market value. Kids find that this value goes up or down as a function of how they did on their last exams or their last report card. They find, too, that the important people in their lives can barely see them through the facade of their grades. Many of their other talents and traits are overlooked. First and foremost, they are judged on the continuum of A through F. The child who has chronic difficulties in making his way through the educational maze finds this scale of judgment devastating to his evaluation of himself. He gets the message that he is just not worth very much. Even the successful scholar is probably injured by this process. He discovers that his worth hangs on the slender thread of what his school has to say about him. He is haunted by the possibility that tomorrow he will fail that next big test and be toppled.

We are not voicing opposition to the use of tests and grades in school, but only to the exaggerated importance assigned to them by parents. We have worked therapeutically with several families in which parents behaved destructively toward their kids because they could see them only within the one-dimensional framework of school success. They undermined the children's self-concepts and their sense of worth by being unwilling to accept them as persons no matter what their scholastic worth. In this respect, parents are probably victims themselves of a culture in which success is often tied to accredited completion of degrees and courses of training that depend on getting good grades. They are persuaded that you are only as good as your ability to compete in the educational arena.

We have seen kids resort to all sorts of desperate strategies in an attempt to cope with the one-sided ("You are worth only what your grades say you are worth") approach to them. They get so angry that they do everything they can to sabotage the school. They are uncooperative, attack other students, mock teachers, and clearly declare that they are through with the system. Or they accept complete defeat, view themselves as worthless, become passive and depressed, and resign from life at an early age. In their Rorschach inkblot responses, they picture themselves as "clowns," "coyotes," and "skunks." Or, even more extremely, they develop dramatic symptoms that permit them to step out of the system. For example, some begin to have chronic stomach-aches and vomiting symptoms, some develop fears and phobias, and some are seized by pains and discomforts that drift from one body area to another. Parents are then forced to see that behind the grades are human beings with other feelings and sensitivities.

Parents should explicitly put themselves on the spot to find out if they are going too far in equating their kids with their school grades. They should ask themselves whether they assign as much importance to things like a child's sense of humor or his ability to be at ease with people as they do to his grades. Do they find that their attitudes toward their children keep shifting up and down as a function of how well they did on the last test? Do they find that around report-card time their children act as if they could potentially be "wiped out" if their grades fell below a certain level? Do mothers and fathers find that, in discussing their children, they focus most of all on their roles as students and rarely on how they are making out in life in general? It is paradoxical that the times when children are doing poorly in school (and are thus viewed by parents as defective grade-making machines) are the times when they most need recognition as persons whose worth goes beyond school performance. The apparent shortest path to a destination may be deceptive. Parents who are obsessively concerned with improving and doing "something" about the school image of their child might be surprised to find they eventually get better results by addressing themselves to the whole child. They have to let that child know that their esteem for him genuinely is not defined by a graph of his grades.

CHAPTER 6

Becoming an Adult:
Adolescence,
Bridging the Generations,
The Dating Game

THERE ARE ALWAYS dramatic anecdotes circulating about fierce encounters between adolescent protagonists and their parents. There are endless stories about adolescents who run away, fatalistically inject themselves with drugs, loudly embrace sexuality, and cultivate a variety of other defiant strategies. But despite such stories, it is probably not true that the average adolescent is more disturbed than the average child in any other age group. A number of studies have failed to detect a measurably greater level of pathology in the adolescent than the nonadolescent. This is not to imply that the adolescent may not have special problems and conflicts unique to his stage of life. But we would hasten to add that adolescence is not a ''stage'' of life in the sense that it suddenly appears and represents something completely new in the child's development. It comes on gradually and is anchored in the whole previous development of the individual. What is unique about this period is that it puts the child on the threshold of becoming a responsible grown-up person. Things happen to him that tell him, ''You are no longer a child. The day is coming when you will have to take full responsibility for yourself. You will have to decide what you want, where you are headed, and how you are going to get there.'' What makes this phase particularly difficult for parents is the fact that their ''little girls'' and ''little boys'' emerge in grown-up bodies and speak in the language of the adult rather than of the child. To some it is quite upsetting to have to acknowledge that their children are so close to being adults. However, to others it is much less of a problem; to still others it is a pleasure.

The Old Versus the New

What is happening inside of your offspring as he gets well into adolescence? On the basis of the overall scientific literature, one thing that can be said with certainty is that he is struggling to harmonize his active and passive feelings (10, 12, 17, 19, 37). On the one hand, he finds a lot of security in being the child who is taken care of. It feels safe to nestle in the nest and stay close to Mom and Dad. It is reassuring to have constant support and guidance. On the other hand, it is confining and demeaning to be dependent and to be treated like a child. The adolescent is stirred by the urge to prove that he is growing up and that he is an individual in his own right. He is thrilled by the idea of making his own decisions, being his own boss, and seeking out his own adventures. He stands between two powerful magnets: one deep inside the family home, the other just beyond the horizon ''out there.'' So he begins to move to and fro, shifting from pole to pole. He is often bewildered by his own fluctuations and tries to figure out ways to stabilize himself.

One of the adolescent's big problems is how to blend the values he has learned at home with those he encounters outside of his family. He ponders how to integrate home values with the new ones implicit in the novel roles he is called upon to assume ''out there.'' If Mom and Dad have taught you that obedience is important, how does this square with the fact that you have to be aggressive in order to win leadership in your local gang or school group? If sexual restraint has been emphasized at home, how do you harmonize that with proving you are a sexually competent person when you begin to date someone seriously? If being safe and cautious has been drilled into you by your parents, how does that fit with showing your friends that you are not afraid to drive fast or hitch a ride with strangers or parachute out of an airplane? How well such contradictions can be blended will depend, first of all, on the adolescent's own basic stability. He needs to have a solid base to stand on in order to competently integrate the contradictory forces that vibrate him. If he has not come up to adolescence with a sense of being at least moderately strong and competent in his own right, he will doubt his ability to harmonize what is happening to him. If he cannot count on himself, he does not have a platform from which to launch himself.

Equally important in this process is the behavior of the adolescent's parents. If they go too far in siding with either of the opposing choices that confront him, they may seriously handicap him. For example, if they encourage him to retreat from the challenge "out there" and to return to the bosom of the family, they will magnify the infantile elements in him. They will slow his development for a long time. If they push him too sharply out of the family by announcing suddenly: "We declare that you are now grown up and that you better not count on us any more for help," they may scare the heck out of him. In his fright, he may not be able to move toward further independence and instead may cling to less mature habits. Or he may react to their announcement with dramatic bravado and launch himself into certain adult roles before he is capable of handling them. He may, for example, suddenly leave home and run off to a distant city. He may want to prove he is capable of surviving without help from the family. Of course, he usually discovers that this is an empty gesture, and he suffers a painful comedown in self-esteem. Parents of adolescents have to find ways of steering a balanced course between the child-like and adult qualities of their offspring. Also, they have to accept, with style, their zig-zags from the one extreme to the other. There are no scientific studies to diagram how to accomplish such aims. However, we would like to offer several suggestions based on our knowledge of the scientific literature and our observations of families ripped by adolescent turbulence.

To begin with, we would underscore the need for parents to approach their adolescent offspring in a spirit of compromise. They should give the message, "We know you have ideas and beliefs that differ from ours. That's O.K. You have a right to construct your own views. But we value our views too. Let's discuss our differences and try to understand each other." This message *if seriously given,* reassures the adolescent that you are not blocking him from his efforts at independence. At the same time it indicates you think there is solidity in the values that you have provided and that have framed his life up to that point. This can be reassuring to the adolescent, even if he vehemently denounces them. If you simply surrender your values because he is opposed to them, you will probably leave him with an underlying feeling that the world is a pretty unstable place. It will seem to him that what is real one day does not survive to be real the next day. Of course, an attitude of compromise also means that you actually would shift your own position closer to that of your offspring, if it seems fair to do so. Let us illustrate the attitude of compromise we have in mind. Consider the following conversation:

ADOLESCENT SON: I don't want to go to church. Religion is a bunch of bunk. I don't believe in God.

FATHER: You know that your mother and I respect the church. But I do respect your right to make up your own mind about your religious beliefs.

SON: I hate going to church. It's a waste of time.

FATHER: You don't have to go today. But some time this week I would like to sit down with you and explain in detail why I think religion is important.

Consider another conversation in which an attitude of compromise is maintained:

ADOLESCENT DAUGHTER: Why can't I stay out later than one o'clock when I go out on dates with my boyfriend? I'm old enough to stay out as late as I want.

MOTHER: Yes, you are older and wiser. Why don't we discuss the one o'clock rule and decide if it's reasonable?

DAUGHTER: I am going out tonight. Is it all right if I stay out late?

MOTHER: Let's make the limit 1:30 tonight. But tomorrow let's sit down and discuss the problem. Your father and I do believe there should be some reasonable rules about when it's time to come home from a date.

By way of contrast, consider the noncompromising attitude in this exchange:

ADOLESCENT DAUGHTER: Why can't I stay out later than one o'clock when I go out on dates with my boyfriend? I'm old enough to stay out as late as I want.

MOTHER: You know the rule. Your father and I have decided that you have to be home by one.

DAUGHTER: You treat me like a baby. You don't trust me. I hate this family. (Begins to cry.)

MOTHER: Young lady, you will do what we expect of you. That's all there is to that. (Her voice sounds determined but is filled with tense overtones.)

When parents give adolescents who are trying to expand their life horizons the message that there is no room even to discuss such expansion, they are, in effect, telling them they will not tolerate their efforts to become more adult and self-responsible. It is usually not so much the specific issue or rule in dispute that is important, but rather the vision the parents communicate concerning what growing up means. Unless that vision includes room for the adolescent's self-shaping and self-fashioning, tense pressures will build up in the family. We have seen again and again that when the adolescent feels trapped into an unreasonably small life space, he usually becomes expert at battering his way out. If necessary, he will step completely outside the value system of his parents. He will invent an entirely new set of rules in which only his views and those of his peers count. We have been consulted by a number of parents who awakened one day to discover that their adolescent offspring were doing exactly what they pleased and were completely ignoring the family's expectations. The parents discovered that they had lost all control over their children. To aggravate matters, it was also often true that the children chose to dramatize their revolt by doing things that were unlawful and led to trouble with the police. The adolescent with radically unreasonable parents may convert himself into a living sacrifice in order to shatter their control. He is "willing" to be arrested and to fail miserably if only the end result will be to show them he cannot be pushed around.

Another important point we would propose about dealing with adolescents relates to what we would call the "rule of decreasing control." This simply refers to the idea that you should be willing to relinquish power over your adolescent offspring as quickly as he grows and proves his abilities. If the adolescent gets the message that you honestly plan to let him make more and more of his own decisions, he will experience his future as full of self-expressive possibilities (but also full of scary new responsibilities). If you give up power over him reluctantly and convey the impression you will rigidly hold on as long as possible, he will conclude that a painful power struggle lies ahead of him. This means he has to be angry and cantankerous. It is surprisingly painful for many parents to surrender power. They act as if it were a sign of weakness, as if it meant a loss of face. They behave as if they were generals who would no longer have enlisted personnel to obey commands. There is no question but that many of the most furious parent-adolescent battles are simply power struggles.

One other general suggestion we would like to offer about dealing with adolescents: clearly confront yourself with the fact that they are in contact with an outer reality in which they are bound to learn things that contradict what you have taught them. Conflict and disagreement are inevitable. The adolescent will acquire ideas from his friends that are alien to you. Every new generation has disagreements with the previous one. Historically this has proven to be unavoidable. It is a source of trouble but, of course, it is also a source of creative innovation. If you adopt this perspective, it will come as no shock when your adolescent kids challenge and oppose you. They are not deviants for doing so. They are simply displaying sensible flexibility in coping with a changing world. Your aim should be to help them bridge between the old and the new. Your intent should be not to prevent disagreements but rather to create an atmosphere in which they are clearly defined and then possibly integrated. It is true that not all disagreements can be integrated. There will inevitably be times when you and your adolescent offspring stand in stark opposition to each other. Your ability to cope with such opposition without becoming panicky or acting as if a catastrophe had occurred will provide an important model. In years to come this model may determine how your children deal in turn with the heresies of their kids.

While differences between parents and their adolescent children are prominent, we may have exaggerated them. The popular press may have fallen into the same exaggeration. It is important to point out that there are actually wide areas of agreement between the generations. Systematic surveys have shown that there are fairly substantial positive correlations between the beliefs of parents and their children (8, 12, 32, 33, 34, 40). One clever study asked the various members of a large number of families (in which there was at least one adolescent) to answer, independently, a variety of questions about themselves and the others. For example, they were asked to describe political beliefs, ways of making decisions, dissatisfactions, and so forth. The results indicated a good deal of agreement among the members as to what was going on in the family. But there were some areas of difference between the adolescents' perceptions and those of their parents. The adolescents did not see that things were as quiet and peaceful as the parents reported. They saw a bit more tension and strife. They also saw more distance and detachment between themselves and their parents than the latter acknowledged. They felt there were more definite disagreements than their parents could see. One of the biggest discrepancies occurred with reference to whether the adolescents were getting along as well "now" with their parents as they had in past years. Parents described things as fairly stable, but their adolescent children felt that things had moved in a negative direction. Apparently there were tensions and difficulties that parents dismissed as not being very important but that their children regarded negatively. It is interesting to compare what parents and their offspring said when they were asked to describe the topics or issues that created the most disagreement between them. There was a trend for the offspring to exceed their parents in mentioning their "social life," "future plans," and "politics." Parents more often attributed disagreements to "home life." There was no difference between parents and their children in how often they mentioned "morality" as a divisive issue.

Several surveys have shown that the vast majority of adolescents are not in a state of revolt. They are concerned about certain conflicts and "injustices," but they do not favor a radical revision of the existing order. It is also interesting that when conflicts exist between the values of the family and the adolescent's peer culture, the conflicts are not always in the direction of the family demanding greater restraint or self-control. For example, there are many instances in which adolescents who are poorly disciplined at home and who have few limits set on them find that when they are with their peers, they are expected to show more self-control. The adolescent who can throw tantrums at home discovers that he is rejected and ejected if he tries out the same tantrums on his friends. Incidentally, as might be expected in terms of current norms, girls have been found to be less concerned about conflict with their parents than are boys. When they do disagree with parental standards, they are more likely than boys to get around them quietly and inconspic-uously. They less often make a big issue of their disagreement. Indeed, many seem to get a sense of safety out of parental rule-making. They are inclined to identify with the parents as people who guide them and show them the way. Of course, many boys, even when they put on a facade of gross disagreement, find comfort in knowing that their parents will enforce certain rules and principles. They may value guidance even when they appear to disown it.

Adolescent boys are more concerned than the girls with problems of self-control (12). Girls have been found to be less worried that they will "let go" in some wild, unpredictable way. Boys are fairly preoccupied with the possibility that their anger will get them into trouble. They wonder if they will be able to stick to the rules spelled out by their fami-lies and other sources of authority. Some of their anxiety stems from the fact that they want to remove themselves from parental control and prove they can govern themselves. But if they move away from parental control, the question arises whether the self-control they can bring to bear will prove to be adequate. They are more worried about this matter than their parents realize. This is another reason why mothers and fa-thers should make it clear they are willing to communicate with and guide their adolescent offspring, even when they appear to be com-mitted to angry alienation and separation. This will help them to feel less potentially out of control and more capable of combining the old and the new.

One of the favorite ploys of the adolescent when he wants to sway his parents not to oppose something he wants is to accuse them of being old-fashioned and not aware of the modern thing to do. He tries to make them feel they are behind the times. In so doing, he plays on the sensi-tivity of Americans about being up to date and not standing in the way of progress or change. He portrays himself as the spokesman for "the modern." He is the authority who will tell the family how it has failed to progress and will rescue it from stagnation. It is difficult for many fa-thers and mothers to resist the call to be more modern. This is especially true if they already feel they are not well acculturated or are out of touch with American ways, as might be true of certain immigrant or minority ethnic groups. The adolescent further pleads his case by complaining that if his parents do not do the modern thing and yield to his requests, he will fail at something important and be ridiculed by his peers. There is no doubt that in many instances the adolescent, in his role as the representative of what is up to date, functions creatively in getting the family to be more flexible. But in this role he can also stir up a lot of confusion and tension. His parents may feel he is being manipulative for his own selfish purposes. Or they may feel puzzled and confused about how to fit what they believe with what he is advocating. Most families evolve a game plan which involves being skeptical of the claims of the adolescent. He is told that he is exaggerating, that he is too influenced by what his friends say, that he should have more loyalty to the old, established ways of looking at things. He rarely expects that his parents will really yield fully to his claims and requests. He usually expects small compromises and small gains. He recognizes that his father and mother stand for stability and caution. In fact, it is their relative caution which gives him the leeway to experiment and to advocate trying way-out alternatives. Parents should be aware of this typical game that goes on in so many families. The game, in its broad form, provides a balance between the old and the new. It becomes a source of serious trouble only when the participants overreact to any one episode or dialogue. The parents and the adolescent offspring have to maintain enough perspective to refrain from an overly extreme response to each other.

What do we know about adolescents who take extreme "anti-Establishment" positions? Several investigations have looked at older adolescents who were involved in open and sometimes violent protests against the Establishment (14, 18, 26, 27, 36, 39). Surprisingly, it was found that they did not come from families in which they had been maltreated. They had a particularly warm and friendly vision of mother. They were often brought up in fairly affluent surroundings by liberal parents whose values were opposed to authoritarianism. The parents seemed to be rather humanitarian people who had a romantic vision of life as a place where people were treated justly and without discrimination. They were also interested more than the average in aesthetic and intellectual matters. They were opposed to many conventional moral standards. They advocated a liberal, flexible attitude with respect to morality. Their anti-Establishment adolescent children were not in revolt against them. Their offspring were not protesting how they had treated them. On the contrary, they were trying to apply their parents' standards to the institutions they had encountered. They reacted to these institutions as not humanitarian and as overly rigid. So they set out to oppose them. There are suggestions that they became preoccupied with issues of injustice and unfair aggression quite early in life. They seemed to feel a personal responsibility to do something about injustice. Indeed, they perceived themselves as "special" and obligated to put themselves on the line to make things better.

Incidentally, it is intriguing how the problems of the adolescent male—with regard to proving his independence and his masculinity—find expression, night after night, in the images that dominate the television screens. There are endless television stories about males who tire of a subordinate role and who then revolt and prove they are heroically capable. We are regaled, too, with multiple episodes about males who are part of a group or who owe allegiance to a special cause but who, after a period of tortured self-doubt, decide to break away and form radically new attachments. We are also frequently bombarded with stories about men who get terribly angry about the way they are treated and who build up explosive emotions they fear they may not be able to control. By way of contrast, the typical problems of the female adolescent rarely seem to find their way to the screen. This may be because they are perceived as less potentially explosive and therefore less exciting.

While adolescence is usually thought of as a time of dramatic psychological change, there are great individual differences in this respect. Some children really do not show much change. Others undergo dramatic reorganization. Parents are usually puzzled about how to interpret the alterations they witness. If there is little change, they wonder if their child is maturing sufficiently. If there are extreme shifts, they get concerned about possible instability. One extraordinary investigation that followed children from birth to adulthood probed the significance of the amount of personality change occurring during adolescence (4). It found quite different results for boys as compared to girls. Consider first the results for the boys. The big changers turned out somewhat paradoxically to be rather careful, inclined to avoid new experiences, and somewhat dependent in their orientation. The nonchangers were described as rather uncomplicated, "radiating confidence," and "quick and eager." It is intriguing that by the time the big adolescent changers arrived at age 40, they showed signs of being very unsure of themselves. They were tense, vulnerable, and guarded. Contrastingly, those showing little adolescent change showed themselves in their 40s to be resourceful, vigorous producers, at ease with the world. Turning to the results obtained from the study of the girls, things look quite different. Those who were big changers during adolescence were described as "in a hurry," dissatisfied with their parents, devoted to achieving independence and selfhood. The nonchangers were depicted as "passive," thoughtful, and somehow fearful. They seemed to make less trouble for their parents than did the changers. When they reached their 40s, the differences between the two groups were even clearer. The changers emerged as "competent" and "comfortable" and had a well-defined idea of who and what they were. The nonchangers seemed to be disappointed in the way things had turned out. They were moody, felt open to threat, and adopted a "hyper-feminine" style of behavior. It would be an exaggeration, though, to say that they were seriously maladjusted. One point to underscore is that although the changers resented their parents during adolescence and made a fair amount of trouble for them, their behavior in this area when they reached adulthood was radically different. They shifted to communicating more frequently with them. Also, they thought back fondly on the fact that their parents had insisted on enforcing their standards and setting achievement goals, instead of just giving in to opposition.

The New Body

The changes that surface in the child's body at puberty are the result of a long maturational process, but they transform his appearance fairly radically once they occur. In a period of a year or two, the boy takes on the visible secondary sex characteristics associated with a man's body. The girl likewise develops the visible breasts and shape of a woman. Each becomes aware of a new capacity to do sexual things and to reproduce. It is surprising how well most adolescents adapt to the radical alterations in their bodies—and, indeed, they gradually learn to take pride in them. But the majority do go through a period of feeling unsettled about what has happened. They experience their mirror reflections as vaguely alien. Studies have shown that adolescence is a time of increased anxiety about the body (12, 17, 19, 24). There are unusual doubts, shame, feelings of inferiority, and a generalized concern about whether the body changes that have occurred are up to normal standards. Boys worry about their muscular strength, their masculinity, and their penis size.

Girls consider the adequacy of their breast dimensions. They ponder whether they are attractive and try to master the sensations that go along with their repeated menstrual bleeding. There is accentuated awareness of the difference between being male as compared to female. The male focuses on the phallic qualities of his body. He becomes hyperaware of his body as an instrument of aggression and as a means for moving swiftly and independently in space. The female entertains intensified images of her body as a potential container for producing a child and as being "open" for linkage with the male body. Despite changing norms about what is proper male and female behavior, these are basic masculine and feminine body attitudes that have persisted in our culture. Such awareness of feminine and masculine qualities is often a source of pride; it is clearly important, too, in defining who you are.

Parents have problems in adjusting to the body changes in their offspring. A mother may be taken aback by her "little boy's" whiskers. A father may be amazed that his "little girl" is displaying breasts that he associates with grown-up women. Such changes signify that big shifts in the parent-child relationship are in the offing. They also magnify the importance of the child's sexual drives, which in most families have remained fairly camouflaged until then. Parents are suddenly reminded: "My child has sexual organs and sexual desires. He will want to do sexual things with his body. Maybe he will get a clearer idea of what I do sexually with my body." In other words, the level of sexual awareness in the household is raised. Therefore, certain kinds of anxieties and embarrassments are energized. Parents not infrequently discover, too, that their children's new sexual equipment casts them in the role of sex objects. A father may be chagrined to discover that his daughter's new sex development makes her attractive, and he may suddenly have images about her as a sexual person. A mother may likewise find that she entertains erotic images that involve her son. Not too much is directly known about how much thought parents give to such images, but there is a fair amount of indirect evidence that it is far from uncommon. The emergence of erotic feelings toward one's children as they develop attractive adult bodies can be alarming to some parents. They confuse fantasy with deed. They feel sinful and bad. Their guilt may drive them to all sorts of unreasonable defenses. They may, in their horror of what they experience, maintain a cold ("See, I am not interested in you") distance from the attractive offspring. Or they may, in their need to purge themselves of blame, perceive the offspring as wickedly sexual and therefore try to suppress all his erotic outlets. Many unreasonable strategies can be found that parents have invented to deal with this problem. It may be helpful to know that there is nothing unique or crazy about parents entertaining erotic fantasies about their children. However, if such fantasies become highly intense and persistent, this probably reflects a breakdown in the relationship between the mother and father and a consequent need to use the children as substitutes for affection and warmth that are not being obtained in marital contacts. In cases of incest that have been studied, the need for such substitute love has frequently been detected.

Mothers and fathers typically are puzzled about how to relate to the body alterations of their adolescent children. They wonder whether they should comment on these alterations. They wonder about the right way to bring up the topic. They don't want to embarrass their kids, and they don't want their own quasi-embarrassment to be exposed. Should a mother comment on the growth of her daughter's breasts? Should a father refer to the new crop of hair on his son's face? The matter is complicated by the fact that various experts have issued statements about what is proper parental behavior in this area. Mothers and fathers may do this or that out of guilt or a sense of obligation inspired by the expert's declarations. Actually, there is no scientific information to provide solid guidance in this area. We would only suggest that extremes be avoided. To evade any references to the adolescent's body transformations is to imply that the topic is somehow too charged or disturbing. On the other hand, to dwell on the topic is to risk the possibility of being intrusive and arousing painful self-consciousness. Another factor to consider is your own emotional tone when you get onto the topic. If you find that you get awfully uptight, there is no great reason to press yourself. Your tension will, in all likelihood, only complicate your child's problem of interpreting what is happening to him. Of course, if you detect that he is experiencing unpleasant anxiety about his body changes, you should provide him with a chance to get some relief by talking. One thing evident in the psychological literature is that clear communication with parents is particularly important when a child is struggling with an issue or conflict that is really upsetting him.

The differences in speed with which children mature physically has consequences for their personalities. Some boys develop pubic hair and other secondary sex attributes long before many of their peers. Some girls begin to menstruate years before other girls. The concept of the early and late maturer is now well established (12, 19, 24). Researchers have been interested in the psychological consequences of being an early or late maturer. The boy who matures well ahead of others has been found to gain a number of advantages as a result. He is regarded as more manly, possesses more than average physical strength, and is assigned a position of superiority by his peers. The boy who is a late maturer has to wait longer to develop the badges of masculinity. He lags behind in physical prowess, which is valued among boys. However, it should also be noted that he is less suddenly called upon to cope with the pressing biological drives that accompany full entry into adolescence. He can fairly gradually adapt to the idea of being a full-fledged man biologically. If you are an early maturer, on the other hand, you are plunged much earlier than others into the experience of possessing a man's body and sexual urges. There is less opportunity to prepare yourself for the powerful body forces that emerge.

Long-term investigations of early and late maturers have revealed a variety of psychological differences between them. The former have typically been found to be more poised, relaxed, and good-natured. As adults they are more often described as objective, rational, conventional, condescending, and satisfied with their appearance. The latter are more often labeled as expressive, buoyant, and also tense. They are depicted as having more tolerance for ambiguity, being more playful, and exhibiting more egalitarian attitudes. Some of these differences have been interpreted in the context of the need to be careful and self-controlled, as compared to being free and imaginative. It has been proposed that the early maturer is so unprepared for the new feelings that arise within him as the result of the abrupt changes in his body that he emphasizes keeping them under control. He tries to control what is happening to him by becoming conventional and by identifying with clear-cut social roles. He is interested in being popular, approved, and accepted. The late maturer is said to be more comfortable with the new feelings in his body because they come on more gradually. So, he can be less conventional and more imaginative and less rigid. Similar differences between early- and late-maturing girls have been described by some psychologists, but other reports have been contradictory; it is probably not safe yet to offer any firm conclusions about this matter that would apply to girls.

It can be helpful to parents to realize what their early- or late-maturing sons may be experiencing. In fact, just knowing some of the basic facts about this phenomenon may prevent unnecessary worry. The boy whose adolescent development is delayed probably stirs the most concern in parents, especially fathers, who are so sensitive to whether their kids are properly masculine or feminine. There may be anxiety about why he is not like other boys. Or there may be questions about whether he is sufficiently masculine, and whether his future sexual development will be adequate. The existing information about such matters, however, is quite reassuring. While the late-maturing boy is delayed in the initiation of his secondary sex characteristics, once the process starts it moves with unusual speed. Furthermore, follow-up studies have shown that he eventually turns out to be just as mature, manly, and sexually competent as the early-maturing boy. Incidentally, it has been reported that in families where the mother has set up an unusually close, intimate relationship with her son, this may prove to be especially threatening to him if he is an early maturer. Apparently the combination of her special intimacy and the early awakening of his sex drives creates upsetting (Oedipal) conflicts within him. These conflicts may constrict him, for example, by discouraging a wide range of interests or even by interfering in some ways with his using his intellectual capacities efficiently.

Dating

The dating game occupies a central spot in adolescence (12). It is an elaborate ritual that takes on intense meaning for the adolescent in defining self. Dating provides girls and boys with their first serious chance to explore "getting together" with the opposite sex. It is an opportunity to learn about the complications of sexualized contacts. Actually, early dating is not very sexualized. It is hemmed in with all sorts of rules and prohibitions that make it possible for girl to meet boy in a situation that is defined as sexual but that is really "safe." Each can find out what it is like to relate to another in a sexual context, while knowing that the amount of sexual feeling expressed will be quite controlled. In early dating, especially, boys and girls play artificial roles rather than being themselves. They say certain expected things to each other, and even say them in a certain sequence. They maintain a good deal of psychological distance. Rarely is there deep or serious commitment. In a sense, one can say that in early dating the important thing is that one has "a date" rather than the fact that "the date" shows specific qualities.

As boys and girls get older, dating becomes more intensive and sexualized. Conventionally, boys take the more aggressive role and try to get maximum sexual contact. Girls are usually expected to impose restraint on boys. They are supposed to stop them before they go "too far." In our culture where boys and girls go off on dates alone and often in very private places, the burden is usually placed on the girl to be the "gate keeper." She finds herself in the very difficult role of not wanting to go "too far" and yet not wanting to alienate her date by being too hostile or rejecting. Recent surveys have shown that girls are less and less willing to be the voice of self-restraint (42). There has been a sharp increase in the amount of serious sexual involvement (including intercourse) in the transactions between boys and girls in the age range of 15, 16, and 17. However, it is still basically true that, on the average, girls see themselves as needing to block the overzealous sexuality of their dates. Several psychologists have suggested that this pattern of interaction between girls and boys during the dating phase has serious repercussions on their sexual relationships when they marry. They indicate that the female becomes so accustomed to thinking of herself as the one who is being pursued and who needs to guard herself sexually that she extends this mode into her married sexuality. That is, when, in the married state, it no longer makes sense to maintain such a self-guarding stance, she continues to do so. This is said to interfere with married intimacy and to make husbands feel their wives are distant and even rejecting.

Obviously, parents have a great influence on how their children behave in the dating game. For example, the anxious mother or father who feels that the woman is inevitably exploited in a sexual relationship will stir the same kind of anxiety in their daughter and push her into an "I've got to defend myself" stance. The same parental attitude may give their son the vision that the only way to relate to a girl sexually is to be extremely aggressive and exploiting. Thus, the daughter acts out one extreme of their attitude and the son the other extreme. It seems to be generally true that the sexual behavior of adolescents becomes difficult to predict when their parents adopt extreme attitudes toward sex.

Adolescents measure themselves ruthlessly through the dating process. They are highly sensitive to the reactions they get from dating partners. They keep careful score on their successes and failures. They microscopically examine every bit of each dating sequence. Each time they fail or succeed in going out with someone considered to be a desirable date, the event has vivid meaning to them. Many adolescents are convinced that their whole future as sexual persons can be predicted from how well their dating career proceeds. They overreact dramatically to the significance of an isolated dating event. Actually, no one really knows, in detail, the relationship between early dating success and later success as a sexual person. However, there is scientific evidence that the ability of a woman to enjoy sex and to attain orgasm is unrelated to the frequency of her early dating. Girls who were quite delayed in their dating careers turn out to be just as sexually responsive as those who began to date early and intensively.

At the same time, interesting information has been collected concerning what differentiates girls who are slow to begin dating from those who commit themselves to serious dating at an unusually early age (12). The girl who is dating rarely or not at all at age 16 has been observed, in a number of different ways, to be slow in her social development. She is more dependent on her family than the average. She has difficulty in visualizing a warm or close relationship between a girl and a boy. Further, she has similar difficulty in visualizing closeness in her ties to other girls. Emotional interaction and mutuality play a relatively small part in her concept of friendship with others. There is a tendency to be self-absorbed and really to be concerned with why things are not developing normally in her social relationships. She is inclined to attribute her difficulties to not being sufficiently physically attractive or to some superficial deficiency such as not being a good conversationalist. But it is not true that she is particularly unattractive. She belongs to fewer social groups and organizations than the average. She doubts herself and has relatively low self-esteem. Her dependence on adults is above average. She expects a good deal of guidance from authorities and is especially concerned about whether she is obeying "the rules." Generally, she is more oriented toward adults than are her peers. Less of conventional femininity is found in her outlook. For example, few feminine themes appear in her daydreams, in her ideals, and in her reasons for preferring certain jobs. On the other hand, she does not display masculine qualities, and she is interested in marriage as a future goal. While the pattern just described has a negative ring to it, we would underscore that no one has shown that girls who are late in getting into the dating game are grossly maladjusted or likely to end up more unhappy than the average as adults.

The preadolescent girl who begins early to date intensively ("go steady") shows some of the same immaturity that seems to typify the girl delayed in her dating. She has been found to be rather inactive socially. She belongs to a limited number of organizations. Less of her leisure time is devoted to social activities than is true for the average. Her interests are more self-oriented, but she is inclined not to be very introspective or imaginative. On the other hand, she does emerge as well-organized and integrated. She is also unusually oriented to adult feminine goals. She is interested in the role of being a wife and a mother. She is conventionally feminine and has limited interest in achievement and success. She does not aspire to an advanced education. Yet she is often a purposeful, energetic individual. There are suggestions that her early intense commitment to a relationship with a boy insulates her from certain experiences with other girls and from other situations that may be important ingredients in future feminine maturity. But this is merely a speculation.

We have the impression that mothers and fathers get highly involved as they witness the dating-game adventures of their children. They identify closely with what is happening. They overreact to each round of dating triumphs and failures. Like their children, they assume that dating behavior foretells the likelihood of being successful as a grown-up sexual person. Of course, they find themselves in the strange position of wanting their kids to be successful in their dating, but not too advanced in what they learn to do sexually. They typically want them to wear the badge of dating popularity, but they want the sexual elements in their dating contacts to be muted. Parents whose kids seem not to be doing well in the dating competition are usually at a loss as to what to do. They are curious about why they are not doing well, but they hesitate to ask them direct questions. The greater the anxiety about sexual matters in the family, the more confused will be the communications exchanged about such issues. Actually, we are skeptical that there is much point in parents directly asking questions like, "Why are you having trouble in your dating?" There is fairly good evidence that the adolescent who is slow in dating is already hyperaware of his problem and does not need to have it called to his attention. He has probably exaggerated its significance and launched ruthless attacks upon himself for his failures. One thing he definitely does not need is for those close to him to show equivalent alarm. That will only reinforce the unrealistic, negative view he has of what is happening. In several families we know, the problem has been especially intensified because one or both parents reexperienced in their offspring's dating failures some similar failures in their own childhood. Old wounds were opened up. Parents who over the years had proved to themselves that they were sexually adequate felt old doubts reactivated. Their highly personalized responses quickly registered on their already troubled offspring and made him feel that there were great, mysterious things linked to his dating experiences that were beyond his understanding.

Once again we would urge parents to examine their own behavior. If they detect exaggerated responses in themselves to the child's dating career, they should ask themselves if this has anything to do with old failures in their own past. If the answer is in the affirmative, this calls for some careful thinking about ways in which they may be overloading the child with their personal anxiety. For example, are they indirectly giving messages like, "You are a disappointment to me" or "You are making me uncomfortable with your failure, and I hold you responsible for the way I feel"? It is often difficult to detect the ways in which one may be giving such messages, but if one looks, the chances of discovering them are significantly greater than if one does not look at all.

Vocation and Career Choice

Rather parenthetically, we would like to introduce a few words about vocational choice (12, 20, 21, 30). By the time boys and girls get into their last few years of high school, they show a new serious interest in career plans. They begin to ask themselves specific questions about where they are headed. One intensive study observed that there are actually three major phases in the individual's process of deciding on a future vocation. Up to age 11 his vocational choices are largely a matter of fantasy. He toys with this or that possibility without real concern about whether he has the necessary talents or whether his choice is economically sound. From age 11 to 17 he becomes increasing aware that his own talents and training will shape his vocational possibilities. Toward the end of his 17th year, as he moves into advanced adolescence, he focuses seriously on his abilities, his preferences, and the problems of synthesizing the two.

Apparently a good part of choosing a career path involves eliminating the things you don't like. Over a period of time the adolescent decides that one choice and then another and still another are not for him. Little is known about what shapes each individual's choices. It is known that children from families of high social-economic status set their sights higher than do those of lower status. It is known, too, that fathers in certain occupational slots—for example, farmers and physicians—are especially likely to serve as vocational models for their sons. Attempts have been made to trace vocational attitudes to the emotional climate in which children grow up. For example, one psychologist has proposed that persons raised by parents who are cold and distant will avoid service occupations that involve doing things for people. Other relationships between parents' behavior and their children's vocational choices have also been suggested. Some of these ideas have shown promise scientifically. Unfortunately, at this point there is little that can be said that will assist parents in facilitating reasonable vocational choices in their adolescent offspring. There is little they can do beyond the general strategy of fostering success in their schoolwork and encouraging them to explore fully their own interests and talents before making final vocational decisions. It should be added, though, that the example parents provide with regard to the value they attach to work and achievement provides a framework for their children's future work behavior.

Defense Techniques

Although the average intensity of conflict between parents and adolescents has been overstated, it is typical to find persistent low-level antagonism. The adolescent has needs for independence and for trying out new approaches to the world, and they motivate him to push and test. His mother and father sense and also directly experience the cutting edge of his orientation. So it is customary to find a certain amount of underground antagonism between the parties concerned. This shows itself in friction about a range of apparently minor things. At one moment it surfaces in a disagreement about the proper loudness at which to play the stereo set. At another time it pops up in a satirical exchange about beards and long hair. There is no end to the number of minor issues that get drawn into the fray. Although many parents find this chronic tension exasperating, we wonder whether it does not serve a useful purpose in helping the adolescent to feel he is maintaining his independence. By conducting himself as someone who is not easily agreeable, he proves he is an individual. He proves that he sets his own limits. It's like drawing a circle around yourself and daring people to cross the line. This can be an important face-saving mechanism and a sensible substitute for more violent forms of self-expression. In our culture where the adolescent is often interminably dependent on his parents (due to the need for extended education, for example) despite his adult body and adult drives, he builds up a lot of angry resentment. He needs ways to drain off this resentment, and there are a lot worse techniques he could use than being stylistically oppositional about minor issues. Parents who do not realize this and who make a major confrontation out of each minor skirmish are asking for unpleasant complications. They are demanding quiet submission, but it is likely they will, in time, create a feisty opponent. We would add, purely as our own impression, that some parents interfere with this process of being self-assertive through minor complaints by taking a passive but mocking stance. They respond to the adolescent drawing a circle around himself by refusing to take him seriously. They tease and kid him and give the message, "You are just a little person who is play-acting at being assertive." They do not treat him as a worthy challenger, but rather as a minor character in a comedy. It is our view that parents should respond to the antagonism of the adolescent as something real that deserves serious consideration but not alarming confrontation.

The pressure the adolescent feels he is under to prove that he is in charge of himself gets him involved in all kinds of enterprises. We have compiled a series of examples we have witnessed in the course of our work:

> A 16-year-old girl in a well-to-do family who felt put down by her mother suddenly decided she wanted to get a job. She wanted to prove she was capable. She obtained employment in a grocery store and enthusiastically devoted herself to it. At the same time, she made it clear she was too busy to carry out any of her usual household duties.
> A 17-year-old boy who felt humiliated after an argument with his father

went out and stole a car and drove it at high speed until he attracted the attention of the police.

A 15-year-old girl whose mother said she was too young to accept a date with an older boy began to come home late from school. The time of her return home became unpredictable and she angrily resisted explaining how she was spending her time.

An 18-year-old boy who was about to enter college and who realized he would have to depend on his father for financial support began to bait him provocatively. He opposed him, questioned his motives, and generally tried to provoke rejection.

A 17-year-old girl whose parents treated her as if she were still a child began to smoke heavily. She insisted on her right to smoke in the house. She insisted she "couldn't help it."

A 16-year-old boy who was overprotected by his parents developed a strong interest in religion. They were somewhat disdainful of formal religion. But he began to attend church regularly and in the course of time adopted the role of the virtuous religious one who was superior to his sinful parents.

Such defensive strategies may seem vital to an adolescent at a certain stage in his attempts to shape an identity. We are not suggesting that parents cannot resist and refuse to go along with them. But if they do, they should respond to the specific piece of behavior rather than to the desire for individuality that lies behind it. How to do this is hard to put into words, but most parents will be able to grasp what we mean and to translate this into gesture and tone.

Disciplining the Adolescent

The problems of disciplining the adolescent are complicated not only by the fact that he is half-child–half-adult, but also the reality that he usually spends so much of his time away from home that his parents have limited information about what he is doing that may call for disapproval (9, 12, 19, 37). One survey of the forms of discipline used by American parents vis-à-vis their adolescent children found that they range across a broad spectrum. Parents use physical punishment (for example, spanking), deprivation (for example, reducing allowance), and psychological techniques (for example, inducing guilt). Deprivation is the most widely used method, and within this category the most common is forbidding mobility (for example, denying the use of the family car or confining the adolescent to the home in the evening). The study examined the traits of adolescents who receive more of one of these three types of discipline than the others. Several trends were picked up. It turned out that girls who were physically punished were especially likely to be submissive. They relied a great deal on authority. They seemed to be particularly tied to their parents. In response to a question about whether a girl who has a good job should give it up and return home if her lonely mother asked her to do so, they were the ones who most often said "yes." They described their family atmosphere as one in which the idea of independence is played down. But while they were rather submissive in attitude, they seemed to be more tempted than the average to deceive their parents. They may have felt that it is difficult to get things directly from the parents, and that they have to "get around" them.

Adolescent boys who are often physically punished by their parents were observed to have dependently submissive attitudes toward them. When asked to answer a series of questions about how one should make personal decisions, they were more likely than boys who do not receive much physical punishment to declare that they would give great weight to parental advice. They exceeded the other groups of boys, too, in their belief that it is harder to be close to a friend than to a member of your own family. They more often assented to statements like, "I wouldn't disobey my parents." But along with this submissive orientation one found that they felt greater resentment. Underneath their facade they harbored a good deal of anger toward their parents. This was revealed when they were asked to express feelings about parent-child relationships in a context where they were not aware that they were exposing their own inner feelings. When they were asked to concoct imaginative stories about children and parents who are involved with each other, they portrayed the interactions as full of friction, tension, and deception. They portrayed the parents as acting in unpleasant and unfriendly ways. Even further, it was found that the physically punished adolescent boys were least likely to build up a consistent set of moral standards for which they felt responsible. They were inclined to see rules as imposed from the outside and to be obeyed only as long as there is the threat of outside punishment. Boys who were disciplined mainly by psychological means were likely to internalize moral standards and to be self-enforcers. Those disciplined mainly by deprivation techniques turned out to be midway between the other two groups in their degree of self-enforcement. It is important to add that the physically punished boys were found to be slowed up in their social development. They dated less than other boys. They had relatively fewer ways of spending their leisure time, they were less interested in reading, and infrequently joined organizations. Those who interviewed them described them as low in self-confidence. One of the conclusions of this study was that physical punishment has more negative effects on adolescent boys than girls. The boys seemed to be moved by it more fundamentally. We have presented this research information in some detail so that parents can draw their own conclusions about the possible consequences of disciplining their adolescent offspring in certain ways as compared to others. Admittedly, the information is limited, but it emerged from an excellent investigation. Also, it fits broadly with the results we reviewed earlier of other studies of discipline in other age groups.

This Could Be Me

Some of the special delights and difficulties of having an adolescent in the family relate to the fact that you can so easily identify with him. As he takes on grown-up features and adopts the style of the adult, it is easy to equate yourself with him. Your memories of your own adolescence will be fresher and more vivid than your recall of your earlier childhood. This makes it more feasible to compare what is happening to your adolescent offspring with what happened to you at a similar point in life. In his budding adult shape you can see your own features with focused clarity. In his increasing preoccupation with adult plans and goals you can detect parallels to your own life pattern. When he is doing well this may be keenly delightful, because you can, in your heightened sense of identification, share in his glory. However, when he is doing poorly this may for the same reason sting you doubly. His failure may signify that a part of yourself has failed. These observations are impressions we have evolved. They do not have scientific backing. But we have noticed in our contacts with families containing adolescent members that the parents tend to grow either too close or too distant in their style of relating to them. They are tempted to treat them as prizes or as aliens. Either of these extremes is sharply troubling to adolescents, because they are already anxiously confused about the proper emotional distance to maintain between their parents and themselves. Such extremes are threatening because they introduce, either positively or negatively, parental attitudes of over-identification at a time when adolescents are trying to define their own boundaries. Parents sense that they are overreacting to their adolescent offspring and are puzzled at how powerfully they get sucked in. They feel deeply immersed. Their offspring detect their over-intense reactions and, in turn, get sympathetically heated up. It is probable that the theme that dominates most exchanges between parents and adolescents has to do with setting their self-boundaries at just the right distance from each other.

CHAPTER 7

The Child Alone: Working Mothers, Absent Fathers, Divorce, Loss

AS A PARENT, you have to make judgments about how much alone-ness is good for your children. If you are a mother who wants to take on a job away from home, you will wonder whether it is good for them not to have their mother around for large parts of the day. If you are a father whose work keeps him away from the house for long periods, you may feel concerned about the impact this is having on them. If you are contemplating divorce, you may wrestle with the question of how much harm it will do to them to be deprived of one of their parents. If your spouse has just died, you may anxiously ponder how this gap in the family will affect them. In all of these instances, the central question has to do with how much contact children need with one or both of their parents to thrive psychologically. We will probe this matter and try to spell out what conditions determine whether the absence of the father or mother will be harmful.

The Working Mother

It is well known that mothers who take on work outside of the home are inclined to feel guilty about doing so. They worry that their absence from the household will do bad things to their children. This is much less true today than it was twenty years ago, when it was less acceptable for women to have other than housewife roles. But even now many women who have jobs outside of the home feel uneasy about whether they are neglecting their motherly duties. Such uneasiness is based in part on the uncertainty of not knowing what the facts are. The average mother does not know what is true or untrue in this area. Therefore, she may unrealistically dream up all sorts of negative and unpleasant consequences of her going to work. Of course, she can also deceptively reassure herself that there is absolutely nothing to worry about. As a matter of fact, the scientific literature indicates that simple "yes" or "no" answers (to the question of whether mothers who take jobs outside of the home will adversely influence their children) are not sensible. The influence will depend on a lot of things. It will depend on the mother's motivation for working and whether she likes her work. It will also relate to the social class of her family and the ages of her children. Daughters may be affected differently from sons. Obviously, too, the quality of the substitute caretaker who takes over the mother's duties while working may well be very important. We think it is worthwhile to consider some of the facts that have been uncovered about these matters (13, 21, 36, 37, 48, 50, 56, 58, 67, 68, 80, 85).

The working mother is usually a person who does not accept the traditional definition of a woman's role. She can see herself as stepping out of the housewife mold. She can invest in a role that expands the range of activities open to a woman. One of the well-documented effects of a mother working is to alter her daughter's ideas about what it means to be a woman. As shown by several studies, her daughter differs from the daughter of the nonworking mother in having more respect for female competence and in seeing women as having a wider range of potential careers. She also tends, as she grows up, to be more oriented toward achievement and to be more interested in working outside of the home. There are hints that she may develop a more positive opinion of herself as a person and, furthermore, may have a more positive image of her mother. Less is really known about how the working mother affects her son. But there are two sets of findings worth mentioning. First, it would appear that when mothers in lower-class families work, their sons have less respect for the father than do sons in lower-class families in which the mother does not work. It may be that within the context of lower-class values that picture the husband as the "breadwinner," the shift in role of the wife from housewife to joint "breadwinner" means a loss of status and power for the husband. An interesting second finding is that when mothers in middle-class families work, their husbands are seen by their sons as more nurturant. This may reflect the fact that when middle-class mothers move into the working world, their husbands often pick up some of their duties and responsibilities within the home. Caring for the kids may be among these new responsibilities. As a result, the father takes on special "I am willing to take care of you" qualities.

As we explore the topic of the working mother, keep in mind that her *feelings* about working inescapably color her behavior. If she feels guilty about neglecting her kids or if she feels overstrained by having too much to do, this is bound to affect her. The mother who takes outside employment because she has to, rather than because she wants to, may build up a lot of angry resentment which she lets out on her kids, who represent one part of her overburdened life. The working mother who likes what she is doing differs from her dissatisfied counterpart in being more sympathetic toward her kids and in using less severe forms of discipline. It is not surprising that there is proof that children of satisfied working mothers feel more positively about their mothers' outside employment than do children of working mothers who are dissatisfied. A paradoxical effect has been noted with respect to the working mothers who feel guilty about being away from their kids "too much." It has been found that such mothers often lean over backwards to give them extra attention, and in quite a few instances this results in their giving their kids even more support than many nonworking mothers provide. However, their leaning over backwards can create other problems and difficulties, such as overindulgence and encouraging too much dependency. There is an overall trend for working mothers to feel they may not be doing quite as good a job in rearing their kids as nonworking mothers do. But at the same time it is interesting that nonworking mothers who are dissatisfied with their lot entertain the most serious doubts of all about their maternal competence. Apropos of the matter of feelings about self, it should be mentioned that working mothers tend to have a greater general sense of personal competence and higher self-esteem than do nonworking mothers.

Does the fact that a mother is working make her feel unusually tense? Does the double role of mother and worker adversely affect her health? What influence does her working role have on the sharing of family power with her husband? These questions are all really focused on the issue of whether the wife's employment has bad effects on her or her husband. The observations of numerous researchers indicate that the working mother's health is as good as and perhaps even a little better than that of her nonworking counterpart. She does not exhibit an unusual amount of strain or tension. She does not seem to be unusually nervous or to have developed an elevated number of psychosomatic symptoms. However, there is no question but that when a mother goes to work, this calls for sizable readjustments within her family. It can create fairly serious conflict with her husband and with her kids. There are individual cases we have seen where such has been the case. But we have also seen instances in which the wife's employment had such positive effects on her that the end result was to buttress the entire family.

The overall research findings indicate that working wives and their husbands get along just about as well as do nonworking wives and their husbands. But there does seem to be a small but significant trend for working wives in the lower classes to have more marital conflicts than their nonworking counterparts. No one knows why this is so. It may reflect the fact that the lower-class husband has a relatively rigid concept of how husbands are supposed to act and therefore may be somewhat unwilling to take on additional burdens within the family when his wife starts to work. This would leave her with an extra load that would make her feel unsatisfied. An analysis of the research literature suggests that the wife's employment is most likely to have a positive rather than negative effect on her marriage if the number of children at home is small, if she enjoys her work, if her husband is not antagonistic to the idea of her employment, and if she and her husband have advanced education.

It may be helpful to look at a few detailed examples of the different ways in which the mother's employment can interact with what is happening in her family. If nothing else, they will make it clear how complex such interactions can be. We would first call your attention to a family we studied in which there was a chronic problem over closeness-distance. The members of this family were inclined to be distant and cool toward each other, but then would begin to feel lonely and isolated, would subsequently accuse each other rather angrily of being too distant, and would try to establish greater intimacy. During one of the ''I need to be independent and not too attached to the others'' phases of the family cycle, the mother, who had never worked before, decided that it was important to her to secure outside employment. When she did so, this was followed by great family upset. Her children interpreted her behavior to mean that she did not want intimacy with them, and they began to display a great deal of angry resistiveness toward her. This angered and disturbed her, and she turned away from them even more and placed still greater importance on her work. The whole process eventuated in a crisis that required outside therapeutic intervention. It was only after the mother's interest in work was disentangled from the irrationalities in this group about closeness-distance, in the course of a series of therapeutic discussions, that it could finally be sensibly integrated into the life of the family. In another family we know, the mother and father were highly competitive with each other; this resulted in considerable tension that affected their children negatively. It particularly disturbed a son who experienced his mother's competition with father as a more general negative attitude toward masculinity. When an opportunity arose for her to take outside employment, this was at first viewed by her husband and son as part of an enlarged competitive campaign on her part. However, when she began to work and found satisfaction and self-realization in what she was doing, she became softer in her attitudes at home. There was a dramatic decrease in competitive tension, and her son obviously felt more comfortable psychologically. The two examples we have just cited point up the tricky ways in which a mother's work aspirations are actually embedded in the dynamics of her family situation.

Let us look in more detail at what is known about how working mothers impinge on their children. Do they treat them differently than nonworking mothers do? Are they stricter or more demanding or less indulgent? It is difficult to make unequivocal statements about such matters. There does seem to be a trend for working mothers in the lower classes (but not the middle classes) to expect their kids to learn to be independent more quickly than nonworking mothers do. They apparently push them a bit more. They expect them to take on more household duties. They exert more control over them and demand more conformance to rules and instructions. It does not seem to be true, on the whole, that working mothers provide inadequate supervision for their children. This issue has been examined in several studies, and no one has been able to find evidence that the working mother is generally a neglecting one. Relatedly, no one has been able to show convincingly that working mothers are unusually likely to produce delinquency in their children.

What is the effect of maternal employment on the child's school career? The observations of psychologists concerning this issue have turned out to be rather complicated. They have found, first of all, that in lower-class families both the sons and daughters of working mothers do better in school than do those of nonworking mothers. They have reported, too, that the college-educated daughters of working mothers set their career goals higher than do college-educated daughters of nonworking mothers. They are more likely to want to get into higher-prestige occupations that women have been reluctant to enter. However, in contrast to such findings, it has also been shown that in the middle classes the sons of working mothers do less well in school than do sons of nonworking mothers. No adequate explanation for this pattern of findings has yet been offered. It does seem to be clear that lower-class and middle-class women often have different reasons for working and also different reactions to their work status. The differences in their attitudes and feelings reflect back on their kids.

One important question that remains unanswered is whether a woman who has a child of infant age can be absent from that child for long periods without negative results. Can a woman leave her child who is two years old or less in the care of others for a major part of the day and not harm it in the process? The scientific answer to this question is not yet known. But it is known that very young children need warmth, consistent handling, and stimulation in order to thrive optimally. Thus the effect upon her infant of a mother working will obviously depend to some extent on who substitutes for her while she is away. If the substitute is indifferent or unfriendly or unpredictable in her behavior toward the child, one may probably anticipate trouble. If it is necessary to have a series of substitutes, each with a different style of caring for the child, one would be concerned about the effects of such shifting and inconsistency. Several psychologists have provocatively pointed out that one of the most serious problems that may evolve as the result of an infant's mother working is that she will not develop the proper feelings of attachment to it. They suggest that a mother's sense of closeness to a child evolves as she intimately cares for it during infancy. They speculate that the working mother who does not have responsibility for caring for her infant for long periods of time cannot build up an adequate maternal attachment. Two researchers, Yudkin and Holmes, who generally approve of maternal employment felt it necessary to offer the following warning:

> We would consider this need for a mother to develop a close and mutually satisfying relationship with her young infant one of the fundamental reasons why we oppose full-time work for mothers of children under three years. We do not say that it would not be possible to combine the two if children were cared for near their mothers so that they could see and be with each other during the day for parts of the day, and by such changes in households as will reduce the amount of time and energy needed for household chores. We are only stating that this occurs very rarely in our present society and is unlikely to be general in the foreseeable future and that the separation of children from their mothers for eight or nine hours a day, while the effects on the children may be counteracted by good substitute care, must have profound effects on the mother's own relationship with her young children and therefore on their relationship in the family as they grow older (85, pp. 131–132).

As we indicated, the real problem is that there is not yet enough scientific information available to say with any assurance whether it is good or bad for mothers to be absent from their infants for extended time spans. We think it is important for mothers with infants who are contemplating working outside the home to have a realistic understanding of this uncertainty. Once they decide to undertake such work, it obviously becomes terribly important that they exercise wisdom and caution in their choice of a substitute caretaker. We realize this is easier said than done. But in the long run it will pay for a mother to set the most exacting standards for herself in how she goes about finding a substitute. Furthermore, in harmony with views we have expressed throughout this book, we would recommend that each mother, day by day, monitor how her infant is faring with the substitute caretaker. If she detects that her child is persistently irritable or troubled or suffering physiological upsets, she should take this as a warning that something is significantly wrong with the caretaking arrangement.

Parent Loss

It is no exaggeration to say that a major cause of misery in children is losing one or both parents. A fairly large percentage of kids find themselves struggling to master the fear and confusion that seize them when their miniature family world is fractured by such events as parent death, divorce, and absence. It is estimated that in 10 percent of the families in the United States, children are living with only one parent (usually the mother). There is no doubt that mother and father are the central pillars of a child's life, and he is damaged if either of them disappears. Very early, for example, one can see how important the mother's presence is to the young child. Mother need only leave the room and he breaks out into pained cries of protest. A baby who finds himself separated for a longer period—for example, because she has to go to the hospital—may show signs of intense distress for the entire time that she is absent. Separation anxiety is a powerful force that sits threateningly at the edge of every child's life. All kinds of statistics suggest that children who do not have a full complement of parents will probably have a tougher time growing up than do those who have both a mother and father. For example, there are significant trends for those who lose parents to show increased psychological disturbance and delinquency and less adequate performance in school. However, they represent statistical averages; it is, of course, perfectly possible that in many individual cases such negative things will not come to pass. As we shall discuss later, this depends in part on what is done to soften the impact of parent loss on the individual child. Actually, the effect of parent loss is a function of a lot of things. It will depend on how early in the child's development the loss occurs, whether it is mother or father or both that disappear from his world, how much substitute support he gets after the separation experience, whether the loss is due to death or divorce or desertion, and so forth. The whole matter is complicated and therefore difficult to predict.

Let us begin by considering what is known about the effects of a child losing his mother (4, 7, 11, 20, 42, 66, 70, 77, 79, 84). It is surprisingly hard to detail how the loss of a mother through death will register on her kids. There is no question but that it makes them painfully unhappy and uncertain. Since the mother is the one who usually takes responsibility for taking care of the children's needs during a large part of the day, her death is more likely to disrupt their routine than does the death of father. It is not easy for a father to find a quick substitute who will provide the children with even an approximate facsimile of the life routine to which they are accustomed. It is not unusual for children who have lost a mother to cry a great deal, to show depression, to have difficulty sleeping, and so forth. There is fairly good evidence that if a mother's death occurs before a child is five years of age, it will have a greater disturbing effect than if it happened at a later point in his life. Long-term appraisals of persons who have lost mothers at an early age suggest they are apt to be more vulnerable than the average to depression and emotional upset. They seem to be uncertain about whether people and relationships are dependable. It is fairly well documented that babies who lose their mothers and who are provided with little in the way of substitute maternal care (for example, when placed in an institution with poor resources) are inclined to develop serious apathy and other forms of shocked response. Incidentally, the apathy is sometimes wrongly interpreted as a sign that the child is no longer acutely disturbed about his loss and has "settled down," but nothing could be more incorrect. It cannot be too much underscored that a man whose wife dies and who has very young children must make certain they get reasonable replacement for the warmth, support, touching, and closeness that mothers usually provide.

Interestingly, quite a lot of information has been published about the particular ways in which losing their father affects children (6, 8, 18, 24, 32, 33, 41, 44, 45, 47, 55, 61, 69, 78). Just as was true for the mother, a father's absence usually means bad news for his kids. It can be said, first of all, that fatherless families are less stable and more prone to develop trouble than are families in which father is present. For example, fatherless families produce more than their share of delinquents and the emotionally disturbed. It has also been shown that the absence of the father results in children developing deficiencies in intellectual performance. One of the main special effects of a father's absence has to do with how well his kids learn their sex roles. It can now be said with reasonable confidence that boys who grow up without a father find it hard to be masculine. They have a blurred picture of what being a man involves. They often feel more feminine than boys who grew up with a father. Careful observation has shown also that they are inclined to be less forceful and aggressive and more submissive in their style of dealing with others. They are more dependent and more willing to accept authority. At the opposite extreme, it is also true that their uncertainty about their masculinity can express itself in hyperaggressive acts. They may try to cover up their uncertainty by being rough and tough. By acting hypermasculine, they seek to camouflage their sensations of femininity. As we mentioned earlier, this motive seems to lie behind the destructive behavior of a sizeable number of delinquent boys who were raised only by their mothers. If a boy loses his father before the age of four or five, he will usually have a greater amount of difficulty in learning how to fill a male role than one whose father disappeared when he was older than five.

The sex-role problems of the boy without a father probably reflect a number of factors. Obviously, they relate in part to the simple fact that he has not had a man around to provide a model of manliness. Indeed, when there has been a surrogate male living in the family—for example, in the form of an older brother or a grandfather—the fatherless boy usually has less trouble in building up a masculine image. But another reason boys who have lost fathers suffer sex-role problems seems to be related to the fact that fathers are more interested than mothers in whether the children in the family act properly masculine or feminine. As we mentioned earlier, mothers are inclined to look at their children as "my children" and to minimize the differences in their sex classification. Fathers are more sensitive to sex differences and devote more energy to giving their kids feedback as to whether they are acting properly like boys or girls. Without such fatherly sex-role monitoring, the children seem to feel less confident about their sexual identity.

So it is not surprising that girls without fathers also run into sex-role difficulties. There does seem to be a trend for the fatherless girl to be less feminine than her counterpart who grew up with a father around the house. One study found that young women who lost father at an early age due to death felt particularly uncomfortable around men and were slow to develop love relationships with them. They were reluctant to date and felt inhibited about sex matters. Some evidence exists too that the woman who has difficulties in being sexually responsive (for example, reaching orgasm) is especially likely to have had a father who either died early or was psychologically unavailable to her. Father is important to a girl's sex-role development not only because he is particularly interested in sex typing, but also because he provides her with an opportunity to relate intimately to a man and to learn what it is like to invest emotionally in a male. By the same token, it would be expected that a boy who loses his mother early might later have sexual problems because he did not have an adequate chance to learn how to invest emotion and feeling in a woman. But little is really known about this point.

Despite all of the destructive effects resulting from the death of the father that have been mentioned, it is also true that other effects have been observed that probably have positive adaptive value. One major study of adolescents who grew up in homes in which the father had died some years earlier showed that they were unusually concerned about the issue of security. This was true of both boys and girls. They were especially conscious of money matters and were interested in ways to bolster their financial future. Their level of affluence tended to be lower than that of families in which the father was still living. They were accustomed to being economical and to carrying a load of chores and extra responsibilities. They often held part-time jobs. Less of their time was spent in leisure activities. Their seriousness was expressed even in their reading habits. Compared to children in families with a father, they were less likely to read comic books, travel or adventure stories, or books about sports. Serious nonfiction books more often drew their attention. Even their daydreams were found to be less romantic and more directed to solving problems. Although one could interpret such behavior to mean that they were unusually burdened, one could also say they had developed traits and habits potentially useful in coping with life problems.

It is far from easy to replace fathers or mothers who have disappeared. Many men and women remarry rather quickly after the death of a spouse because they want to fill the gap in the family and make sure their kids do not miss out on fathering or mothering. But this is not as effective a solution as would appear at first sight. A number of studies have found that kids do not generally respond very favorably to stepfathers and stepmothers. While these studies do not provide us with ultimate answers, they do suggest that kids whose mothers remarry may actually be a bit more maladjusted than those who do not remarry. Children are inclined to feel angry and unaccepting of stepfathers, and negative feelings toward stepmothers are even more intense, according to these studies. The picture of the cruel stepmother that pops up so often in folklore is matched to some extent by the feelings children exhibit toward their new "mother" when their fathers remarry. One researcher suggested that the reason why stepmothers stir up more antagonism than stepfathers do is because they are more likely to bring about radical changes in the new households they enter. A stepmother is more likely to persuade her new husband to her view of how the children should be treated than a stepfather is to pull his new wife in his direction. This probably reflects the fact that stepmothers and mothers are more involved in the care of the children. Their responsibility in this area gives them greater authority and decision-making power. One of the implications of the findings about stepfathers and stepmothers is that a man or woman who has lost a spouse and subsequently met someone who seems to be a prospect for remarriage should carefully consider how that person will fit in with the children in the family. This is a critical issue and one that can be sensibly evaluated by observing how the children and the prospect get along with each other in a variety of situations. If, after weeks of contact between them, you repeatedly detect tension and unpleasant feelings, this is a bad sign and bodes ill for the children—not to mention the strain it will impose on the prospective spouse and finally upon you.

It may be helpful to classify and briefly discuss certain core problems that are faced by any husband or wife whose spouse dies and that are likely to rub off on the children. Consider the following:

1. There is a surging sense of being alone and lonely. This is accompanied by feelings of anxiety and insecurity. The result is a parent who feels unusually inadequate and uncertain about how to cope. The children will quickly detect this and become more uncertain themselves. They may, as a result, huddle closer to the remaining parent and expect increased affection and support. This, in turn, is often experienced by the parent as an extra burden which may intensify his sense of having too much responsibility for someone who is so alone. We have seen cases in which this resulted in the parent turning to his children for support and psychologically demanding that they take up the burden of comforting him. This may be done in various ways. For example, the parent may draw unusually close to his children in an apparently comforting stance but in so doing really give the underlying message, "I want you to keep very near to me. Don't try to be independent. Your place is close by. I don't want to find myself alone."

2. There is an abrupt interruption of the continuity and program of the family group. So often, especially in middle-class families, the goals being pursued represent a compromise between the needs of the two spouses. Therefore when one of them leaves the scene, there will be

a shift away from the compromise and toward the values of the remaining parent. For example, a man who is highly ambitious and who can see work and accomplishment as the only worthwhile activities in life may have compromised with his less ambitious wife in such fashion that a balanced amount of leisure and relaxation was also admitted into the family agenda. But when the wife dies, he may shift back to his extreme position. Of course, the children will quickly detect this shift when they find themselves pressured to be more active and productive. The shift in family continuity also applies to disciplinary practices. Parents typically support each other in their disciplinary decisions. The setting and enforcing of standards in the face of the children's resistance is much easier when it derives from two adults who have reassured each other they are doing the "right thing." The parent who is left alone will usually be less consistent and firm in disciplinary practices. This seems to be especially true of the mother whose husband has died. It is also true that the remaining parent may react to a sense of not being as much in control of discipline as usual by becoming unduly harsh. The harshness is a warning to the kids that might be paraphrased, "Don't think that just because I am alone you don't have to obey me. I'll show you who is boss."

3. One of the biggest things that happens is a reshuffling of family roles. As soon as you remove one member of an intimate group, there may be radical changes in how the remaining members react to each other. A child who has been the favorite of the parent who died may suddenly find himself pushed aside because the remaining parent who now possesses more power has a different favorite. Or the eldest child in the family who had a rather dependent role in the family may suddenly find that he has to move up and take a lot of new responsibilities previously handled by the parent who died. Such demands for role change are stressful and create dissonant family static. The surviving parent should be aware that his or her kids will be exposed to new role demands; in recognizing this, he or she will be better prepared to understand certain of their discomforts and protests.

4. Still another crucial matter concerns the nature of the outside contact sought by the remaining spouse. Actually, a breakdown in old contacts will occur for both wives and husbands because, as "singles," they will usually be less accepted by other married couples. But more importantly, the spouse who is left will turn more to outside groups in which potential new sex partners and potential new spouses can be en-

countered. In mentioning this, we are leading up to the point that when a spouse dies, the family becomes an incomplete unit. There is suddenly a chilling possibility that a new parent will be formally added through remarriage or in substitute form, if the remaining spouse gets involved in a new intense sexual relationship. The children are vividly affected by this process because they are given a sense that things are temporary. If a new major figure can be added to the family at any time, the future is not predictable. The children may imagine various extreme unpredictable changes, with jealousy prominently coloring their images ("I will not be able to get close to my parent any more because the new one he is bringing in will get between us"). They have to cope with feelings that things are transitory and that there cannot be dependable stability even within the family.

Divorce

Children suffer a special form of loss when their mother and father get divorced (15, 19, 25, 43, 63, 76, 83). One of their parents, usually father, withdraws from the household and becomes an outsider whom they see only infrequently. There is no doubt that divorce creates serious problems for them. About 70 percent of all divorces involve fairly young children. It is also striking that about 80 percent of divorced persons remarry and then about 40 percent of this group eventually embark on a second divorce. So, quite a number of children are exposed to the divorce experience more than once as they are growing up. There has usually been a long period of battle and name-calling between parents before the decision to divorce is made, and their kids have had to absorb great quantities of tension and conflict. Sometimes the divorce comes almost as a relief to them because it puts an end to overwhelming tension. There are suggestions that children whose parents are highly incompatible with each other but who do not get divorced may suffer more psychological damage in the long run than do children with incompatible parents who decide to separate. However, with respect to this matter there are complications. Although divorce is supposed to end the relationship between the two spouses, surveys have shown that in a great many instances a long period of intimate dissension persists after the divorce. The child's mother and father may continue for years to battle each other personally and in the courts about alimony, visitation rights, custody, and so forth. The child is witness to this and swims in the bitterness and dissension for what must seem like an interminable time.

Studies of children in divorced families indicate that they are often terribly angry at both of their parents. They see the divorce as a betrayal. They do not understand why their parents "gave up" and did not try harder to solve their differences. They feel bitter that their parents were so selfishly involved with their own problems that they were willing to let the family be wrecked. Not infrequently they become highly involved in fantasies and schemes to reunite mother and father. It is a rare child who wants the split to become permanent; instead he imagines the magical things he might do to reconcile the two most important people in his life. Even after divorce has occurred, kids may work hard at trying to get their parents back together. When the finality of a divorce can no longer be denied, there are a fair number of children who, strangely, feel guilty and blame themselves for what has happened. They feel they should have done *something* to stop it all. Their unrealistic sense of guilt is actually reinforced by the fact that parents at the edge of divorce do express a lot of their dissension in disagreements as to how their children should be treated and disciplined. The children hear these differences loudly aired and can easily get the feeling "I am the one who should be blamed for what is going wrong." The child's sense of being to blame and his parallel intense resentment at his parents for breaking up the family unleash sharp turmoil in him. Children in the midst of the divorce process not infrequently show symptoms such as somatic distress (stomach-aches, bowel problems), temper tantrums, running-away behavior, unusual apathy and passivity, and so forth.

We have worked therapeutically with a number of families caught up in divorce. The one thing that has most impressed us about the children in such families is their feeling that the world as they know it is coming to an end. They seem to feel that if their family can be broken up, anything can happen. They see themselves as drifting and not having a safe home base. In their responses to Rorschach ink blots, they project such images of insecurity as "people falling off a cliff," "a house burning down," and "a tank breaking through the walls of a house." Some express their tension in nightmares in which they find themselves lost in strange places or being attacked by alien monsters. They become concerned with keeping track of where their parents are. Some develop transient phobias about going out of the house. For example, there may be unusual hesitation about going off to school in the morning. Generally, such disturbances subside within several months after the divorce, but underground rumblings continue for quite a while.

A number of experts have warned that a frequent problem that arises after divorce is that the parent who has custody of the child may unreasonably cast him in the substitute role of the parent who has left and in so doing inflict psychological damage. A favorite example of this, cited in the literature, is the mother who has broken off with her husband in the midst of great bitterness, but who in her loneliness after the divorce paradoxically misses him. If she has a son, she may use him as a substitute to take the place of her former husband. She may expect him to assume some of the father's previous responsibilities, and she may psychologically impose upon him for emotional intimacy. But at the same time, because he is a male and is an easily available target, she may unreasonably vent upon him the anger she feels toward her former husband. So he finds himself simultaneously pulled toward mother, deprived of his own identity, and irrationally attacked. This would obviously disconcert anyone. It certainly jars a young child. He just can't make any sense out of what is happening to him.

How might a mother know whether she was casting her son in an ambivalent substitute role? Here are some warning signs:

Does she expect him to do a variety of things father used to do?

Does she find herself shifting back and forth frequently between getting him to draw close and then angrily attacking him?

Is she often tempted to say, "You act just like your father"?

Does she frequently criticize him for the same failings and faults she used to attribute to her husband?

Does she find herself chronically irritated when he is around, even though he is not doing anything wrong?

Does she find that her son is increasingly saying things that indicate he is drawing away from her and identifying with an aggressive image of his father?

We think it is possible for a parent to become aware of such irrational role casting. It may not be easy to do something constructive about it, but in the act of becoming aware there is at least the possibility of making a decision that will lead to a change. Without such awareness, things will just drift along in the same irrational pattern.

One large-scale study of adolescent boys and girls found that if they lived with a mother who was divorced, they had an unusual amount of negative feeling about being overcontrolled. This was especially true for the boys, but it also applied to the girls. They perceived their mother as someone who was too strict and too invested in making up rules. The boys were usually tempted to revolt in some way. The girls were more likely to acquiesce and to feel little strain about mother's apparent authoritarian stance. The heightened strictness of the divorced mother often seemed to be inspired by her anxiety about whether she could properly control her family. It was as if she felt that without the support of her husband she was in a position of weakness and therefore could not for a moment risk relaxing her authority. She had to make a point of staying in command so that her kids, especially her sons, would not find an opening to challenge her.

A good deal of devaluation of both parents and the children may be a by-product of the divorce conflict. In the case where a parent dies, the surviving one usually encourages positive memories of him. There is a tendency to idealize the departed one. The children in the family find it easy to construct enhanced "nice person" images about the dead parent and also to view the surviving one as brave in the midst of suffering and turmoil. There is quite an opposite tendency when divorce enters the picture. The parents denounce each other in front of the children. Each tries to win their loyalty by emphasizing the badness of the other. Each is inclined to destroy the virtue and credibility of the other. This undermines the children's respect for their parents and reduces the possibility of thinking of them as people who are strong and capable of guiding them through adversity. This may, in turn, make children feel less competently protected and therefore more unsure of themselves. They may feel less capable. Their decline in self-esteem is increased by the sense of being part of a failing enterprise. It should be added at this point that one study found that many children interpret divorce as a sign that they themselves, in the future, may not be able to become competent marriage partners and parents. They reason that if their parents have failed at maintaining a viable family, they too will fail when they grow up. Suddenly it becomes painfully real to them that it is possible to fail in marriage. The sense of failure children experience about divorce is indirectly obvious in their embarrassment about the whole matter and their concern about whether other people outside the family know about the breakup between their parents.

We would like to underscore that although divorce is an ordeal for almost all children, they do learn to adapt. Scars undoubtedly remain. But it is interesting that no one has been able to show scientifically that children from divorced families are generally more disturbed than those from intact families. This is a credit to their resilience. It is also a credit to the fact that most parents involved in divorce are somewhat aware of the potential damage that can result to their kids and try hard to do compensatory things that will protect them. At least one of the parents involved often invests extra time in being with the kids, tries to explain and make sense out of what is happening, and gives the message that he will provide help when it is really needed.

Dealing with Death

Death is not an easy thing to understand (3, 5, 22, 23, 31, 49, 54, 60, 82). It takes children a fairly long time to comprehend what it is all about. The young child up to the age of nine or so finds the concept highly confusing. He finds it hard to disentangle death from things like people going away for a long time or creatures not showing spontaneous movement. He is also puzzled by the idea that death is irreversible. He expects dead things to come back alive again. He may tell stories in which people and animals are "killed" at one moment and then resume their activity the next. Piaget, the Swiss psychologist, suggests on the basis of his studies that the child's ideas about death cannot become accurate until he develops rather complex intellectual skills. He feels that true understanding of death does not really crystallize until pre-adolescence. Incidentally, he also thinks that the child's great curiosity about death and his desire to understand what causes it serve as a powerful stimulus to learning about the nature of causation in general. Several studies have involved talking to young children about death (3, 54). Here are a few quotes from these studies that illustrate a child's confusion:

I'm killing the orange. I'm cutting it—that is killing it, isn't it?
If people don't go out for a walk, they die.
The dead close their eyes because sand gets into them.
Mother lay down on the floor and went to sleep, so I went to sleep too.
   (Said by a young child who found her mother dead on the floor and
   went to sleep beside her.)

The problems children have in comprehending death are magnified
because their parents are so reluctant to discuss the topic with them.
Parents are probably even more "uptight" about explaining death than
they are about sexual matters. Many parents still respond to questions
about death by using vague phrases like "gone to sleep," "carried
away to Heaven," and "God took him." Also, they carefully shield
their kids from the sight of death. It is confined to hospital rooms and
the body is quickly whisked off to the undertaker. Kids rarely see anyone dead in real life. In many other cultures the situation is quite different, and children get a chance to witness death as a natural phenomenon. We do, though, give our children spectacularly aggressive visions
of death. Every night the television screen is bursting with images of
people being bumped off by all of the incredibly violent means ever invented. Death is typically tied to being murdered. Often, too, it is associated with being destroyed by some esoteric disease in a "medical
center." The child's television experiences probably add to his confusion by linking all death to murder and terror.

   It is the existence of such conditions that makes it all the more important that parents give their kids simple and honest answers about what
dying means. They must make it clear, as far as the child's intellectual
development permits, that death involves the breakdown of body functioning, that it is irreversible, that it is not due to magical forces, that it
is universal, that it involves permanent disappearance from the current
scene, and so forth. They should use naturally occurring opportunities like the deaths of insects and animals, or the loss of relatives to illustrate what the state of death is. When parents are evasive and unclear
about the nature of death, two things happen: (1) their kids get the impression that they are so scared about the topic that they can't bear to
talk about it, and they assume they ought to be just as scared; and (2)
their kids get confused because they have to make up their own fantasies
and "facts" to explain what must seem like a chilling mystery.

   Researchers who have monitored what happens to families in which one parent dies have found that weeks sometimes go by before young children are given a reasonable idea of what has actually happened. For example, in one instance a mother waited two months before telling her young daughter that her dead father had not recovered from an illness for which he had been hospitalized. Finally, she did tell her that he had died and "gone away." But in this atmosphere of denial and barely understandable communication, the child reacted minimally to what was said and continued to speak of her father as if he were still alive. In another family a young girl who had been informed that her father was dead and "gone to Heaven" wanted to know if she could send her father a Christmas gift. Her mother answered "no" and discouraged further discussion of the matter. Her daughter persisted in trying to find out what was happening to her father by asking questions about what people wear and eat in Heaven. Her mother replied that she didn't know but would try to find out. In so doing she reinforced her daughter's notion that her father was still alive in another place.

Some parents delay for years informing their kids that the deceased parent's body is buried in the ground. They put off or evade taking them to the cemetery for fear that this elementary state of affairs will be revealed. In some instances young kids do go to the cemetery but do not understand the link between the death of the parent and the place called "cemetery." They may act as if they understand, but they are so intimidated by the obvious unwillingness of the surviving parent to talk about death that they do not ask the questions that would reveal their true puzzlement. Many parents admit they do not adequately explain death events to their kids because they are afraid they cannot do so without breaking down and crying or losing control of self. They are so uncomfortable with their own grief that they experience it as something that can only be embarrassing. It is a mistake to assume that not talking to a child about the death of one of his parents will shield him from that event. Every child is shocked by such death, even if he does not appear on the surface to be much affected. The result of not communicating with him is not to shield him but to enhance his sense of being caught up in something that is mysterious, unbearably threatening, and to be borne in pained isolation. To block a child from talking and asking questions about a significant death in his life is to prevent him from grieving and mourning. There is a fair amount of evidence that people do not adapt well in the long run to the death of a loved one unless they get a chance to express their sadness, their regrets, and their sense of loss.

The problem of dealing sensibly with a child's grief is complicated by the fact that he often expresses it in ways hard for an adult to understand. Several studies have shown this. A child may vent his disturbance about a death by an outburst of silly mirth that helps him to deny how bad he feels. He may show absolutely no feeling at all. Or he may simply become irritable and hyperactive. An adult perceiving such behavior in the context of the death of someone dear to the child may interpret it as callous and cold. But one must remember that young children have had so little opportunity to experience grief that they have yet to learn the most effective and acceptable ways to express such emotion. They are amateur grievers, and this is all the more reason for adults to provide sensible examples of how to mourn. The surviving parent who cries and expresses suffering in the presence of his children may be helping them by setting an example that declares, "It's all right to admit you feel hurt and down because of what has happened. It's all right to admit that something terrible and disturbing has occurred and that you are scared."

We would like at this point to offer some examples of sensible and not-so-sensible dialogues that might take place between a parent and a child shortly after the other parent has died. Consider the following:

YOUNG CHILD: Where is Mama?
FATHER: She will be gone for a long, long time.
CHILD: I want Mama (begins to cry).
FATHER: She has gone away.

This exchange illustrates the frequent error of trying to conceal from the child that the dead parent is irrevocably gone. The father attempts to comfort the child by referring to Mama as "gone" and thereby pretending there is still a chance she will return at some future time. But this will only create complications, confusion, and a delay in the mourning process.

Let us replay the dialogue in a more sensible form:

YOUNG CHILD: Where is Mama?
FATHER: She is dead. She will not be with us any more.
CHILD: Will I ever see her again?
FATHER: No, Sweetheart. I will take care of you. I love you.

Father gives his child a clear and realistic picture of the fact that mother is gone. But he also makes it clear that he loves the child and that he wants to protect and comfort him.

Now consider another example:

YOUNG CHILD: I want Daddy. I want Daddy. (Cries and acts very emotional about his or her dead father.)
MOTHER: Stop crying. You're getting too upset.
CHILD: (Continues to cry and act very agonized.)
MOTHER: I said stop it. Right now!

The mother is mistaken in her attempts to cut off her child's emotional display. It is perfectly natural for the child to feel hurt and to express mourning openly. The child who cannot mourn openly is the one who is most likely to get in trouble. It might be speculated that the mother in the present dialogue cannot stand the child's unleashed emotions because they tempt her to let go in the same way. But this kind of loss of control frightens her.

Let us consider still another dialogue:

MOTHER (to her young son): Father is dead. He's gone, but I know I can count on you to help me.
SON: I'll help you, Mom.
MOTHER: You're brave just like your father. He'd be proud of you.
SON: Don't worry, Mom.

In this scene the mother appears to be giving her son a comforting pat on the back as she communicates about the death of father. But reading between the lines, it is fairly obvious that she is doing other things that will probably disturb him. First of all, she is really focusing on the fact that she and not he needs help and support. She is assigning to her son the role of provisioning her. She turns away from the fact that he also needs special comforting and that as his parent she should be doing something about it. Secondly, she makes a point of referring to how similar he and his father are ("You're brave just like your father"). This may not be a good idea during the immediate period following the death of a parent, because children, especially very young ones, sometimes have a problem in distinguishing their own identity from that of the one who has died.

Indeed, several expert observers of mourning behavior have focused on the struggle many children have in separating themselves from the identity of the departed parent. In its simplest and rather distorted form this difficulty may show itself when a child, shortly after the death of his parent, develops symptoms which are an obvious imitation of the illness of that parent. For example, a child whose father had a brain tumor producing intense headaches began to complain a few days after father's death that his head was hurting. He expressed his feeling of being like his father by hurting like father had. It is not surprising that a young child who was closely identified with a parent should have trouble distinguishing himself from the parent even though he has died. But to be identified with someone who is dead, especially when you are mixed up about what "dead" means, can be awfully frightening. Until a very young child has had a chance to reach an understanding that the death of one of his parents does not mean that an equally bad thing is about to happen to him, he may be panicked. It is up to the surviving parent to give each of his children the focused attention that will convince him he is an individual in his own right. The child who may have the hardest time separating himself from the dead parent is one whose surviving parent cannot tolerate having lost his spouse and therefore converts his child into a substitute by treating him as if he were like the dead one. We would like to point out that one of the reasons kids are half trapped into holding onto the dead parent is that they have such limited chances to transfer their affection and trust to another. An adult who loses someone has opportunities to interact with numerous other adults and in the process to find new persons to love, but the young child has a much narrower choice of replacements. He is in no position to "look around." He has only the remaining parent to whom he can transfer what he had invested in the other parent. This may not be enough for him.

The psychological condition of a child just prior to the death of his mother or father will either magnify or cushion the impact of that death. Obviously, if he has been coping adequately with his problems and feeling secure he will be less upset by the death than if he were already struggling with disturbing dilemmas. One of the factors most likely to sharpen the impact of death is pre-existing anxiety about loss and separation. This would be illustrated by the child who has a history of being unusually sensitive to separation from his parent. He may have shown his sensitivity by much crying whenever baby sitters were brought in, by his resistance to going to nursery school, or by his need to have someone sit with him when falling asleep at night. Death is an ultimate separation, and one can predict that the child with an unusual amount of separation anxiety will show exaggerated discomfort when a death crisis arises. One study of young children was actually able to demonstrate that the greater their anxiety about being separated from their parents, the greater was their general fear of death. It should also be mentioned that there is a tie-in between a child's fear of death and how much anxiety he has about getting hurt. Death has significance as a force that destroys the body. If a child has exhibited a good deal of alarm about protecting his body (for example, avoiding body contact sports or becoming highly emotional about minor cuts and bruises) he will probably overreact to death in the family. Further, there are clinical reports that suggest the overreaction may be painfully reinforced if the death of a parent occurs under mutilating conditions such as a car or industrial accident. The sensitized child then has to cope with images of body destruction, which stir up his dread in this area.

We would like to close this discussion by simply pointing out that the child's poise in the face of death is, in all likelihood, crucially influenced by how well his surviving parent has come to terms with the threat of death. It is that parent's actual behavior (verbal and nonverbal) under fire that will tell the child how tough he can expect things to get.

CHAPTER 8

---

*More Problems and Puzzles:
Sex Differences, Family
Size, Watching Television,
God, Family Theme*

THIS CHAPTER will range across a variety of topics. Several issues
and puzzles concerning children and parents remain that we would like
to consider, at least briefly.

How Different Are Girls and Boys?

Every parent approaches the job of raising children with certain fixed
ideas about how males and females differ from each other. These ideas
undoubtedly influence how they treat their sons and daughters. If you
assume that girls are passive and dependent, you will probably foster
just such traits in your daughter. If you are convinced that boys cannot
be nurturant and gentle, this may turn out to be a self-fulfilling proph-

ecy. Fortunately, there is now available excellent and dependable information about the ways in which male and female children are alike and different.

INTELLECTUAL DIFFERENCES

Let us begin by considering what is known about the intellectual abilities of the two sexes (50). As many people have noticed informally, girls are superior to boys in verbal skills. They have larger vocabularies, speak more fluently, understand language better, read better, and generally excel in doing things with words. It is around 11 years of age that their verbal superiority becomes especially clear, thereafter continuing to increase through high school and perhaps beyond. But there are two areas in which boys do consistently better than girls. First, they are superior in mathematical ability. This becomes apparent about the age of 12 or 13. Boys show greater ease in dealing with numbers, they grasp numerical concepts faster, and generally are better able to think in mathematical terms. Secondly, around the time of adolescence males begin to reveal an advantage over girls in their spatial ability. They are able to reproduce spatial patterns better, perceive relative distances more accurately, and find their way better through complicated spatial mazes.

Many people believe that girls do not cope as well as boys with problems calling for independent analytic thinking. It is said that girls have special difficulties in grasping complex networks of facts and breaking them down into fundamental concepts. It is further assumed that girls are better than boys at simpler, repetitive intellectual tasks. The overall implication is that boys are superior at the more complex forms of thinking and analysis. The scientific findings do not support such a view. Many studies have looked at this matter, and they have largely discredited the old assumptions about males being analytically superior.

The intellectual differences that do exist between the sexes can obviously lead to variations in school performance. Girls may have relatively more difficulty with subjects like arithmetic and algebra. Boys may have more trouble in learning to read well or to write fluently. As you watch your male and female children grow up, the intellectual differences you detect between them may make more sense if you look at them in the context we have just reviewed. We do not mean to imply that individual girls may not be outstanding in their mathematical or spatial abilities. Similarly, we do not mean to suggest that individual boys may not be outstanding in their verbal skills. What we have described refers to averages. There is actually much overlap between the two sexes. Some girls do better than most boys in mathematics, and some boys have greater verbal facility than most girls. However, there are average differences that are a fact of life, and parents will encounter them in the relatively good or poor performances of their children in various intellectual settings.

PERSONALITY DIFFERENCES

One of the favorite stereotypes known to guide parents is that girls are lackadaisical and not as interested in achievement as boys are. It is widely assumed that girls are relatively low in their desires to be successful and to push ahead. The existing research does not support this assumption as it might be applied to children (50). For example, it is interesting that, on the average, girls get higher grades in school than do boys. Also, when girls and boys are asked to make up imaginative stories, themes of achievement are, if anything, more prominent for the former than the latter. It may be true that boys and girls aim their achievement interests at different goals, but there is no difference in the amount of drive each has to do well. Obviously, as our culture is currently set up, the achievement drives of the two sexes tend to move into divergent channels. Males are more likely to achieve in business, the professions, the sciences, and so forth. Females more often turn their aspirations in the direction of doing well at such things as raising children and managing households. But this situation is changing. There are now increasing numbers of women able to channel their achievement energies into areas previously reserved for men. In short, the female has as much zest for achievement as the male, but she has been given messages to express this zest in certain ways that camouflage it.

It does seem to be true that boys are more power-oriented than girls. There may be a biological basis for the male to act in a tougher, more aggressive fashion. Both in animals and in cultures throughout the world, the male is especially typified by his aggression. He seems to be more aroused be competition and by the question of who is to be dominant. Boys fairly quickly exceed girls in their sense of being tough and potent. While they *generally* do not have more self-confidence than girls, they do think of themselves as possessing more strength and power. They are more preoccupied with proving they are high on the dominance ladder. They are quicker to struggle and fight to prove their potency. They more often challenge the authority of adults. They are less willing than girls to admit weakness or to express fear and uncertainty. There is some question whether boys are less anxious and disturbed than girls when they encounter threats. A number of studies have found that boys are more ashamed of showing fear than girls, and so they try harder to conceal it. For example, when they are asked to respond to "anxiety questionnaires" which contain questions designed to detect whether there is lying or undue "covering up" in the answers given, it has consistently been found that they are more defensive than girls. They more often lie about and camouflage their fears. Of course, since girls have more sanction to be open about their anxieties, they also feel freer to show them publicly. The boy, in his pursuit of potency, is ashamed to show fear in front of others, and probably conceals it more from himself. This difference in behavior results in teachers generally rating girls as more timid and anxious than boys.

It needs to be underscored that girls do not have a lower opinion of themselves than boys. They simply attach importance to different values and strengths than boys do. It is not at all clear that girls allow boys to dominate them. They are less likely to use direct aggression and physical strength in their encounters. But they make use of other qualities and assets to exert influence. Actually, in early childhood the sexes are relatively segregated in their play, so tests of dominance are fairly infrequent. As children mature and begin to observe all of the complexities of social interaction and bargaining, the balance between the male and female becomes equal. The female develops her own effective ways of influencing what happens in a relationship with a male. Most experimental studies indicate that girls have as much to say as boys do about what will happen when they begin to interact with each other. While girls are more compliant than boys when dealing with adults, they do not yield to the wishes of boys their own age any more frequently than the boys yield to them.

One other related point we want to discuss is whether girls are more influenced by what people expect of them than are boys. Do girls have greater sensitivity to "social" stimuli? One of the most knowledgeable authorities in this field has emphatically said "no." Boys are just as concerned as girls about how others perceive them. They are also just as interested as girls in finding closeness, approval, friendliness, and intimacy. Actually, boys tend to form larger friendship groups than girls. They move in larger aggregations. Girls are more likely to relate to friends one or two at a time. While boys and girls may be sensitive to different social cues in certain situations, they are both equally influenced by what the people who are important in their lives expect of them.

How Differently Do Parents Treat Daughters and Sons?

How do parents' ideas about the masculine and the feminine find their way into their treatment of their sons and daughters? What contrasts exist in their treatment of boy versus girl offspring? A good deal of thought has been given to this topic by psychologists (50). A quick survey of what they have learned may be useful to any parent who is interested in understanding his own behavior in this area. Obviously, there is plenty of evidence that mothers and fathers cue their kids in thousands of ways as to the differences in the ways boys and girls are supposed to act. One need not go into detail about the differences in the clothes, the toys, the activities, and the goals they choose for them. It should be pointed out, though, that parents are more insistent that boys conform to sex-role stereotypes than that girls do so. A daughter may act like a tomboy without getting much criticism, but a boy who acts like a sissy gets severely depreciated. In any case, let us look at other areas in which parents might behave differently toward their male and female offspring. It might be well to begin by asking the simple question: do parents spend more time with, or give more attention to, their male as compared to their female children? The answer is "no." Careful monitoring of parents' contacts with their young children in a variety of situations has not revealed that they focus more or less attention on their daughters than their sons. They do not speak more to one sex than the other. Nor do they show more emotional warmth toward one sex than the other. But there are a few interesting sidelights that have come out of such monitoring. It was noted that parents respond more to the "gross motor behavior" of sons than that of daughters. Parents give special attention to the muscle movements of sons. They handle their bodies more vigorously and stimulate muscular reaction. At the same time, they seem to handle their young daughters more carefully, as if their bodies were fragile and could be easily hurt. This last finding obviously reflects an unrealistic bias, in view of the fact that the health of the female is at least equal (and probably superior) to that of the male.

Do parents restrict one sex more than the other? It is difficult to say with assurance, but there are suggestions that parents apply restrictions more severely to their young male than to their female offspring. Psychologists report that mothers and fathers use firmer enforcement with sons than daughters. When once they issue an order, they are especially likely—in the case of the boy—to follow it up and make sure it has been obeyed. However, one important study did find that when a daughter reaches about the age of seven, parents become more conscious of needing to give her an extra bit of protection, and so they are more likely to chaperone her than they do their son. Their concern that an adult accompany the daughter when she moves into novel situations is likely to place an extra load of restrictions on her mobility and also upon her sense of being free to do things on her own. But returning again to the generally more restrictive disciplinary attitude taken toward sons, it should be added that they are also more likely to be physically punished and to be the target of other negative sanctions. Quite consistently, it has been found that parents spank sons more often than daughters. This is true over a wide age range. Boys are more often on the receiving end of power plays and force emanating from their parents. Mothers are more likely to say "no" to a son than to a daughter. When they do say "no" to a daughter, they are more likely to suggest an alternative possibility.

In speculating on why boys are punished more severely, two possibilities have been mentioned. One relates to the fact that girls are seen as more fragile than boys and less able to tolerate pain. Perhaps parents feel that it would be "too much" to inflict tough punishment on a girl's body. It might hurt her too much. A second possibility relates to the observation that it simply takes more effort for a parent to make boys stop doing something than it does to stop girls. Detailed studies have detected that when parents think their children are doing something wrong and they tell them to cease and desist, daughters will usually do so after one or two warnings. Sons do not comply so easily. Therefore, it may be necessary to use more forceful methods, like spanking, to get compliance within a reasonable time. No one really knows why boys should be more difficult to control. Perhaps their heightened aggressive drives play a role. Incidentally, there is reason to believe that fathers exceed mothers in their extra severity toward sons' aggressive acts as compared to daughters'. But mothers may be a bit biased against daughters. We have, in the course of our own personal work with families, been struck with how often tension erupts because a father sees the mother as showing favoritism toward their son, or a mother feels the father favors their daughter. The tension may reflect jealousy. The one parent interprets the favoritism to mean that it is at his or her expense that the other is giving an extra inappropriate amount of affection to the favored child. At this point we will not go into the details of how such feelings are tied to the Oedipal attachments and rivalries that exist among parents and their kids.

Returning again to the greater negative sanctions parents apply to boys, it has paradoxically been observed that praise and positive feedback are also more often addressed by parents to boys than to girls. In other words, boys get more negative *and* more positive parent reactions. No one really knows why this is so. But it has been suggested that boys are somehow under more parental surveillance than girls. Parents are more set to respond to them in an extreme way, either positively or negatively. This may mean that boys are more expert in stirring responses in adults. It may mean that boys have some special value or significance to adults. If you are concerned that your daughter not feel that you are less invested in her than her brother, this is a point to keep in mind. Her perception of how much importance you ascribe to her may be influenced not only by the number of positive reactions you send her way but also the negative ones. On a common-sense basis, it does seem to be true that we have the strongest reactions, whether positive or negative, to the people who are most significant to us.

We would like to emphasize that parents have the power to shape their sons and daughters into practically any image they think is appropriately masculine or feminine. There are few biologically determined differences in personality or style. Most of the contrasts in male and female behavior in our culture probably result from the expectations of parents. Mothers and fathers expect sons and daughters to behave in specific ways, and they will make it clear to them how well they are conforming to the expected model. In one interesting study, experimenters made videotapes of a very young child doing various things; when adults who viewed the tape were told the child was a boy, they evaluated what he was doing quite differently from when they were told the child was a girl. Analogously, parents may pay no attention if a girl does a certain thing, but react strongly if a boy performs exactly the same act. Day by day, parents tune their children finely to fit their sex-role stereotypes. We have been impressed that when these stereotypes are too extreme or unreasonable they incite children to adopt sex-role styles that will disconcert their parents.

Family Size and Family Position

A child's fate is partially decided by the size of the family into which he is born. It is also influenced by the order in which he enters the family. If you are the first born, you will probably have different experiences with your parents than if you are born second or third or fourth down the line. Certain conditions are created in families just because they are small or large or because the kids joined them in a certain sequence. It may be helpful to mothers and fathers to become acquainted with some of the things that have been discovered about such phenomena (see 1–34).

If the size of a family did not prove to have an impact on children, it would be amazing. The only child is obviously in a different role than the child who has numerous brothers and sisters. One cannot imagine that the only child would not receive more attention and more individualized consideration. Research findings have actually isolated a series of differences in the way kids are treated in small as compared to large families. (The term "small" applies to families with two or fewer children, and "large" refers to the presence of three or more.) One of the most prominent differences between the small and large family has to do with the exercise of power. On the average, parents in large families are more authoritarian than those in small families. They lay down more rules and expect greater obedience. They seem to maintain more distance between themselves and their kids and to define their relationships more in terms of rules and less in terms of feelings. Overall, they are more traditional, strict, and punitive in the way they wield authority. Also, they use physical punishment more often. As a result, their children feel more distant from them than do those raised in small families. Their children have more difficulty in identifying with them and in using them as role models. It is interesting that children from small families are more likely to spend their leisure time with their parents and to make their rules part of their selves, rather than laws to be obeyed out of fear of punishment. But their acceptance of parental values does not mean they are more dependent. In fact, they absorb parental values in a context of warmth rather than anxiety, and this leaves them with a sense of autonomy—of not having been forced into conformity. The child from the large family is more inclined to feel that he cannot really make his own decisions and that he has to find out what external authorities expect of him before he can safely act. He is left with quite an ambivalent attitude. He sees authority figures as people who push him around, and he would like to push back. At the same time he feels he must adhere to their rules. But to complicate things, his sense of being distant from his parents motivates him to turn to other people for ideas and support. So he attaches more importance to the values of his peers than does the child from the small family. He is more likely to turn to his friends, rather than his parents, for advice. The conditions in large families incite tension. Children in large families do seem to be more tense and dissatisfied than those in small ones. They tend to feel less positively toward their parents. There is even evidence that being born into a large family may prove to have negative effects on intellectual abilities. For example, intelligence test scores of those from large families have been found to be significantly lower than those from smaller families. Incidentally, this finding is complicated by the fact that the spacing of children plays a role in intelligence level. Generally, the wider the spacing between children, the higher their intelligence quotients.

We have seen a few disturbed children from large families in which the size factor itself seemed to be involved in their disturbance. The families we have in mind all included ten children or more. The symptoms shown by the children who were brought in for treatment were, on the surface, rather varied, but we detected a common theme that might be paraphrased as follows: "Am I an individual? Do I have an identity of my own? Am I just an inadequate appendage of someone else?" In one instance this concern was expressed in repeated episodes of running away. The child felt that he had to prove that he could get along as a person with no attachment to his family. In another instance the concern was expressed in an adolescent's obsessive feeling that he did not look like a real man and that he was too feminine. That is, his basic perception of himself as not being a viable individual was transformed into anxiety that he would not be able to achieve manhood. As we studied the families from which these children came, we detected two contradictory disturbing forces. On the one hand, the very size of the families made it almost mandatory that the parents deal with their kids in an impersonal, rule-oriented way. They could not give serious concentrated attention to any one of them. This created feelings of isolation and distance. On the other hand, the concentration of so many people into one house ruled out genuine privacy. It was impossible to be alone. Someone was always near you, asking questions, being competitive, and minding your business. So, there were extremes of distance and closeness that made it difficult for the children to develop a consistent way of relating to others and defining themselves. Their personal boundaries were strained by having to adapt to great emotional isolation (vis-à-vis their parents) and great intrusiveness (initiated by their brothers and sisters). The need to keep adapting to such extremes was troubling to all the kids in the family. The majority learned to get along in this atmosphere, but there were a few who could not stand what was happening and finally expressed their hurt in symptomatic ways that alarmed their parents. We are aware that the material we have reported in this section sounds pretty negative for the large family as a place to raise children. We can only say that we are reporting what seems to be true.

People tacitly believe that whether you are the eldest child in the family, or the youngest, or somewhere in between helps to explain your behavior. For example, they assume that being the eldest may result in learning to take a good deal of responsibility. Or they may assume that being the youngest encourages babyish, dependent attitudes. A vast concentration of scientific effort has gone into trying to understand this matter. Many scientific papers have probed links between birth order and a gamut of things like feelings toward one's parents, success in school, ability to deal with stress, and fear of getting hurt. The findings have turned out to be quite controversial. It is difficult to find consistent or unanimous agreement, but after carefully sifting through a good part of the published findings, we concluded there were certain observations worth describing.

We would first call your attention to some conditions that apply to the first-born. Almost everyone agrees that mother and father feel differently about their first-born than the other children who follow. The first-born is a unique experience for them. They are unpracticed in child care when they initially encounter him. They learn how to be parents in their trial-and-error efforts with him. Because of their inexperience they probably feel especially insecure in dealing with his problems. They probably react in a more extreme way to him than to their later-born kids. While there is fair agreement on these points, it is also true that no one has been able to isolate the particular practices parents adopt toward their first-borns that they do not apply to their later-borns. For example, no one has been able to show that they are either tougher or more lenient toward first-borns. Similarly, no one has demonstrated that they actually pay more attention to the first-borns. But even so, first-borns do behave in certain special ways. One of their most outstanding traits is a tendency to be conforming and to adopt the roles their parents expect of them. They are oriented to doing well, to being conscientious, and to attaining conventional success. A consistent finding is that an unusually high percent of first-borns manage to reach the college level. Among males, first-borns have also shown a trend to be more intellectually complex and creative than are later-borns. In a way, one might say they are especially attracted to the values and goals of adults. They are more turned in the direction of the way their parents see the world. It can also be said that they operate with a heightened load of tension and anxiety. While studies have not been unanimous on this point, there are quite a lot of positive results that add up impressively. First-borns seem to be a bit more timid than later-borns. They seem to feel more tension. They are more inclined to avoid taking risks, especially if they might lead to physical injury. For example, they avoid sports involving rough body contact. They are also probably more loath to experience pain.

A few words should be given to the topic of the middle child. Little can be said with assurance. One of the reasons for this is that the definition of a "middle child" is bound to be rather vague and variable. One middle child may have two older and two younger sibs, while another may have only one sib on either side of him. Obviously, too, there can be complex variations in the sex of his sibs, their spacing in relation to him, and so forth. It has been theorized that he should have stressful adjustment problems because he not only has to compete with older sibs but also suffers from being displaced from the baby position by his younger sibs. One of the better studies concerned with the middle child has found that he has trouble setting high goals. He tends to think of his future not as a time when he will rise above his family origins, but rather will fall below them. Another finding that should be mentioned is that he is reluctant to accept the values of his parents. He is less likely than the first-born to internalize his parents' rules. He probably finds it easier to break family rules. However, we should quickly add that there are no solid data indicating that when the middle child grows up he does less well or is more unhappy than children in other ordinal positions in the family.

The last-born (youngest) child in the family grows up in his own special set of conditions. He has one or more older sibs. There is no one in the family younger or weaker than he is. His parents have already had a good deal of experience in child rearing and no longer find the process novel. Adding another child may not mean that much to them. Also, the mother, who would at the time of his birth be in the last phases of her child-producing career, may already be turning her attention to new areas of interest. She may be building up strong urges to take a job outside of the family. The father may typically be distracted by the need to provide financial support for his expanded family. In other words, both the mother and father of the last-born may have limited energy available to give to him. He will probably not be as much in the center of their lives as most of the earlier-born were. So, it should not be surprising that one study of adolescents who were the youngest in the family reported that they differed from adolescents in other ordinal positions by being less attached to their parents. They seemed to be more interested in looking outside of the family for social contacts. They spent relatively more of their leisure time with friends. They expressed more loyalty to friends and placed more value in maintaining good relationships with them. Their self-esteem was more often tied to how their peers treated them. In some ways, these findings contradict popular ideas about the youngest in the family being the ''baby'' who is most dependent on mother and father. Apparently, his behavior is quite the opposite of dependent clinging. Of course, it could still be argued that his apparent movement away from mother and father is a compensation, a way of denying desires to be the little one.

It is certainly worthwhile for parents to hold in mind a rough outline of the facts we have just summarized concerning ordinal position. They can, from time to time, take a look to see if their style of dealing with their older and younger kids fits with known patterns. Are they encouraging their first-born to be unusually conforming and conventional? Are they giving their youngest the message that they are not as interested in him as they are in their other kids? If they are alert to such matters, they can more quickly detect biases in their own behavior and try corrective maneuvers.

Absorbing Television Input

Everyone knows that watching television can produce strong emotions. If you spend several hours absorbed in the TV screen, you will experience a gamut of sensations: tension, excitement, anxiety, anger, sadness, and triumph. No one doubts any longer that TV input into the human viewer can be powerful. Just about every parent has seen one of his kids scared out of his wits by a monster program. Many have had to give up sleep in order to comfort a child as he grappled with his TV-induced monsteritis. For very realistic reasons it has become common for parents to worry about what TV is doing to their children. They know that, on the average, their children are spending two or three hours a day absorbing TV images. They wonder whether they are doing less serious reading and spending less time in active play as the result of their devotion to TV. However, it should be mentioned that the loss in time devoted to such activities as the result of TV watching is quite a bit less than most parents imagine. The loss comes mainly from devoting less time to radio-listening, movie-going, and reading comic books and pulp magazines. Parents worry that their kids will become passive blobs as the result of sitting immobile and chained to the TV set day after day. They wonder if the everlasting violence of the TV world will infect their kids and encourage them to do aggressive, unpredictable things. They worry, too, about whether watching TV is bad for their health, whether it can ruin their eyes, whether it can interfere with their digestion right after eating a meal, whether it causes too much loss of sleep, and so forth.

The social importance of the question whether TV has bad effects has stimulated a good deal of sophisticated research (see 51–56). As we have immersed ourselves in the findings we have been impressed, first of all, that no one has shown convincingly that watching TV is, on the average, bad for your child's health. It apparently does not produce significant eye strain except under the most extreme, unfavorable conditions. No special health problems seem to be tied to TV viewing. Surveys have suggested that even with reference to losing sleep, the average child may go to bed only about 15–25 minutes later than usual as the result of his devotion to TV programs.

How does TV input affect your offspring psychologically and emotionally? As is so often true, a complex answer is the only valid one. We would preface the answer by saying that the research findings bearing on it have sometimes been in disagreement. However, they are coming together more and more. It might be well to make it clear that no one has seriously demonstrated that children who spend long hours absorbing TV stuff are particularly likely to become delinquents or to develop gross symptoms of psychological distress. But there is reason to believe that TV input can have psychological repercussions about which parents would want to know. These repercussions depend on a number of things, such as the sex of the child, how well he gets along with his parents, and his social class.

One of the main questions that has been studied is whether TV viewing makes kids more aggressive or hostile. This is a natural question to ask in view of the unbelievable saturation of TV fare with murder and gore. Systematic surveys have shown that themes of killing, assault, rape, and torture fill the average evening of commercial programs. One survey that compiled the content of 100 hours of TV presentations recorded 12 murders, 16 major gun fights, 21 persons shot, 21 other violent incidents, 37 hand-to-hand fights, a stabbing in the back with a butcher knife, 4 suicide attempts, 4 people falling off cliffs, 2 attempts to run people down with cars, a psychotic loose in an airliner, 2 mob scenes (one involving the hanging of an innocent man), a horse crushing a man, and miscellaneous other violence (robberies, falling from trains, guillotining). What happens to children who endlessly watch such a parade of sado-masochistic fantasies? First of all, quite a number of them get scared. They build up tension and they feel uneasy. They feel threatened. One study refers especially to the fear engendered by weird, dark scenes in which unspeakable forms of cruelty are being perpetrated. The threat intensifies for very young children who are just in the process of sorting out the difference between the real world and the TV world. The tension produced in kids by TV viewing has been documented in the laboratory. Recordings of physiological reactions have been obtained from four- and five-year-olds as they watched various kinds of TV shows. Those involving human violence elicited the biggest reactions and were also rated by the kids as the "scariest." Secondly, the children's level of irritability and aggression is affected. The input of hostile TV imagery does seem to make them do more hostile things. They are stimulated to act more aggressively toward their friends. They become more intolerant of being blocked or inhibited. They are more resistive to obeying rules. They are less willing to accept delay in getting the things they want. One research project was able to show in a sample of children who were followed for many years that chronic exposure to TV aggression, while in the age range of eight through nine, resulted in heightened displays of hostility ten years later. The reinforcement of aggression produced by TV exposure seems to apply especially to kids who are already above average in aggression. They are the ones who show the largest increase in hostile behavior as the result of contact with TV's angry models. It should be added that there is some hint that girls may be less likely than boys to act out anger as the result of TV violence.

While it has been shown that TV images, especially those focusing on violence, can incite negative psychological vibrations, it may also be true that they can have positive effects. For example, several psychologists have found that when people get very angry and do not have ways to discharge their tension, they may find it comforting to immerse themselves in fantasy material that wishfully fulfills what they would like to do. In other words, if you are terribly angry and would like to slug someone, you may get some vicarious relief out of watching a TV program in which the hero knocks someone out. Scattered scientific reports have observed just such an effect in some groups of children whose anger was measured before and after exposure to violent TV material. The possible comforting role of TV watching has emerged, too, in studies that indicate that the greater the conflict between children and parents in middle-class families, the more time the children spend in front of the TV set. One may speculate that immersion in the TV world helps them to forget their conflict and gives them fantasy outlets for their resentments. It is extremely interesting that in lower-class families the findings go, if anything, in the opposite direction. In that instance, the greater the parent-children conflict, the less inclined are the children to watch TV. No one knows why this difference occurs. We would add that while the greater absorption in TV of the child in conflict with his parents can be interpreted as being comforting to him, one could also argue that it encourages an unrealistic approach to problem solving.

One may reasonably suggest that it only delays settling conflicts if refuge is taken in fantasy rather than directing energy into more active channels.

The potential for TV to do good for the family has been underscored by many commentators. Obviously, it could be a rich source of educational information for kids. Surveys have shown that pre-school children who watch TV probably enter school with enhanced vocabularies as the result of the range of verbal material they have experienced. But this advantage from TV input quickly fades as books and other reading material gain dominance as sources of facts and vocabulary. The potential value of TV was pointed up in an experiment in which pre-school children in a nursery school were exposed to a series of educational TV programs that emphasized the importance of being cooperative, friendly, and helping. When they were later compared with nursery school children who were not exposed to such programs, their behavior was found to be "improved" in a number of ways. They were more likely to persist at tasks they undertook. This was particularly likely to happen if they were above average intellectually. They were also more likely to obey rules and to tolerate frustrating delays. In lower-class children the TV programs led to an increase in cooperative play, nurturance, and expression.

We conclude that television can do both bad and good things for children. It can provide information and educational input. It obviously provides entertainment, and it can offer substitute fantasy outlets for gripes and frustrations. It has a potential for teaching constructive attitudes that encourage cooperation and problem solving. But at the same time, the high concentration of violence and tragedy transmitted by the networks can be very scary. Some kids obviously do get seriously frightened by what they see on the TV screen. There is fairly good reason to believe that repetitive TV violence can incite violent fantasy and aggressive acting out, particularly in those who have the most serious problems in coping with their own hostile feelings. The savage sadists who inhabit TV scripts can become seductive models for the young. It is possible that some psychotic adolescents may be pushed to bizarre exploits by their TV experiences. They (and also very young children) may have difficulty in distinguishing the TV fantasy from the real world. Of course, one should keep in mind that other kinds of fantasy material besides the TV form sell weird violence. There is a high saturation of aggression in the old classic fairy tales, in children's books, in comic books, and in movies. TV has not introduced a unique theme. It has only increased the amount of persistent exposure to it.

Parents have to take the responsibility for gauging the plus or minus impact of TV on their own children. They should not blindly assume that TV is bound to have this or that effect. It is probably irrational for them to make up arbitrary rules about how much TV and the types of TV their kids should watch, without first finding out what TV actually does to them. The research findings make it clear that children respond differently to TV input as a function of such variables as their intelligence level, social class, and amount of conflict with their parents. Each mother and father has plenty of opportunity to learn what TV is doing to each of his children. He can tell whether TV violence scares the child and makes him feel insecure for a period of time. He can determine whether several hours of TV bloodshed render the child irritable and oppositional, or even downright hostile. He can see plainly whether the child is using the TV set to escape responsibility, dodge problems, and avoid communication. He can also tell whether the shy kid who is afraid of anger is getting a chance to "practice" having angry images and ideas by following the angry action on the TV screen. He can detect whether the introverted kid is using TV as a window on the world to find out more about the varieties of people and situations that exist "out there." He can perceive whether the high-achieving, rigidly dutiful child who always does his work on time finds relaxation in the zest and passion of TV events. It is on the basis of such observations that parents should make their decisions about the TV viewing careers of their children. They may want to limit the viewing time for one but encourage an increase for another. Unless they detect obvious negative effects, it may be the wisest course to let each child make his own decisions about how much he wants to open himself to TV input. The parent who is arbitrarily restrictive on the child's TV behavior may simply come across as a censor who does not trust his offspring to make decisions for himself. It is a rather interesting paradox that one study discovered that parents who are most consistent in screening the ideas and experiences to which their children should be exposed are the ones who apparently create conditions that eventually (by the time of high school) result in those children spending an unusually great amount of time watching TV for entertainment purposes. It may be of interest to add that the parents' own TV viewing habits do not seem to have much influence on their offspring's habits. The relationships between the two are greater than

223

chance, but they are very small. Also, there is a hint that children's TV habits are a bit closer to those of mother than of father.

We have noticed that tensions between parents and children frequently surface in disagreements about TV. Parents tell their kids that it is bad for them to watch certain programs, and they in turn get mad. Or parents take away "TV privileges" as a form of punishment. Or a lot of bad feeling develops because parents and children can't agree on which of two favorite programs to watch. Relatedly, kids in the family get into conflict about which program to watch, and their parents get dragged into their TV vendetta. There are also a good many struggles that involve pulling the kids away from the TV set so that they will go to sleep or finish their homework or complete their household chores. At the other extreme, we have been struck with the fact that sometimes there is a reversal; the parent-child conflict gets expressed in the child interfering with the parents' TV watching. For example, a child wanting attention wanders into the room where his parents are entranced with a TV program and somehow manages to keep blocking their view of the screen, or makes so much noise they can't hear the program. The fact that so much conflict crystallizes around TV issues dramatizes the central role that TV has taken on in many, many families.

In closing this section, we would simply like to list a number of irrational ways in which parents incorporate the TV set into the family:

It is often used as a mechanical baby sitter. Children learn to sit quietly absorbed in TV images and not bother their parents by trying to communicate with them.

It is used primarily as an apparatus for meting out punishment. Pretty soon the kids think of TV as a device for maintaining control over them by rationing how much time they can spend looking at it.

There may be a tendency to depend on TV to provide excitement and stimulation. Instead of generating new ideas and activities on their own, the family members are given the message by their parents to turn to TV images to whip up their fantasies.

The TV set is assigned the role of the house villain. Everything "bad" the kids do is blamed on their TV habits.

The TV set is cast in the role of having great powers far beyond its real potency. It is portrayed to the children as capable of exaggerated influence, whether for bad or good.

The parents link the TV set with vulgarity, low status, and lack of intellectuality. They give the impression that watching TV is low-class and should be colored by guilt.

In some instances parents are so obviously in need of watching TV and so upset by anything which interferes that their kids get the impression that TV is necessary for one's security. The TV box becomes a security blanket for the household.

We have listed a random sample of the TV irrationalities we have encountered. There are others. They probably all intrude into the rationality of parent-child encounters.

Religion, Church-Going, Conformity

We keep hearing from children about the frustrations religion visits upon them. They complain that they are tired of going to church. They do not understand why they have to get dressed up to go to services on Sunday. They protest the burden of having to attend religious classes on top of their regular school responsibilities. They depreciate certain religious customs that seem outmoded or impractical. Young children are inclined to see religion as restrictive and forcing demands upon them. This relates partially to the fact that parents who value the role of belief in God and affiliation with the church try hard to imprint their kids with their values. They feel that religion is central and that it is their duty to transmit religious faith to the next generation. They are sure their children cannot be virtuous or moral without becoming obedient followers of the church. We have noticed that even parents who are personally irreligious wonder from time to time if it is fair to deprive their offspring of religious training. They may feel downright guilty about this.

As a matter of fact, it is known that a sizeable percentage of offspring, as they move into adolescence and beyond, deviate from their parents' religious views (see 35–49). They may join other denominations or give up religion altogether. Or, at times, if their parents are irreligious, they may go to the opposite extreme and become conforming churchgoers. Not much is known about what determines whether a child will follow in his parents' religious footsteps. One of the most thorough investigations in this area did come up with some interesting generalizations. First, it was shown that college students are most likely to conform to their parents' religious ideology if both of the parents have similar religious beliefs. If they are both devout, their offspring are likely to be devout. If they are both religious skeptics, their offspring will probably adopt skepticism. Secondly, offspring are most likely to conform to the parents' religious ideology if that ideology is closest to the most widely accepted religious position in that cultural group. In other words, if parents hold deviant religious positions, their kids are less likely to follow along. Thirdly, if parents disagree religiously, their offspring will probably adopt the ideology of the parent who is closest to the most widely accepted religious position. Finally, if parents disagree religiously, their offspring are a bit more likely to move in the mother's, rather than father's, direction.

The religious household is usually typified by certain qualities. It is on the conservative side. Its values emphasize the traditional. There is a belief in the value of authority, obedience to parents, clear distinctions between male and female roles, and the importance of father-power. Restraint, obedience, and conformity are put forward as guiding principles. Autonomy and independence are played down. It is well established that children from religious homes show lower levels of nonconformity and deviance than those from nonreligious homes. They are less likely to engage in extreme forms of activism. They less often engage in premarital sex or make use of various illegal drugs (such as marijuana). It has been widely believed that highly religious families produce children who are emotionally handicapped. For example, it is presumed that the religious atmosphere somehow renders children so repressed and rigid that they cannot adequately deal with their biological drives and erotic wishes. However, most psychologists who have looked into this matter have not detected unusually high or low maladjustment in those from religious homes. Mental illness and religiosity are not reliably tied together in any way.

Although there has been a noticeable decline in religiosity and in church attendance among the young men and women in the United States, it still remains true that religion is of real importance to a large segment of them. Several surveys have discovered that when college students are asked the role of religion in their lives, they attribute genuine significance to it. There is a trend for 70 percent or more to say they feel a rather strong "need for religion" to help them in coping with their life problems. More women than men assign such importance to religion. Careful questioning of young adolescents reveals that they are often concerned about religious themes. They wonder whether God exists. They worry about sin. They speculate about the sources of creation. They wonder if there is order and sense in the universe. They question why there is evil in the world. At another level, they struggle with feelings that have mystical overtones. They experience awe and sensations of revelation that have, through the ages, been identified with religiosity. Their search for purpose and meaning leans strongly at times on the vocabulary of religion. The broad integrative envelope provided by religious belief is very attractive to many as a way of mastering the confusion and contradictions of their evolving life trajectories. The intensity with which adolescents can find meaning in religion is revealed in their conversion experiences. No one knows how common such experiences are, but there may be a sizeable minority of young people who are seized by the dramatic feeling that they have "found God" and who see themselves as thereby acquiring a new identity. The conversion process is accompanied by vivid emotion, a sense of the world being reorganized, and a feeling of relief that the pieces finally fit together. Similar conversions may also occur outside of the religious realm, in the context of becoming a revolutionary or the adherent of some new social doctrine.

Anthroplogists have shown that in every culture there is a need to express certain basic attitudes through religion. Similar needs also exist in our culture, and the children growing up in it reflect this in their behavior. The religious concepts that children evolve will, of course, be shaped strongly by the specific concepts of their parents. If their parents are Catholic, they will probably have different notions about God than if they are Protestant or Jewish. The formal doctrines of each religious denomination offer specialized religious images. But there is also anthropological evidence to suggest that some basic attitudes about the friendliness of the gods, the amount of evil in the world, and the pervasiveness of sin are influenced by the way an individual has been treated by his parents. Significant statistical correlations have been shown to exist between some child-rearing practices and the kinds of religiously tinged attitudes just mentioned. These correlations have been based primarily on cultures outside of the Western countries, so it is impossible to draw conclusions that can be applied on a one-to-one basis to children in our society. But speaking generally, one can say that the harsher the ways in which one treats a child, the more likely he is to view religious forces and figures as harsh. The child who has had a tough life will be inclined to visualize the spiritual world in forboding terms. Whatever formal religious doctrines he learns will probably be superimposed on the "gut-level" image of the universe he has constructed while growing up in his family. Religion is obviously not something that a child learns only in his church. His ultimate religious convictions are a composite of what his parents say and do about religious matters, how they treat him as a human being, and also his own needs to make sense out of what he has witnessed.

Family Themes

Early in this book we pointed out that each family is a small but complicated organization. Its members have intertwining ties. In order to exist reasonably as a group, they have to balance and counterbalance the strong feelings they entertain toward each other. Things that happen to one of them cannot fail to spread out and have effects upon all. The internal intimacy of people living in families extends to wrestling in common with certain core dilemmas.

Several different investigators have noticed that each family is often preoccupied with a central theme or problem, and its members are invested in this problem each in his own way. We first became interested in this phenomenon a number of years ago when we observed that the individual fantasy responses of family members to ink blots and pictures contained striking parallels. Even though these responses were secured in a way that prevented any family member from influencing what any of the others would say when asked to look at blots and pictures, amazing similarities appeared. As we explored these similarities through interviews and other procedures, we could see that they usually reflected a major focus of concern in the family. We became aware that most families are typified by a central preoccupation. For example, in one family everyone is struggling with the problem of proving he is not weak and "down" but rather strong and "up." In another family the theme may relate to the issue of feeling foreign and alienated and wanting to find ways of getting closeness and acceptance from other people. In another family the central theme focuses on the question of how one can survive in a world that is too tough and in which love and nurturance are so scarce. In yet a further instance, a family may be caught up in a struggle to master anxieties linked to sexual drives and the differences between the male and female roles.

Typically, each member of the family is involved with the family theme in his own special fashion. Let us consider a family group in which the theme concerns being strong and "up" versus weak and "down." The father may show his concern about this issue in his strenuous efforts to get ahead in his job and in his need to be sure that everyone in the family acknowledges his authority. The mother may register her concern in her need to have the biggest and fanciest home in the neighborhood and to be accepted in superior social circles. The daughter may reveal her preoccupation with the theme in her dedication to getting high grades and in an unusual sensitivity to being criticized. The son may reflect the theme in his endless efforts to fashion his body in the Superman image through exercise and sports and by his bullying of the weaker kids on the block. Within the family itself, the theme may be powerfully evident in the way the various members jockey for positions of power and superiority. We have seen many families in which one member is finally overwhelmed by the problem or threat confronting them all and breaks down with a spectacular psychological symptom. For example, in the family struggling with the theme of superiority versus weakness, the daughter might suddenly begin to report sensations of weakness and futility and tearfully plead to withdraw from school for a while. Or the son might dramatically get caught stealing a neighbor's car and thereby obtain widespread publicity as to what a daring and aggressive fellow he is.

It has been intriguing to us that the equivalent family theme may often be detected in multiple generations of one family (69, 70, 76, 77). We participated in a study in which psychological tests were administered to five different generations of the same family, and it was possible to demonstrate that the same theme was prominent throughout. Each generation dealt with the theme in its own way. In this particular instance the family members were all struggling to master their sexual fantasies and wishes. In one generation the solution might take the form of clamping down and being extremely puritanical, while in another it might take the reverse form of wild eruptions of sexual acting-out. Most of the troubles that occurred over the five generations had to do with either over-control or under-control of sexual impulses. It would be scientifically premature to say that every family wrestles with its own central theme for generation after generation. This may not be true in some families. A good deal of research will be required before this question can be settled. We would simply like to emphasize that a fair amount of evidence exists that family members share similar problems and conflicts (see 67–82). This has been a guiding assumption in our therapeutic work with disturbed children. It has also, for many years, been widely accepted by others dedicated to helping troubled boys and girls. In the course of helping children, it is usually theorized that they cannot be healed adequately unless the key people in their family life—mother and father—are also treated. It is almost universally accepted by child therapists that the disturbed child mirrors what is, at some level, also fulminating in one or both of his parents. The view is also held by many that the disturbed child is merely the visible representative of a troubled family. He is simply the weakest link in the chain at that moment. Or he is the scapegoat upon whom the other family members are unloading their tensions about the central family problem. Indeed, it has been observed that when you follow a disturbed family over a period of years, one member may first surface with symptoms that label him as "the patient," but after he "gets better" a second member may pop up with symptoms, and so forth down the line. Each member successively dramatizes what is bothering everyone in the group.

It is not by accident that we have chosen to discuss the matter of family interdependence as one of the last topics in this book. In so doing, we want to close on the same message we highlighted at the beginning. Essentially, this message asserts that parents and children are part of a complicated social system, and that the things that go on between them have to be interpreted in the context of that system.

CHAPTER 9

Final Thoughts

WE HOPE we have made it clear that achieving success as a mother or father is not easy. It has been fashionable for certain experts to reassure parents that all they have to do is "act natural" and trust to their own instincts in order to do the right thing. This notion is soothing to people who do not want to face up to the fact that skill and hard work are just as important in raising children as in any other human enterprise. There are few areas of life where energy and expert knowledge do not help to solve problems. The more you know about a task you tackle, the greater the likelihood you will be successful. We see no reason to assume that the problems encountered by parents should be an exception. Actually, we have witnessed many instances in which parents were able to cope better with child-rearing dilemmas by acquiring pertinent information. Of course, they had to be willing to act on the basis of the information. We have seen parents who, after being briefed on the bad effects of overly severe forms of punishment, began to use a more moderate approach, and who were rewarded by less antagonistic behavior from their kids. We have seen parents who became much more calm and reasonable toward their so-called "hyperactive child" when they could accurately understand that his "symptoms" did not mean that he was seriously flawed or "sick." We have seen parents who pulled their kids out of the acute phase of a phobic dread of attending school by assimilating and applying certain facts we communicated to them about the relationship between the child's fear and the effects of mothers and fathers being overly possessive and overly intrusive. We have observed young boys whose disturbance decreased significantly when their mothers learned that getting too intimately close to them was feminizing and injurious.

We do not mean to imply that knowledge is all that it takes for parents to cope with child-rearing problems. There are many instances in which acquiring the facts does not do parents much good, because they are motivated by irrational feelings that get in the way. If you don't like one of your kids and can't change your negative attitude, this means an antagonistic relationship with him is inevitable no matter how much information you store up about child rearing. If you are painfully scared of life and have to hold onto your children the way some people hold onto a life preserver, this will ultimately cause a compensatory reaction in them. Your stock of child-rearing information will be of little utility when matched against your fear. Undoubtedly, deep emotions and unconscious wishes play an important part in how we treat our children. This has been well established scientifically. But it is also true that there are large areas of behavior in which rationality and knowledge are still important. Knowing what is true can help many parents to master crises and behave more sensibly. Accurate information can assist them in more effectively deciding such things as how early to wean a child, how much independence to allow him, when to toilet train, and how much emphasis to place on formal sex education.

One of the most demanding things we have proposed throughout this book is that parents monitor, day by day, what is actually going on with their children. We have suggested that they watch to see if their children continue to act unusually unhappy or tense or depressed or angry. If they find this to be so, they are probably doing something damaging, and there is reason to plan remedial action. By being conscientious observers they can detect early if things are going wrong. In so doing, they increase the chances of finding a solution. When parents allow disturbed reaction patterns in their children to go on for years, these patterns become almost irreversible. Research has shown that early intervention and trouble-shooting can dramatically help a child who is becoming disturbed. Parents who detect persistent signs of distress in their children can launch corrective maneuvers on their own. They can scan themselves and try to see how they may be contributing to the problem. They can use the information they pick up from such self-examination to experiment with new ways of relating to their kids. If they have been too tough, they can soften their stance. If they have been too inconsistent, they can work hard at harmonizing their expectations. If they have been too intrusive, they can back off. If they have not been communicating clearly, they can pour a lot more energy into what they say. They often manage to initiate constructive changes because they have the powerful motive of wanting to relieve the pain they see in their children. They are so worried about the discomfort of their disturbed kids that they are willing to work hard at potential cures. We would speculate that most problems between parents and children get settled in this self-initiated way. However, in a small proportion of cases, parents find that no matter how hard they try they are not able to bring about changes that will relieve their children's disturbance. It may then be sensible to call in outside consultation. This may range all the way from sitting down with a wise friend and discussing the problem to contacting a professional expert like a psychologist or psychiatrist. Consultation with an expert does not necessarily mean that a long period of expensive therapy is inevitable. It is possible that after parents are given an understanding of what they are doing wrong, they may be able to muster corrective action on their own. But such action may be difficult if rigid attitudes based on anger or weakness or fear are involved.

We would like to return again to the matter of mothers and fathers staying alert to what is happening in the family. Part of this process should include their monitoring their own feelings. We suggested that they should regularly stop and take stock of how they *feel* when they are close to their children. If they find over and over that they feel anger or tension or any other negative emotion when they interact with them, they should ask why. If they are uncomfortable when they are at close quarters with them, this probably means the kids are similarly uncomfortable. As earlier mentioned, there are also more localized problem areas in which mothers and fathers can check themselves to see if they are causing trouble. We have offered miniature check lists that a parent might use to decide if he is manipulating his offspring in unfair ways. For example, if he finds he is repeatedly doing things such as restricting the child's movements or encouraging him to be overly dependent, he should wonder whether he is preventing him from learning how to be a real individual. In other instances, we proposed ways in which parents could monitor such things as whether they are too distant, too suspicious, too pushy, too over-identified, too inclined to give contradictory messages, and so forth. We see the sensitive parent as tuned into his own feelings and capable of using them to get an advanced sighting on what is happening between his children and himself.

Another theme we would simply like to mention is the importance of avoiding extremes. Many of the difficulties mothers and fathers get into evolve from going too far in one direction or the other. The scientific literature contains many illustrations of how parents who move too far from a middle ground force their children into untenable positions. It will be recalled that children do not fare well if their parents usually inflict punishment either with great severity or with unrealistic lightness. Also, extremes in behavior about achievement do not work. If mothers and fathers push too hard to make their kids come out on top, or if they set their expectations far too low, the result is that the kids adopt a distorted and usually troubled approach to achievement demands. We have specified, in various places in this book, the value of parents taking a middle position on a number of other major issues.

Finally, no matter how hackneyed it may sound, we must emphatically repeat that there is no substitute for just plain friendliness and warmth. We have cited scientific evidence that children do well in so many ways if they feel their parents like them and are willing to give of themselves. Illustratively, it has been shown that in an atmosphere of friendliness they have a better chance of arriving at a clear sense of identity, forming good and stable personality defenses, and doing well in school. Friendliness cannot be faked. However, the hostile parent need not remain entangled in his own anger permanently. If he faces up to his real feelings and explores the reasons for them, he may be able to shift. But if he cannot muster the will to do so, he will probably be faced with progressively more warlike behavior from his kids.

We have, in essence, dramatized the idea that being an effective parent calls for knowledge and hard work. It does not come "naturally." It requires, also, a willingness to keep updating your understanding of how the people in your family feel about each other. But perhaps most important of all, it demands a willingness to keep in touch with your own attitudes and biases toward your children.

⋙REFERENCES⋘

Chapter 1

1. Alexander, J. F. (1973). "Defensive and Supportive Communications in Normal and Deviant Families," *Journal of Consulting and Clinical Psychology* 40: 223–231.

2. Alkire, A. A. (1969), "Social Power and Communication within Families of Disturbed and Nondisturbed Preadolescents," *Journal of Personality and Social Psychology* 13: 335–349.

3. ——— (1972). "Enactment of Social Power and Role Behavior in Families of Disturbed and Nondisturbed Preadolescents," *Developmental Psychology* 7: 270–276.

4. Becker, J., Tatsuoka, M. M., and Carlson, A. R. (1965). "The Communicative Value of Parental Speech in Families with Disturbed Children," *Journal of Nervous and Mental Disease* 141: 359–364.

5. Becker, W. C., Peterson, D. R., Luria, Zella, Shoemaker, D. J., and Hellmer, L. A. (1962). "Relations of Factors Derived from Parent-Interview Ratings to Behavior Problems of Five-Year-Olds," *Child Development* 33: 509–535.

6. Birtchnell, J. (1969). "The Possible Consequences of Early Parent Death," *British Journal of Medical Psychology* 42: 1–12.

7. Block, J. (1969). "Parents of Schizophrenic, Neurotic, Asthmatic, and Congenitally Ill Children," *Archives of General Psychiatry* 20: 659–674.

8. Block, Jeanne, Patterson, V., Block, J., and Jackson, D. D. (1958). "A Study of the Parents of Schizophrenic and Neurotic Children," *Psychiatry* 21: 387–397.

9. Bronfenbrenner, U. (1961). "The Changing American Child—a Speculative Analysis," *Merrill-Palmer Quarterly* 7: 73–95.

10. Ciarlo, D. D., Lidz, T., and Ricci, J. (1967). "Word Meaning in Parents of Schizophrenics," *Archives of General Psychiatry* 17: 470–477.

11. Cowen, E. L., Huser, J., Beach, D. R., and Rappaport, J. (1970). "Parental Perceptions of Young Children and Their Relation to Indexes of Adjustment," *Journal of Consulting and Clinical Psychology* 34: 97–103.

12. Duncan, P. (1971). "Parental Attitudes and Interactions in Delinquency," *Child Development* 42: 1751–1765.

13. Frank, G. H. (1965). "The Role of the Family in the Development of Psychopathology." *Psychological Bulletin* 64: 191–205.

14. Gassner, S. and Murray, E. J. (1969). "Dominance and Conflict in the Interactions between Parents of Normal and Neurotic Children," *Journal of Abnormal Psychology* 74: 33–41.

15. Gelfand, D. M. and Hartmann, D. P. (1968). "Behavior Therapy with Children: a Review and Evaluation of Research Methodology," *Psychological Bulletin* 69: 204–215.

REFERENCES

16. Golfarb, W., Goldfarb, N., and Scholl, H. H. (1965–66). "The Speech of Mothers of Schizophrenic Children," *American Journal of Psychiatry* 122: 1220–1227.

17. Goldin, P. C. (1969). "A Review of Children's Reports of Parent Behaviors," *Psychological Bulletin* 71: 222–236.

18. Goldstein, M. J., Gould, E., Alkire, A., Rodnick, E. H., and Judd, L. L. (1970). "Interpersonal Themes in the Thematic Apperception Test Stories of Families of Disturbed Adolescents," *Journal of Nervous and Mental Disease* 150: 354–365.

19. Granlund, E. and Knowles, L. (1969). "Child-Parent Identification and Academic Underachievement," *Journal of Consulting and Clinical Psychology* 33: 495–496.

20. Green, A. H., Gaines, R. W., and Sandgrund, A. (1974). "Child Abuse: Pathological Syndrome of Family Interaction," *American Journal of Psychiatry* 131: 882–886.

21. Hall, C. L., Jr. (1965). "Maternal Control as Related to Schizoid Behaviors in Grossly Normal Males," *Journal of Personality* 33: 613–621.

22. Handel, G. (1965). "Psychological Study of Whole Families," *Psychological Bulletin* 63: 19–41.

23. Hoffman, M. L. and Hoffman, L. W. (eds.) (1964). *Review of Child Development Research* Vol. 1. New York: Russell Sage Foundation.

24. Jones, M. C. (1968). "Personality Correlates and Antecedents of Drinking Behavior in Adult Males," *Journal of Consulting and Clinical Psychology* 32: 2–12.

25. Klein, M. M., Plutchik, R., and Conte, H. R. (1973). "Parental Dominance-Passivity and Behavior Problems of Children," *Journal of Consulting and Clinical Psychology* 40: 416–419.

26. Lidz, T. (1969). "The Influence of Family Studies on the Treatment of Schizophrenia," *Psychiatry* 32: 237–251.

27. Matarazzo, J. D. and Saslow, G. (1960). "Psychological and Related Characteristics of Smokers and Nonsmokers," *Psychological Bulletin* 57: 493–513.

28. McClelland, D. C., Davis, W. N., Kalin, R., and Wanner, E. (1972). *The Drinking Man* New York: Free Press.

29. McCord, W., Porta, J. and McCord, J. (1962). "The Familial Genesis of Psychoses: a Study of the Childhood Backgrounds of Twelve Psychotics," *Psychiatry* 25: 60–71.

30. Mishler, E. G. and Waxler, N. E. (1965). "Family Interaction Processes and Schizophrenia: a Review of Current Theories." *Merrill–Palmer Quarterly* 11: 269–315.

31. ———— (1968). *Interaction in Families* New York: Wiley.

32. Morris, G. O. and Wynne, L. C. (1965). "Schizophrenic Offspring and Parental Styles of Communication," *Psychiatry* 28: 19–44.

33. Murray, E. J., Seagull, A., and Geisinger, D. (1969). "Motivational Patterns in the Families of Adjusted and Maladjusted Boys," *Journal of Consulting and Clinical Psychology* 33: 337–342.

34. Myers, J. K. and Roberts, B. H. (1959). *Family and Class Dynamics in Mental Illness* New York: Wiley.

35. Novak, A. L. and Van der veen, F. (1970). "Family Concepts and Emotional Disturbance in the Families of Disturbed Adolescents with Normal Siblings," *Family Process* 9: 157–171.

36. Odom, L., Seeman, J., and Newbrough, J. R. (1971). "A Study of Family Communication Patterns and Personality Integration in Children," *Child Psychiatry and Human Development* 1: 275–285.

37. Oleinick, M. S., Bahn, A. K., Eisenberg, L., and Lilienfeld, A. M. (1966). "Early Socialization Experiences and Intrafamilial Environment," *Archives of General Psychiatry* 15: 344–353.

38. Palombo, S. R., Merrifield, J., Weigert, W., Morris, G. O., and Wynne, L. C. (1967). "Recognition of Parents of Schizophrenics from Excerpts of Family Therapy Interviews," *Psychiatry* 30: 405–412.

39. Paulson, M. J., Lin, Tien-teh, and Hanssen, C. (1972). "Family Harmony: an Etiologic Factor in Alienation," *Child Development* 43: 591–603.

40. Piety, K. R. (1968). "Parent Perception and Social Adjustment among Elementary and High School Students," *Journal of Clinical Psychology* 24: 165–171.

41. Platt, H., Jurgensen, G., and Chorost, S. B. (1962). "Comparison of Childrearing Attitudes of Mothers and Fathers of Emotionally Disturbed Adolescents," *Child Development* 33: 117–122.

42. Reiss, D. (1968). "Individual Thinking and Family Interaction: An Experimental Study of Categorization Performance in Families of Normals, Those with Character Disorders and Schizophrenics," *Journal of Nervous and Mental Disease* 146: 384–403.

43. ——— (1971). "Varieties of Consensual Experience: Contrasts between Families of Normals, Delinquents, and Schizophrenics," *Journal of Nervous and Mental Disease* 152: 73–95.

44. Riester, A. E. and Zucker, R. A. (1968). "Adolescent Social Structure and Drinking Behavior," *Personnel and Guidance Journal* 47: 304–312.

45. Sanders, S. (1972). "Selective Auditory Perception of Parental Voices by the Disturbed Child," *Genetic Psychology Monographs* 85: 51–112.

46. Schofield, W. and Balian, L. (1959). "A Comparative Study of the Personal Histories of Schizophrenic and Nonpsychiatric Patients," *Journal of Abnormal and Social Psychology* 59: 216–225.

47. Schooler, C. (1972). "Childhood Family Structure and Adult Characteristics," *Sociometry* 35: 255–269.

48. Schuham, A. I. (1972). "Activity, Talking Time, and Spontaneous Agreement in Disturbed and Normal Family Interaction," *Journal of Abnormal Psychology* 79: 68–75.

49. Sherman, H. and Farina, A. (1974). "Social Adequacy of Parents and Children," *Journal of Abnormal Psychology* 83: 327–330.

50. Siegelman, E., Block, J., Block, Jeanne, and von der Lippe, A. (1970). "Antecedents of Optimal Psychological Adjustment," *Journal of Consulting and Clinical Psychology* 35: 283–289.

51. Siegman, A. W. (1966). "Father Absence during Early Childhood and Antisocial Behavior," *Journal of Abnormal Psychology* 71: 71–74.

52. Spinetta, J. J. and Rigler, D. (1972). "The Child-Abusing Parent: a Psychological Review," *Psychological Bulletin* 77: 296–304.

53. Stabenau, J. R. (1973). "Schizophrenia: a Family's Projective Identification," *American Journal of Psychiatry* 130: 19–23.

54. Tallman, I. (1970). "The Family as a Small Problem-Solving Group," *Journal of Marriage and the Family* 32: 94–104.

55. Werner, M., Stabenau, J. R., and Pollin, W. (1970). "Thematic Apperception Test Method for the Differentiation of Families of Schizophrenics, Delinquents, and 'Normals,' " *Journal of Abnormal Psychology* 75: 139–145.

REFERENCES

56. Wimberger, H. C. and Kogan, Kate L. (1974). "A Direct Approach to Altering Mother-Child Interaction in Disturbed Children," *Archives of General Psychiatry* 30: 636–639.

57. Winder, C. L. and Rau, L. (1962). "Parental Attitudes Associated with Social Deviance in Preadolescent Boys," *Journal of Abnormal and Social Psychology* 64: 418–424.

58. Zuckerman, M. (1966). "Save the Pieces! A Note on 'The Role of the Family in the Development of Psychopathology,' " *Psychological Bulletin* 66: 78–80.

Chapter 2

1. Bandura, A. and Walters, R. H. (1959). *Adolescent Aggression* New York: The Ronald Press.

2. Baragona, R. (1964). "The Relationship between Certain Parental Attitudes and Selected Personality Characteristics in Nursery School Children." Unpublished doctoral dissertation, Rutgers, The State University.

3. Barry, H. III (1969). "Cross-Cultural Research with Matched Pairs of Societies," *Journal of Social Psychology* 79: 25–33.

4. Battle, E. S. and Lacey, B. (1972). "A Context for Hyperactivity in Children, over Time." *Child Development* 43: 757–773.

5. Baumrind, D. (1967). "Child Care Practices Anteceding Three Patterns of Preschool Behavior," *Genetic Psychology Monographs* 75: 43–88.

6. ——— (1968). "Authoritarian versus Authoritative Parental Control," *Adolescence* 3: 255–272.

7. ——— (1971). "Current Patterns of Parental Authority," Developmental Psychology Monographs, Vol. 4, 1.

8. Bayley, Nancy, and Schaefer, E. S. (1967). "Maternal Behavior and Personality Development Data from the Berkeley Growth Study," In *Studies in Adolescence,* ed. R. E. Grinder. New York: Macmillan, pp. 141–151.

9. Beckwith, L. (1972). "Relationships between Infants' Social Behavior and Their Mothers' Behavior," *Child Development* 43: 397–411.

10. Bornston, F. L. and Coleman, J. C. (1956). "The Relationship between Certain Parents' Attitudes toward Child Rearing and the Direction of Aggression of Their Young Adult Offspring," *Journal of Clinical Psychology* 12: 41–44.

11. Braginsky, D. D. (1970). "Parent-Child Correlates of Machiavellianism and Manipulative Behavior," *Psychological Reports* 27: 927–932.

12. Bronson, W. C. (1972). "The Role of Enduring Orientations to the Environment in Personality Development," *Genetic Psychology Monographs* 86: 3–80.

13. Bronson, W. C., Katten, E. S., and Livson, N. (1959). "Patterns of Authority and Affection in Two Generations," *Journal of Abnormal and Social Psychology* 58: 143–152.

14. Bugental, D. E., Love, L. R., and Kaswan, J. W. (1972). "Videotaped Family Interaction: Differences Reflecting Presence and Type of Child Disturbance," *Journal of Abnormal Psychology* 79: 285–290.

15. Calhoun, L. G. and Mikesell, R. H. (1972). "Biodata Antecedents of the Need for Approval in Male College Freshmen," *Developmental Psychology* 7: 226.

16. Chorost, S. B. (1962). "Parental Child-Rearing Attitudes and the Correlates in Adolescent Hostility," *Genetic Psychology Monographs* 66: 49–90.

17. Coopersmith, S. (1967). *The Antecedents of Self-Esteem* San Francisco: Freeman.

18. Davids, A. and Hainsworth, P. K. (1967). "Maternal Attitudes about Family Life and Child Rearing as Avowed by Mothers and Perceived by Their Underachieving and High-Achieving Sons," *Journal of Consulting Psychology* 31: 29–37.

19. Davis, W. L. and Phares, E. J. (1969). "Parental Antecedents of Internal-External Control of Reinforcement," *Psychological Reports* 24: 427–436.

20. Dielman, T. E., Barton, K., and Cattell, R. B. (1973). "Cross-Validational Evidence on the Structure of Parental Reports of Child Rearing Practices," *Journal of Social Psychology* 90: 243–250.

21. Douvan, E. and Adelson, J. (1966). *The Adolescent Experience* New York: Wiley.

22. Droppleman, L. F. and Schaefer, E. S. (1963). "Boys' and Girls' Reports of Maternal and Paternal Behavior," *Journal of Abnormal and Social Psychology* 67: 648–654.

23. Epstein, R. and Komorita, S. S. (1965). "Parental Discipline, Stimulus Characteristics of Outgroups, and Social Distance in Children," *Journal of Personality and Social Psychology* 2: 416–420.

24. Gecas, V. (1971). "Parental Behavior and Dimensions of Adolescent Self-Evaluation," *Sociometry* 34: 466–482.

25. ——— (1972). "Parental Behavior and Contextual Variations in Adolescent Self-Esteem," *Sociometry* 35: 332–345.

26. Gordon, J. E. and Smith, E. (1965). "Children's Aggression, Parental Attitudes, and the Effects of an Affiliation-Arousing Story," *Journal of Personality and Social Psychology* 1: 654–659.

27. Heilbrun, A. B., Jr. (1968). "Sex Role, Instrumental-Expressive Behavior, and Psychopathology in Females," *Journal of Abnormal Psychology* 73: 131–136.

28. Heilbrun, A. B., Jr. and Orr, Helen K. (1965). "Maternal Childrearing Control History and Subsequent Cognitive and Personality Functioning of the Offspring," *Psychological Reports* 17: 259–272.

29. Hoffman, M. L. (1960). "Power Assertion by the Parent and Its Impact on the Child," *Child Development* 31: 129–143.

30. ——— (1963). "Parent Discipline and the Child's Consideration of Others," *Child Development* 34: 573–588.

31. ——— (1967). "Child-Rearing Practices and Moral Development: Generalizations from Empirical Research," In *Studies in Adolescence,* ed. R. E. Grinder. New York: Macmillan, pp. 275–293.

32. Hoffman, M. L. and Hoffman, L. W. (1964). *Review of Child Development Research* New York: Russell Sage Foundation.

33. Hoffman, M. L. and Saltzstein, H. D. (1967). "Parent Discipline and the Child's Moral Development," *Journal of Personality and Social Psychology* 5: 45–57.

34. Itkin, W. (1955). "Relationships between Attitudes toward Parents and Parents' Attitudes toward Children," *Journal of Genetic Psychology* 86: 339–352.

REFERENCES

35. Kagan, J. and Moss, H. A. (1962). *Birth to Maturity: A Study in Psychological Development* New York: Wiley.

36. Koenig, F., Sulzer, J. L., and Hansche, W. J. (1971). "Mother's Mode of Discipline and Child's Verbal Ability," *Child Study Journal* 2: 19–22.

37. Kogan, K. L. (1972). "Specificity and Stability of Mother-Child Interaction Styles," *Child Psychiatry and Human Development* 2: 160–168.

38. Koutrelakos, J. (1968). "Authoritarian Person's Perception of His Relationship with His Father," *Perceptual and Motor Skills* 26: 967–973.

39. Lambert, W. W., Triandis, L. M., and Wolf, M. (1959). "Some Correlates of Beliefs in the Malevolence and Benevolence of Supernatural Beings: A Cross-Societal Study," *Journal of Abnormal and Social Psychology* 58: 162–169.

40. Lyle, W. H., Jr., and Levitt, E. E. (1955). "Punitiveness, Authoritarianism, and Parental Discipline of Grade School Children," *Journal of Abnormal and Social Psychology* 51: 42–46.

41. Lynn, R. (1961). "Personality Characteristics of the Mothers of Aggressive and Unaggressive Children," *Journal of Genetic Psychology* 99: 159–164.

42. Lynn, R. and Gordon, I. E. (1962). "Maternal Attitudes to Child Socialization: Some Social and National Differences," *British Journal of Social and Clinical Psychology* 1: 52–55.

43. Madoff, J. M. (1959). "The Attitudes of Mothers of Juvenile Delinquents toward Child Rearing," *Journal of Consulting Psychology* 23: 518–520.

44. Marshall, H. H. (1965). "The Effect of Punishment on Children: A Review of the Literature and a Suggested Hypothesis," *Journal of Genetic Psychology* 106: 23–33.

45. McCord, W., McCord, J., and Howard, A. (1961). "Familial Correlates of Aggression in Non-Delinquent Male Children," *Journal of Abnormal and Social Psychology* 62: 79–93.

46. Minton, C., Kagan, J., and Levine, J. A. (1971). "Maternal Control and Obedience in the Two-Year-Old," *Child Development* 42: 1873–1894.

47. Mosher, D. L. and Mosher, J. B. (1965). "Relationships between Authoritarian Attitudes in Delinquent Girls and the Authoritarian Attitudes and Authoritarian Rearing Practices of Their Mothers," *Psychological Reports* 16: 23–30.

48. Moulton, R. W., Burnstein, E., Liberty, P. G., Jr., and Altucher, N. (1966). "Patterning of Parental Affection and Disciplinary Dominance as a Determinant of Guilt and Sex Typing," *Journal of Personality and Social Psychology* 4: 356–363.

49. Patterson, G. R. (1965). "Parents as Dispensers of Aversive Stimuli," *Journal of Personality and Social Psychology* 2: 844–851.

50. Peck, R. F. (1967). "Family Patterns Correlated with Adolescent Personality Structure," In *Studies in Adolescence,* ed. R. E. Grinder. New York: Macmillan, pp. 133–140.

51. Petrullo, L. and Bass, B. M., eds. (1961). *Leadership and Interpersonal Behavior* New York: Holt, Rinehart & Winston.

52. Sears, R. R. (1961). "Relation of Early Socialization Experiences to Aggression in Middle Childhood," *Journal of Abnormal and Social Psychology* 63: 466–492.

53. Sears, R. R., Maccoby, E. E., Levin, H., and others (1957). *Patterns of Child Rearing* Evanston, Ill.: Row, Peterson.

54. Slater, P. E. (1962). "Parental Behavior and the Personality of the Child," *Journal of Genetic Psychology* 101: 53–68.

55. Slocum, W. L. and Stone, Carol L. (1963). "Family Culture Patterns and Delinquent-Type Behavior," *Marriage and Family Living* 25: 202–208.

56. Symonds, P. M. (1939). *The Psychology of Parent-Child Relationships* New York: Appleton-Century.

57. Unger, S. M. (1962). "Antecedents of Personality Differences in Guilt Responsivity," *Psychological Reports* 10: 357–358.

58. Walsh, R. P. (1968). "Parental Rejecting Attitudes and Control in Children," *Journal of Clinical Psychology* 24: 185–186.

59. Zunich, M. (1966). "Child Behavior and Parental Attitudes," *Journal of Psychology* 62: 41–46.

Chapter 3

1. Arnaud, S. (1959). "Some Psychological Characteristics of Children of Multiple Sclerotics," *Psychosomatic Medicine* 21: 8–22.

2. Baker, B. L. (1969). "Symptom Treatment and Symptom Substitution in Enuresis," *Journal of Abnormal Psychology* 74: 42–49.

3. Bergmann, T. [in collaboration with Freud, A.] (1965). *Children in the Hospital* New York: International Universities.

4. Caldwell, B. M. (1964). "The Effects of Infant Care," In *Review of Child Development,* ed. M. L. Hoffman and L. W. Hoffman. New York: Russell Sage Foundation, pp. 9–87.

5. Centers, L., and Centers, R. (1963). "Body Cathexes of Parents of Normal and Malformed Children for Progeny and Self," *Journal of Consulting Psychology* 27: 319–323.

6. Dow, T. E., Jr. (1965). "Social Class and Reaction to Physical Disability," *Psychological Reports* 17: 39–62.

7. Eisenman, R. (1970). "Birth Order, Sex, Self-Esteem, and Prejudice against the Physically Disabled," *The Journal of Psychology* 75: 147–155.

8. Fisher, S. (1970). *Body Experience in Fantasy and Behavior* New York: Appleton-Century-Crofts.

9. —— (1973). *Body Consciousness* Englewood Cliffs, N.J.: Prentice-Hall.

10. Fisher, S. and Cleveland, S. (1968). *Body Image and Personality* New York: Dover, rev. ed.

11. Fisher, S. and Greenberg, R. (in press). *The Scientific Credibility of Freud's Theories and Therapy* New York: Basic Books.

12. Forrer, G. R. (1959). "The Mother of a Defective Child," *Psychoanalytic Quarterly* 28: 59–63.

13. Gardner, R. A. (1968). "Psychogenic Problems of Brain Injured Children and Their Parents," *Journal of the American Academy of Child Psychiatry* 7: 471–491.

14. —— (1969). "The Guilt Reaction of Parents of Children with Severe Physical Disease," *American Journal of Psychiatry* 126: 636–644.

15. Gelfand, S. (1963). "The Relationship of Birth Order to Pain Tolerance," *Journal of Clinical Psychology* 19: 406.

16. Graham, P. and George, S. (1972). "Children's Response to Parental Illness: Individual Differences," *Journal of Psychosomatic Research* 16: 215–255.

REFERENCES

17. Grayden, C. (1958). "The Relationship between Neurotic Hypochondriasis and Three Personality Variables: Feelings of Being Unloved, Narcissism, and Guilt Feelings." Unpublished doctoral dissertation, New York University.

18. Jacobs, M. A., Spilken, A. Z., Norman, M. M., Anderson, L., and Rosenheim, E. (1972). "Perceptions of Faulty Parent-Child Relationships and Illness Behavior," *Journal of Consulting and Clinical Psychology* 39: 49–55.

19. Johnson, R. (1971). "Maternal Influence on Child Behavior in the Dental Setting," *Psychiatry in Medicine* 2: 221–228.

20. Jordan, T. E. (1962). "Research on the Handicapped Child and the Family," *Merrill-Palmer Quarterly* 8: 243–260.

21. Kuethe, J. L. (1962). "Social Schemas," *Journal of Abnormal and Social Psychology* 64: 31–38.

22. Lax, R. F. (1972). "Some Aspects of the Interaction between Mother and Impaired Child: Mother's Narcissistic Trauma," *International Journal of Psycho-Analysis* 53: 339–344.

23. Lussier, A. (1960). "The Analysis of a Boy with a Congenital Deformity," In *Psychoanalytic Study of the Child,* Vol. 15. New York: International Universities, pp. 430–453.

24. Macgregor, F. C., Abel, T. M., Bryt, A., Lover, E., and Weissmann, S. (1953). *Facial Deformities and Plastic Surgery* Springfield, Ill.: Charles C Thomas.

25. Martin, B. and Kubly, D. (1955). "Results of Treatment of Enuresis by a Conditioned Response Method," *Journal of Consulting Psychology* 19: 71–73.

26. Mechanic, D. (1964). "The Influence of Mothers on Their Children's Health Attitudes and Behavior," *Pediatrics* 33: 444–453.

27. Meissner, A. L., Thoreson, R. W., and Buller, A. J. (1967). "Relation of Self-Concept to Impact and Obviousness of Disability among Male and Female Adolescents," *Perceptual and Motor Skills* 24: 1099–1105.

28. Mercer, R. T. (1974). "Mothers' Responses to Their Infants with Defects," *Nursing Research* 23: 133–137.

29. Michel-Hutmacher, R. (1955). "The Inside of the Body in the Imagination of Children," *Schweizer Zeitschrift für Psychologische Anwendung* 14: 1–26. (German trans.)

30. Money, J. and Ehrhardt, A. A. (1972). *Man & Woman. Boy & Girl* Baltimore, Md.: Johns Hopkins.

31. Nagy, M. H. (1953). "Children's Conceptions of Some Bodily Functions," *Journal of Genetic Psychology* 83: 199–216.

32. Peterson, E. T. (1972). "The Impact of Adolescent Illness on Parental Relationships," *Journal of Health and Social Behavior* 13: 429–437.

33. Petroni, F. A. (1969). "Social Class, Family Size, and the Sick Role," *Journal of Marriage and the Family* 31: 728–735.

34. Richardson, S. A., Hastorf, A. H., and Dornbusch, S. M. (1964). "Effects of Physical Disability on a Child's Description of Himself," *Child Development* 35: 893–907.

35. Rutter, M. (1970). "Sex Differences in Children's Responses to Family Stress," In *International Year Book of Child Psychiatry,* ed. E. J. Anthony and C. Koupernik, Vol. 1: *The Child in His Family* New York: Wiley.

36. Sears, R. R., Maccoby, E. E., and Levin, H. (1957). *Patterns of Child Rearing* Evanston, Ill.: Row, Peterson.

37. Schechter, M. D. (1961). "The Orthopedically Handicapped Child," *Archives of General Psychiatry* 4: 247–253.

38. Schilder, P. and Wechsler, D. (1935). "Short Communication: What Do Children Know about the Interior of the Body?," *International Journal of Psychoanalysis* 16: 355–360.

39. Schoelly, M. L. and Fraser, A. W. (1955). "Emotional Reactions in Muscular Dystrophy," *American Journal of Physiological Medicine* 34: 119–123.

40. Schonell, F. and Watts, B. (1956). "A First Survey of the Effects of a Subnormal Child on the Family Unit," *American Journal of Mental Deficiency* 61: 210–219.

41. Shaffer, J. P. (1964). "Social and Personality Correlates of Children's Estimates of Height," *Genetic Psychology Monographs* 70: 97–134.

42. Siller, J. (1960). "Psychological Concomitants of Amputation in Children," *Child Development* 31: 109–120.

43. Smith, W. I., Powell, E. K., and Ross, S. (1955). "Food Aversions: Some Additional Personality Correlates," *Journal of Consulting Psychology* 19: 145–149.

44. Townes, B. D., Wold, D. A., and Holmes, T. H. (1974). "Parental Adjustment to Childhood Leukemia," *Journal of Psychosomatic Research* 18: 9–14.

Chapter 4

1. Apperson, L. B. and McAdoo, W. G., Jr. (1968). "Parental Factors in the Childhood of Homosexuals," *Journal of Abnormal Psychology* 73: 201–206.

2. Bardwick, J. M. (1971). *Psychology of Women: A Study of Biocultural Conflicts* New York: Harper & Row.

3. Beach, F. A., ed. (1965). *Sex and Behavior* New York: Wiley.

4. Bieliauskas, V. J. (1965). "Recent Advances in the Psychology of Masculinity and Femininity," *Journal of Psychology* 60: 255–263.

5. Biller, H. B. and Weiss, S. D. (1970). "The Father-Daughter Relationship and the Personality Development of the Female," *Journal of Genetic Psychology* 116: 79–93.

6. Conn, J. (1940). "Children's Reactions to the Discovery of Genital Differences," *American Journal of Orthopsychiatry* 10: 747–754.

7. Conn, J. and Kanner, L. (1947). "Children's Awareness of Sex Differences," *Journal of Child Psychiatry* 1: 3–57.

8. DeMartino, M. F., ed. (1963). *Sexual Behavior and Personality Characteristics* New York: Citadel.

9. Douvan, E., and Adelson, J. (1966). *The Adolescent Experience* New York: Wiley.

10. Fisher, S. (1973). *The Female Orgasm* New York: Basic Books.

11. Fisher, S. and Greenberg, R. P. (in press). *The Scientific Credibility of Freud's Theories and Therapy.* New York: Basic Books.

12. Freud, S. (1938). "Three Contributions to the Theory of Sex," In *Basic Writings of S. Freud,* ed. A. A. Brill. New York: Modern Library.

13. Kagan, J. and Moss, H. A. (1962). *Birth to Maturity: A Study in Psychological Development* New York: Wiley.

REFERENCES

14. Kenyon, F. E. (1968). "Studies in Female Homosexuality—Psychological Test Results," *Journal of Consulting and Clinical Psychology* 32: 510–513.

15. Kinsey, A. C., Pomeroy, W., and Martin, C. (1948). *Sexual Behavior in the Human Male* Philadelphia: Saunders.

16. Kinsey, A. C., Pomeroy, W., Martin, C., and Gebhard, P. (1953). *Sexual Behavior in the Human Female* Philadelphia: Saunders.

17. Kohlberg, L. (1966). "A Cognitive-Developmental Analysis of Children's Sex-Role Concepts and Attitudes," In *The Development of Sex Differences,* ed. E. Maccoby. Stanford, Calif.: Stanford University Press, pp. 82–173.

18. Lynn, D. B. (1969). *Parental and Sex Role Identification* Berkeley, Calif.: McCutchan.

19. Masters, R. E. L. (1967). *Sexual Self-Stimulation* Los Angeles, Calif.: Sherbourne.

20. Masters, W. H. and Johnson, V. (1966). *Human Sexual Response* Boston: Little, Brown.

21. ———— (1970). *Human Sexual Inadequacy* Boston: Little, Brown.

22. Money, J., ed. (1965). *Sex Research: New Developments* New York: Holt, Rinehart and Winston.

23. Rainwater, L. (1965). *Family Design: Marital Sexuality, Family Size, and Contraception* Chicago, Ill.: Aldine.

24. Schofield, M. (1965). *The Sexual Behaviour of Young People* Boston: Little, Brown.

25. Terman, L. M. (1951). "Correlates of Orgasm Adequacy in a Group of 556 Wives" *Journal of Psychology* 32: 115–172.

26. Winokur, G., ed. (1963). *Determinants of Human Sexual Behavior* Springfield, Ill.: Charles C. Thomas.

Chapter 5

1. Altus, W. D. (1965). "Birth Order and Academic Primogeniture," *Journal of Personality and Social Psychology* 2: 872–876.

2. Baer, D. J. and Ragosta, T. (1966). "Relationship between Perceived Child-Rearing Practices and Verbal and Mathematical Ability," *Journal of Genetic Psychology* 108: 105–108.

3. Barclay, J. R., Stilwell, W. E., and Barclay, L. K., (1972). "The Influence of Paternal Occupation on Social Interaction Measures in Elementary School Children," *Journal of Vocational Behavior* 2: 433–447.

4. Barry, H., III. (1957). "Relationships between Child Training and the Pictorial Arts," *Journal of Abnormal and Social Psychology* 54: 380–383.

5. Bartlett, E. W. and Smith, C. P. (1966). "Childrearing Practices, Birth Order and the Development of Achievement-Related Motives," *Psychological Reports* 19: 1207–1216.

6. Barton, K., Dielman, T. E., and Cattell, R. B. (1974). "Child Rearing Practices and Achievement in School," *Journal of Genetic Psychology* 124: 155–165.

7. Baruch, G. K. (1972). "Maternal Influences upon College Women's Attitudes toward Women and Work," *Developmental Psychology* 6: 32–37.

244

8. Battle, E. S. and Lacey, B. (1972). "A Context for Hyperactivity in Children, Over Time," *Child Development* 43: 757–773.

9. Bee, H. L. (1967). "Parent-Child Interaction and Distractibility in 9-Year-Old Children," *Merrill–Palmer Quarterly* 13: 175–190.

10. Bieri, J. (1960). "Parental Identification, Acceptance of Authority, and Within-Sex Differences in Cognitive Behavior," *Journal of Abnormal and Social Psychology* 60: 76–79.

11. Bond, G. L. and Tinker, M. A. (1973). *Reading Difficulties,* 3rd ed. Englewood Cliffs, N.J.: Prentice-Hall.

12. Bradburn, N. M. (1963). "N Achievement and Father Dominance in Turkey," *Journal of Abnormal and Social Psychology* 67: 464–468.

13. Bronfenbrenner, U. (1961). "Some Familial Antecedents of Responsibility and Leadership in Adolescents," In *Leadership and Interpersonal Behavior,* ed. L. Petrullo and B. M. Bass. New York: Holt, Rinehart and Winston.

14. Brunkan, R. J. (1965). "Perceived Parental Attitudes and Parental Identification in Relation to Field of Vocational Choice," *Journal of Counseling Psychology* 12: 39–47.

15. Busse, T. V. (1969). "Child-Rearing Antecedents of Flexible Thinking," *Developmental Psychology* 1: 585–591.

16. Chaffee, S. H., McLeod, J. M., and Atkin, C. K. (1971). "Parental Influences on Adolescent Media Use," *American Behavioral Scientist* 14: 323–340.

17. Coleman, J. C., Bornston, F. L., and Fox, J. (1958). "Parental Attitudes as Related to Reading Disabilities in Children," *Psychological Reports* 4: 47–51.

18. Cooper, J. B. and Lewis, J. H. (1962). "Parent Evaluation as Related to Social Ideology and Academic Achievement," *Journal of Genetic Psychology* 101: 135–143.

19. Cross, H. J. (1970). "The Relation of Parental Training to Conceptual Structure in Preadolescents," *Journal of Genetic Psychology* 116: 197–202.

20. Damerson, L. E. (1955). "Mother-Child Interaction in the Development of Self-Restraint," *Journal of Genetic Psychology* 86: 289–308.

21. Davids, A. and Hainsworth, P. K. (1967). "Maternal Attitudes about Family Life and Child Rearing as Avowed by Mothers and Perceived by Their Underachieving and High-Achieving Sons," *Journal of Consulting Psychology* 31: 29–37.

22. Davidson, K. S., Sarason, S. B., Lighthall, F. F., Waite, R. R., and Sarnoff, I. (1958). "Differences between Mothers' and Fathers' Ratings of Low Anxious and High Anxious Children," *Child Development* 29: 155–160.

23. Domino, G. (1969). "Maternal Personality Correlates of Sons' Creativity," *Journal of Consulting and Clinical Psychology* 33: 180–183.

24. Douvan, E. and Adelson, J. (1966). *The Adolescent Experience* New York: Wiley.

25. Dreyer, A. S. and Well, M. B. (1966). "Parental Values, Parental Control, and Creativity in Young Children," *Journal of Marriage and the Family* 28: 83–88.

26. Dubno, P. and Freedman, R. D. (1971). "Birth Order, Educational Achievement, and Managerial Attainment," *Personnel Psychology* 24: 63–70.

27. Eisenman, R. and Schussel, N. R. (1970). "Creativity, Birth Order, and Preference for Symmetry," *Journal of Consulting and Clinical Psychology* 34: 275–280.

28. Feld, S. C. (1967). "Longitudinal Study of the Origins of Achievement Strivings," *Journal of Personality and Social Psychology* 7: 408–414.

29. Franco, D. (1965). "The Child's Perception of 'the Teacher' as Compared to His Perception of 'the Mother,' " *Journal of Genetic Psychology* 107: 133–141.

REFERENCES

30. Freeberg, N. E. and Payne, D. T. (1967). "Dimensions of Parental Practice Concerned with Cognitive Development in the Preschool Child," *Journal of Genetic Psychology* 111: 245–261.

31. Garwood, D. S. (1964). "Personality Factors Related to Creativity in Young Scientists," *Journal of Abnormal and Social Psychology* 68: 413–419.

32. Gerber, G. L. (1973). "Psychological Distance in the Family as Schematized by Families of Normal, Disturbed, and Learning-Problem Children," *Journal of Consulting and Clinical Psychology* 40: 139–147.

33. Gitlin, S. (1958). "A Study of the Interrelationships of Parents' Measured Interest Patterns and Those of Their Children." Unpublished doctoral dissertation, Temple University.

34. Goldstein, K. M., Cary, G. L., Chorost, S. B., and Dalack, J. D. (1970). "Family Patterns and the School Performance of Emotionally Disturbed Boys," *Journal of Learning Disabilities* 3: 12–17.

35. Gordon, J. E. (1959). "Relationships among Mothers' n Achievement, Independence Training Attitudes, and Handicapped Children's Performance," *Journal of Consulting Psychology* 23: 207–212.

36. Grams, A., Hafner, A. J., and Quast, W. (1965). "Child Anxiety: Self-Estimates, Parent Reports, and Teacher Ratings," *Merrill-Palmer Quarterly* 11: 261–266.

37. Hamilton, V. (1971). "Effect of Maternal Attitude on Development of Logical Operations," *Perceptual and Motor Skills* 33: 63–69.

38. Heilbrun, A. B., Jr. (1962). "Parental Identification and College Adjustment," *Psychological Reports* 10: 853–854.

39. Heilbrun, A. B., Jr., Harrell, S. N., and Gillard, B. J. (1967). "Perceived Child-rearing Attitudes of Fathers and Cognitive Control in Daughters," *Journal of Genetic Psychology* 111: 29–40.

40. Heilbrun, A. B., Jr. and Orr, H. K. (1965). "Maternal Childrearing Control History and Subsequent Cognitive and Personality Functioning of the Offspring," *Psychological Reports* 17: 259–272.

41. ——— (1966). "Perceived Maternal Childrearing History and Subsequent Motivational Effects of Failure," *Journal of Genetic Psychology* 109: 75–89.

42. Hermans, H. J. M., Ter Laak, J. J. F., and Maes, P. C. J. M. (1972). "Achievement Motivation and Fear of Failure in Family and School," *Developmental Psychology* 6: 520–528.

43. Hollenbeck, G. P. (1965). "Conditions and Outcomes in the Student-Parent Relationship," *Journal of Consulting Psychology* 29: 237–241.

44. Hurley, J. R. (1967). "Parental Malevolence and Children's Intelligence," *Journal of Consulting Psychology* 31: 199–204.

45. Jackson, R. M. and Meara, N. M. (1974). "Father Identification, Achievement, and Occupational Behavior of Rural Youth: One Year Follow-Up," *Journal of Vocational Behavior* 4: 349–356.

46. Kagan, J. and Moss, H. A. (1962). *Birth to Maturity: A Study in Psychological Development* New York: Wiley.

47. Katkovsky, W., Preston, A., and Crandall, V. J. (1964). "Parents' Attitudes toward Their Personal Achievement and toward the Achievement Behaviors of Their Children," *Journal of Genetic Psychology* 104: 67–82.

48. ——— (1964). "Parents' Achievement Attitudes and Their Behavior with Their

Children in Achievement Situations," *Journal of Genetic Psychology* 104: 105–121.

49. Kellaghan, T. and MacNamara, J. (1972). "Family Correlates of Verbal Reasoning Ability," *Developmental Psychology* 7: 49–53.

50. Kennedy, W. A. and Willcutt, H. (1963). "Youth-Parent Relations of Mathematically-Gifted Adolescents," *Journal of Clinical Psychology* 19: 400–402.

51. Kerckhoff, A. C. and Huff, J. L. (1974). "Parental Influence on Educational Goals," *Sociometry* 37: 307–327.

52. Landers, D. M. and Martens, R. (1971). "The Influence of Birth Order and Situational Stress on Motor Performance," *Psychonomic Science* 24: 165–167.

53. LeMay, M. (1970). "Birth Order and Scholastic Aptitude and Achievement," *Journal of Consulting and Clinical Psychology* 34: 287.

54. Levin, H. (1963). "Permissive Child Rearing and Adult Role Behavior," In *Contributions to Modern Psychology,* 2d ed., ed. D. E. Dulany, Jr. et. al. New York: Oxford University Press, pp. 351–355.

55. Li, A. K.-F. (1974). "Parental Attitudes, Test Anxiety, and Achievement Motivation: A Hong Kong Study," *Journal of Social Psychology* 93: 3–11.

56. Lyle, W. H., Jr. and Levitt, E. E. (1955). "Punitiveness, Authoritarianism, and Parental Discipline of Grade School Children," *Journal of Abnormal and Social Psychology* 51: 42–46.

57. Maccoby, E. E., ed. (1966). *The Development of Sex Differences* Stanford, Calif.: Stanford University Press.

58. Maddy, N. R. (1943). "Comparison of Children's Personality Traits, Attitudes, and Intelligence with Parental Occupation," *Genetic Psychology Monographs* 27: 3–65.

59. Marshall, H. H. (1965). "The Effect of Punishment on Children: A Review of the Literature and a Suggested Hypothesis," *Journal of Genetic Psychology* 106: 23–33.

60. Martindale, C. (1972). "Father's Absence, Psychopathology, and Poetic Eminence," *Psychological Reports* 31: 843–847.

61. Maw, W. H. and Maw, E. W. (1966). "Children's Curiosity and Parental Attitudes," *Journal of Marriage and the Family* 28: 343–345.

62. McClelland, D. C. (1961). *The Achieving Society* Princeton, N.J.: Van Nostrand.

63. McClelland, D. C., Baldwin, A. L., Bronfenbrenner, U., and Strodtbeck, F. L. (1958). *Talent and Society* Princeton, N.J.: Van Nostrand.

64. McClelland, D. C. and Friedman, G. A. (1952). "A Cross-Cultural Study of the Relationship between Child-Training Practices and Achievement Motivation Appearing in Folk Tales," In *Readings in Social Psychology,* 2d ed. New York: Holt.

65. McClelland, D. C., Rindlisbacher, A., and DeCharms, R. (1955). "Religious and Other Sources of Parental Attitudes toward Independence Training," In *Studies in Motivation,* ed. D. C. McClelland. New York: Appleton-Century-Crofts.

66. Murray, C. (1971). "The Effects of Ordinal Position on Measured Intelligence and Peer Acceptance in Adolescence," *British Journal of Social and Clinical Psychology* 10: 221–227.

67. Mussen, P. H. and Parker, A. L. (1965). "Mother Nurturance and Girls' Incidental Imitative Learning," *Journal of Personality and Social Psychology* 2: 94–97.

68. Mutimer, D., Loughlin, L., and Powell, M. (1966). "Some Differences in the Family Relationships of Achieving and Underachieving Readers," *Journal of Genetic Psychology* 109: 67–74.

REFERENCES

69. Norman, R. D. (1966). "The Interpersonal Values of Parents of Achieving and Nonachieving Gifted Children," *Journal of Psychology* 64: 49–57.

70. Oberlander, M. I., Frauenfelder, K. J., and Heath, H. (1971). "The Relationship of Ordinal Position and Sex to Interest Patterns," *Journal of Genetic Psychology* 119: 29–36.

71. Oberlander, M., Jenkin, N., Houlihan, K., and Jackson, J. (1970). "Family Size and Birth Order as Determinants of Scholastic Aptitude and Achievement in a Sample of Eighth Graders," *Journal of Consulting and Clinical Psychology* 34: 19–21.

72. Patterson, G. R. (1965). "Parents as Dispensers of Aversive Stimuli," *Journal of Personality and Social Psychology* 2: 844–851.

73. Patterson, G. R., Littman, R. A., and Hinsey, W. C. (1964). "Parental Effectiveness as Reinforcers in the Laboratory and Its Relation to Child Rearing Practices and Child Adjustment in the Classroom," *Journal of Personality* 32: 181–199.

74. Pearlin, L. I. and Kohn, M. L. (1966). "Social Class, Occupation, and Parental Values: A Cross-National Study," *American Sociological Review* 31: 466–479.

75. Pearlin, L. I., Yarrow, M. R., and Scarr, H. A. (1967–68). "Unintended Effects of Parental Aspirations: The Case of Children's Cheating," *American Journal of Sociology* 73: 73–83.

76. Radin, N. (1971). "Maternal Warmth, Achievement Motivation, and Cognitive Functioning in Lower-Class Preschool Children," *Child Development* 42: 1560–1565.

77. ——— (1972). "Father-Child Interaction and the Intellectual Functioning of Four-Year-Old Boys," *Developmental Psychology* 6: 353–361.

78. Rees, A. H. and Palmer, F. H. (1970). "Factors Related to Change in Mental Test Performance," *Developmental Psychology Monograph* 3: No. 2.

79. Rehberg, R. A., Sinclair, J., and Schafer, W. E. (1970). "Adolescent Achievement Behavior, Family Authority Structure, and Parental Socialization Practices," *American Journal of Sociology* 75: 1012–1034.

80. Rubin, D. (1968). "Mother and Father Schemata of Achievers and Underachievers in Primary School Arithmetic," *Psychological Reports* 23: 1215–1221.

81. ——— (1969). "A Comparison of the Mother and Father Schemata of Achievers and Underachievers: A Study of Primary Grades and Achievement in Arithmetic," *Journal of Social Psychology* 78: 295–296.

82. Santrock, J. W. (1972). "Relation of Type and Onset of Father Absence to Cognitive Development," *Child Development* 43: 455–469.

83. Sarason, I. G. and Koenig, K. P. (1965). "Relationships of Test Anxiety and Hostility to Description of Self and Parents," *Journal of Personality and Social Psychology* 2: 617–621.

84. Sarason, S. B., Davidson, K. S., Lighthall, F. F., Waite, R. R., and Ruebush, B. K. (1960), *Anxiety in Elementary School Children* New York: Wiley.

85. Saxe, R. M. and Stollak, G. E. (1971). "Curiosity and the Parent-Child Relationship," *Child Development* 42: 373–384.

86. Shaw, M. C. and White, D. L. (1965). "The Relationship between Child-Parent Identification and Academic Underachievement," *Journal of Clinical Psychology* 21: 10–13.

87. Siegelman, M. (1973). "Parent Behavior Correlates of Personality Traits Related to Creativity in Sons and Daughters," *Journal of Consulting and Clinical Psychology* 40: 43–47.

88. Solomon, D., Hirsch, J. G., Scheinfeld, D. R., and Jackson, J. C. (1972). "Family Characteristics and Elementary School Achievement in an Urban Ghetto," *Journal of Consulting and Clinical Psychology* 39: 462–466.

89. Stein, R. S., Stein, A. B., and Kagan, J. (1970). "The Effects of Ordinal Position and Identification on the Development of Philosophical Attitudes," *Journal of Genetic Psychology* 117: 13–24.

90. Stewart, M. A., Pitts, F. N., Jr., Craig, A. G., and Kieruf, W. (1966). "The Hyperactive Child Syndrome," *American Journal of Orthopsychiatry* 36: 861–867.

91. Stolz, L. M. (1967). *Influences on Parent Behavior* Stanford, Calif.: Stanford University Press.

92. Strodtbeck, F. L. and Creelan, P. G. (1968). "The Interaction Linkage between Family Size, Intelligence, and Sex-Role Identity," *Journal of Marriage and the Family* 30: 301–307.

93. Tocco, T. S. and Bridges, C. M., Jr. (1973). "The Relationship between the Self-Concepts of Mothers and Their Children," *Child Study Journal* 3: 161–179.

94. Weinstein, L. (1968). "The Mother-Child Schema, Anxiety, and Academic Achievement in Elementary School Boys," *Child Development* 39: 257–264.

95. Werner, E. E. (1969). "Sex Differences in Correlations between Children's IQs and Measures of Parental Ability, and Environmental Ratings," *Developmental Psychology* 1: 280–285.

96. Werry, J. S. (1969). "Developmental Hyperactivity," In *Annual Progress in Child Psychiatry and Child Development,* ed. S. Chess and A. Thomas. New York: Brunner-Mazel, pp. 485–505.

97. Werts, C. E. and Watley, D. J. (1972). "Paternal Influence on Talent Development," *Journal of Counseling Psychology* 19: 367–373.

98. Willerman, L. and Stafford, R. E. (1972). "Maternal Effects on Intellectual Functioning," *Behavior Genetics* 2: 321–325.

99. Willis, J. W. (1971). "Parental Attitudes and Academic Achievement in a Sample of Emotionally Disturbed Children," *Psychological Reports* 29: 866.

100. Wolkon, G. H. and Levinger, G. (1965). "Birth Order and Need for Achievement," *Psychological Reports* 16: 73–74.

101. Worthy, M. and Markle, A. (1970). "Racial Differences in Reactive versus Self-Paced Sports Activities," *Journal of Personality and Social Psychology* 16: 439–443.

102. Wyer, R. S., Jr. (1965). "Self-Acceptance, Discrepancy between Parents' Perceptions of Their Children, and Goal-Seeking Effectiveness," *Journal of Personality and Social Psychology* 2: 311–316.

Chapter 6

1. Adams, J. F., ed. (1968). *Understanding Adolescence* Boston: Allyn & Bacon.

2. Alkire, A. A., Goldstein, M. J., Rodnick, E. H, and Judd, L. L. (1971). "Social Influence and Counterinfluence within Families of Four Types of Disturbed Adolescents," *Journal of Abnormal Psychology* 77: 32–41.

3. Bamber, J. H. (1974). "The Fears of Adolescents," *Journal of Genetic Psychology* 125: 127–140.

REFERENCES

4. Block, J. (1971). *Lives Through Time* Berkeley, Calif.: Bancroft Books.

5. Bronson, W. C. (1967). "Stable Patterns of Behavior: The Significance of Enduring Orientations for Personality Development," In *Minnesota Symposia on Child Psychology,* ed. J. P. Hill, Vol. 2.

6. ———— (1972). "The Role of Enduring Orientations to the Environment in Personality Development," *Genetic Psychology Monographs* 86: 3–80.

7. Cava, E. L. and Raush, H. L. (1952). "Identification and the Adolescent Boy's Perception of His Father," *Journal of Abnormal and Social Psychology* 47: 855–856.

8. Chaffee, S. H., McLeod, J. M., and Atkin, C. K. (1971). "Parental Influences on Adolescent Media Use," *American Behavioral Scientist* 14: 323–340.

9. Chorost, S. B. (1962). "Parental Child-Rearing Attitudes and their Correlates in Adolescent Hostility," *Genetic Psychology Monographs* 66: 49–90.

10. Coleman, J. S. (1962). *The Adolescent Society* Glencoe, Ill.: The Free Press.

11. Dentler, R. A. and Monroe, L. J. (1961). "The Family and Early Adolescent Conformity and Deviance," *Marriage and Family Living* 23: 241–247.

12. Douvan, E. and Adelson, J. (1966). *The Adolescent Experience* New York: Wiley.

13. Engel, M. (1959). "The Stability of the Self-Concept in Adolescence," *Journal of Abnormal and Social Psychology* 58: 211–215.

14. Flacks, R. (1967). "The Liberated Generation: An Exploration of the Roots of Student Protest," *Journal of Social Issues* 23: 52–75.

15. Gecas, V. (1971). "Parental Behavior and Dimensions of Adolescent Self-Evaluation," *Sociometry* 34: 466–482.

16. Goldstein, M. J., Judd, L. L., Rodnick, E. H., Alkire, A., and Gould, E. (1968). "A Method for Studying Social Influence and Coping Patterns Within Families of Disturbed Adolescents," *Journal of Nervous and Mental Disease* 147: 233–251.

17. Grinder, R. E., ed. (1963). *Studies in Adolescence* New York: Macmillan.

18. Hanssen, C. A. and Paulson, M. J. (1972). "Our Anti-Establishment Youth: Revolution or Evolution?" *Adolescence* 7: 393–408.

19. Hoffman, L. W., and Hoffman, M. L., eds. (1966). *Review of Child Development Research,* Vol. 2. New York: Russell Sage Foundation.

20. Holland, J. (1959). "A Theory of Vocational Choice," *Journal of Counseling Psychology* 6: 35–45.

21. ———— (1968). "Explorations of a Theory of Vocational Choice," *Journal of Applied Psychology Monograph Supplement* 52: No. 1, Part 2, 1–54.

22. Hunt, J. V., and Eichorn, D. H. (1972). "Maternal and Child Behaviors: A Review of Data from the Berkeley Growth Study," *Seminars in Psychiatry* 4: 367–381.

23. Johnson, T. F. (1952). "Conceptions of Parents Held by Adolescents," *Journal of Abnormal and Social Psychology* 47: 783–789.

24. Jones, M. C. (1965). "Psychological Correlates of Somatic Development," *Child Development* 36: 899–911.

25. Kandel, D. and Lesser, G. S. (1969). "Parent-Adolescent Relationships and Adolescent Independence in the United States and Denmark," *Journal of Marriage and the Family* 31: 348–358.

26. Keniston, K. (1967). "The Sources of Student Dissent," *Journal of Social Issues* 23: 108–137.

27. ———— (1968). *Young Radicals* New York: Harcourt Brace & World.

28. Konopka, G. (1973). "Requirements for Healthy Development of Adolescent Youth," *Adolescence* 8: 291–316.

29. Liccione, J. V. (1955). "The Changing Family Relationships of Adolescent Girls," *Journal of Abnormal and Social Psychology* 51: 421–426.

30. Mead, M. (1949). *Male and Female* New York: Dell.

31. Medinnus, G. R. (1965). "Adolescents' Self-Acceptance and Perceptions of Their Parents," *Journal of Consulting Psychology* 29: 150–154.

32. Mlott, S. R. (1972). "Some Significant Relationships between Adolescents and Their Parents as Revealed by the Minnesota Multiphasic Personality Inventory," *Adolescence* 7: 169–182.

33. Niemi, R. C. (1974). *How Family Members Perceive Each Other* New Haven, Conn.: Yale University Press.

34. Peck, R. F. (1958). "Family Patterns Correlated with Adolescent Personality Structure," *Journal of Abnormal and Social Psychology* 57: 347–350.

35. Peskin, H. (1973). "Influence of the Developmental Schedule of Puberty on Learning and Ego Functioning," *Journal of Youth and Adolescence* 2: 273–290.

36. Petroni, F. A. (1972). "Adolescent Liberalism—The Myth of a Generation Gap," *Adolescence* 7: 221–232.

37. Sebald, H. (1968). *Adolescence: A Sociological Analysis* New York: Appleton-Century-Crofts.

38. Seligman, R., Gleser, G., Rauh, J., and Harris, L. (1974). "The Effect of Earlier Parental Loss in Adolescence," *Archives of General Psychiatry* 31: 475–479.

39. Smith, M. B., Haan, N., and Block, J. (1970). "Social-Psychological Aspects of Student Activism," *Youth and Society* 1: 261–288.

40. Smith, T. E. (1970). "Foundations of Parental Influence upon Adolescents: An Application of Social Power Theory," *American Sociological Review* 35: 860–873.

41. Solomon, D. (1961). "Adolescents' Decisions: A Comparison of Influence from Parents with That from Other Sources," *Marriage and Family Living* 23: 393–395.

42. Sorensen, R. C. (1972). *Adolescent Sexuality in Contemporary America* New York: World Publishing.

Chapter 7

1. Anderson, R. E. (1968). "Where's Dad?" *Archives of General Psychiatry* 18: 641–649.

2. Anthony, E. J. and Koupernik, C., eds. (1974). *The Child in his Family: Children at Psychiatric Risk,* Vol. 3. New York: Wiley.

3. Anthony, S. (1971). *The Discovery of Death in Childhood and After* London: Penguin Press.

4. Barry, H., Jr. and Lindemann, E. (1960). "Critical Ages for Maternal Bereavement in Psychoneuroses," *Psychosomatic Medicine* 22: 166–181.

5. Becker, D. and Margolin, F. (1967). "How Surviving Parents Handled Their Young Children's Adaptation to the Crisis of Loss," *American Journal of Orthopsychiatry* 37: 753–757.

REFERENCES

6. Benson, L. (1968). *Fatherhood: A Sociological Perspective* New York: Random House.

7. Berg, M. and Cohen, B. B. (1959). "Early Separation from the Mother in Schizophrenia," *Journal of Nervous and Mental Disease* 128: 365–369.

8. Biller, H. B. (1971). *Father, Child, and Sex Role* Lexington, Mass.: Heath.

9. Birtchnell, J. (1969). "The Possible Consequences of Early Parent Death," *British Journal of Medical Psychology* 42: 1–12.

10. Blinder, B. J. (1972). "Sibling Death in Childhood," *Child Psychiatry and Human Development* 2: 169–175.

11. Bowlby, J. (1973). *Attachment and Loss,* Vol. 2. New York: Basic Books.

12. Brill, N. Q. and Liston, E. H., Jr. (1966). Parental Loss in Adults with Emotional Disorders," *Archives of General Psychiatry* 14: 307–314.

13. Burchinal, L. G. and Rossman, J. E. (1961). "Relations among Maternal Employment Indices and Developmental Characteristics of Children," *Marriage and Family Living* 23: 334–340.

14. Cheek, F. E. (1965). "Family Interaction Patterns and Convalescent Adjustment of the Schizophrenic," *Archives of General Psychiatry* 13: 138–147.

15. Cline, D.W. and Westman, J. C. (1971). "The Impact of Divorce on the Family," *Child Psychiatry and Human Development* 2: 78–83.

16. Cohen, L. J. and Campos, J. J. (1974). "Father, Mother, and Stranger as Elicitors of Attachment Behaviors in Infancy," *Developmental Psychology* 10: 146–154.

17. Crook, T. and Raskin, A. (1975). "Association of Childhood Parental Loss with Attempted Suicide and Depression," *Journal of Consulting and Clinical Psychology* 43: 277.

18. Crumley, F. E. and Blumenthal, R. S. (1973). "Children's Reactions to Temporary Loss of the Father," *American Journal of Psychiatry* 130: 778–782.

19. Despert, J. L. (1962). *Children of Divorce* Garden City, N.Y.: Doubleday.

20. Earle, A. M. and Earle, B. V. (1961). "Early Maternal Deprivation and Later Psychiatric Illness," *American Journal of Orthopsychiatry* 31: 181–186.

21. Etaugh, C. (1974). "Effects of Maternal Employment on Children: A Review of Recent Research," *Merrill-Palmer Quarterly of Behavior and Development* 20: 71–98.

22. Fulton, R., ed. (1965). *Death and Identity* New York: Wiley.

23. Furman, E. (1974). *A Child's Parent Dies* New Haven, Conn.: Yale University Press.

24. Goldstein, H. S. (1972). "Internal Controls in Aggressive Children from Father-present and Father-absent Families," *Journal of Consulting and Clinical Psychology* 39: 512.

25. Goode, W. J. (1956). *After Divorce* Glencoe, Ill.: The Free Press.

26. Graham, P. and George, S. (1972). "Children's Response to Parental Illness: Individual Differences," *Journal of Psychosomatic Research* 16: 251–255.

27. Gregory, I. (1965). "Anterospective Data following Childhood Loss of a Parent: I. Delinquency and High School Dropout," *Archives of General Psychiatry* 13: 99–109.

28. ——— (1965). "Anterospective Data following Childhood Loss of a Parent: II: Pathology, Performance, and Potential among College Students," *Archives of General Psychiatry* 13: 110–120.

29. ——— (1966). "Retrospective Data concerning Childhood Loss of a Parent: I:

Actuarial Estimates vs. Recorded Frequencies of Orphanhood,'' *Archives of General Psychiatry* 15: 354–361.

30. —— (1966). ''Retrospective Data concerning Childhood Loss of a Parent: II: Category of Parental Loss by Decade of Birth, Diagnosis, and MMPI,'' *Archives of General Psychiatry* 15: 362–367.

31. Harrison, S. I., Davenport, C. W., and McDermott, J. F., Jr. (1967). ''Children's Reactions to Bereavement,'' *Archives of General Psychiatry* 17: 593–597.

32. Hetherington, E. M. ''Effects of Paternal Absence on Sex-Typed Behaviors in Negro and White Preadolescent Males,'' *Journal of Personality and Social Psychology* 4: 87–91.

33. —— (1972). ''Effects of Father Absence on Personality Development in Adolescent Daughters,'' *Developmental Psychology* 7: 313–326.

34. Hilgard, J. R. and Newman, M. F. (1963). ''Early Parental Deprivation as a Functional Factor in the Etiology of Schizophrenia and Alcoholism,'' *American Journal of Orthopsychiatry* 33: 409–420.

35. —— (1963). ''Parental Loss by Death in Childhood as an Etiological Factor among Schizophrenic and Alcoholic Patients Compared with a Non-Patient Community Sample,'' *Journal of Nervous and Mental Disease* 137: 14–28.

36. Hoffman, L. W. (1974). ''The Effects of Maternal Employment on the Child—A Review of the Research,'' *Developmental Psychology* 10: 204–228.

37. Hoffman, Lois W. and Nye, F. I. (1974). *Working Mothers* San Francisco, Calif.: Jossey-Bass.

38. Hoffman, M. L. and Hoffman, L. W., eds. (1964). *Review of Child Development* New York: Russell Sage Foundation.

39. Kelly, F. J. and Baer, D. J. (1969). ''Age of Male Delinquents when Father Left Home and Recidivism,'' *Psychological Reports* 25: 1010.

40. Koch, M. B. (1961). ''Anxiety in Preschool Children from Broken Homes,'' *Merrill-Palmer Quarterly* 7: 225–231.

41. Kogelschatz, J. L., Adams, P. L., and Tucker, D. M. (1972). ''Family Styles of Fatherless Households,'' *Journal of the American Academy of Child Psychiatry* 11: 365–383.

42. Leifer, A. D., Peiderman, P. H., Barnett, C. R., and Williams, J. A. (1972). ''Effects of Mother-Infant Separation on Maternal Attachment Behavior,'' *Child Development* 43: 1203–1218.

43. Lewis, M. (1974). ''The Latency Child in a Custody Conflict,'' *Journal of the American Academy of Child Psychiatry* 13: 635–647.

44. Lynn, D. B. and Sawrey, W. L. (1959). ''The Effects of Father-Absence on Norwegian Boys and Girls,'' *Journal of Abnormal and Social Psychology* 59: 258–262.

45. Marsella, A. J., Dubanoski, R. A., and Mohs, K. (1974). ''The Effects of Father Presence and Absence upon Maternal Attitudes,'' *Journal of Genetic Psychology* 125: 257–263.

46. Martindale, C. (1972). ''Father's Absence, Psychopathology, and Poetic Eminence,'' *Psychological Reports* 31: 843–847.

47. McCord, J., McCord, W., and Thurber, E. (1962). ''Some Effects of Paternal Absence on Male Children,'' *Journal of Abnormal and Social Psychology* 64: 361–369.

48. —— (1963). ''Effects of Maternal Employment on Lower-Class Boys,'' *Journal of Abnormal and Social Psychology* 67: 177–182.

REFERENCES

49. Miller, J. B. (1971). "Children's Reactions to the Death of a Parent: A Review of the Psychoanalytic Literature," *Journal of the American Psychoanalytic Association* 19: 697–719.

50. Miller, S. M. (1974). "The Effects of Maternal Employment on Sex Role Perception, Interests, and Self-Esteem in Kindergarten Girls," Report No. 53, Developmental Program, University of Michigan.

51. Mitchell, D. and Wilson, W. (1967). "Relationship of Father Absence to Masculinity and Popularity of Delinquent Boys," *Psychological Reports* 20: 1173–1174.

52. Moerk, E. L. (1973). "Like Father Like Son: Imprisonment of Fathers and the Psychological Adjustment of Sons," *Journal of Youth and Adolescence* 2: 301–310.

53. Morrison, J. R. (1974). "Parental Divorce as a Factor in Childhood Psychiatric Illness," *Comprehensive Psychiatry* 15: 95–102.

54. Nagy, M. (1948). "The Child's Theories concerning Death," *Journal of Genetic Psychology* 73: 3–27.

55. Nelson, E. A. and Vangen, P. M. (1971). "Impact of Father on Heterosexual Behaviors and Social Development of Preadolescent Girls in a Ghetto Environment," *Proceedings, 79th Annual Convention, APA*, pp. 165–166.

56. Peterson, E. T. (1961). "The Impact of Maternal Employment on the Mother-Daughter Relationship," *Marriage and Family Living* 23: 355–361.

57. Pollock, G. H. (1962). "Childhood Parent and Sibling Loss in Adult Patients," *Archives of General Psychiatry* 7: 295–305.

58. Powell, K. S. (1961). "Maternal Employment in Relation to Family Life," *Marriage and Family Living* 23: 350–355.

59. Robertson, J. and Robertson, Joyce. (1972). "Quality of Substitute Care as an Influence on Separation Responses," *Journal of Psychosomatic Research* 16: 261–265.

60. Ross, R. (1966). "Separation Fear and the Fear of Death in Children." Unpublished doctoral dissertation, New York University.

61. Santrock, J. W. (1970). "Influence of Onset and Type of Paternal Absence on the First Four Eriksonian Developmental Crises," *Developmental Psychology* 3: 273–274.

62. ——— (1972). "Relation of Type and Onset of Father Absence to Cognitive Development," *Child Development* 43: 455–469.

63. Schlesinger, B. (1966). "The One-Parent Family: Recent Literature," *Journal of Marriage and the Family* 28: 103–109.

64. Schooler, C. (1972). "Childhood Family Structure and Adult Characteristics," *Sociometry* 35: 255–269.

65. Schwarz, J. C. (1968). "Fear and Attachment in Young Children," *Merrill-Palmer Quarterly* 14: 313–322.

66. Seligman, R., Gleser, G., Rauh, J., and Harris, L. (1974). "The Effect of Earlier Parental Loss in Adolescence," *Archives of General Psychiatry* 31: 475–479.

67. Sharp, L. J. (1960). "Employment Status of Mothers and Some Aspects of Mental Illness," *American Sociological Review* 25: 714–717.

68. Siegel, A. E. and Haas, M. B. (1963). "The Working Mother: A Review of Research," *Child Development* 34: 513–542.

69. Siegman, A. W. (1966). "Father Absence during Early Childhood and Antisocial Behavior," *Journal of Abnormal Psychology* 71: 71–74.

70. Skard, A. G. (1965). "Maternal Deprivation: The Research and Its Implications," *Journal of Marriage and the Family* 27: 333–343.

254

71. Sklarew, B. H. (1959). "The Relationship of Early Separation from Parents to Differences in Adjustment in Adolescent Boys and Girls," *Psychiatry* 22: 399–405.

72. Spelke, E., Zelazo, P., Kagan, J., and Kotelchuck, M. (1973). "Father Interaction and Separation Protest," *Developmental Psychology* 9: 83–90.

73. Stayton, D. J., Ainsworth, M. D. S., and Main, M. B. (1973). "Development of Separation Behavior in the First Year of Life: Protest, Following, and Greeting," *Developmental Psychology* 9: 213–225.

74. Stoller, R. J. (1974). "Symbiosis Anxiety and the Development of Masculinity," *Archives of General Psychiatry* 30: 164–172.

75. Suedfeld, P. (1967). "Paternal Absence and Overseas Success of Peace Corps Volunteers," *Journal of Consulting Psychology* 31: 424–425.

76. Sugar, M. (1970). "Children of Divorce," *Pediatrics* 46: 588–595.

77. Tennes, K. H. and Lampl, E. E. (1966). "Some Aspects of Mother-Child Relationship Pertaining to Infantile Separation Anxiety," *Journal of Nervous and Mental Disease* 143: 426–437.

78. Trunnell, T. L. (1968). "The Absent Father's Children's Emotional Disturbances," *Archives of General Psychiatry* 19: 180–188.

79. Vernon, D. T. A., Foley, J. M., and Schulman, J. L. (1967). "Effect of Mother-Child Separation and Birth Order on Young Children's Responses to Two Potentially Stressful Experiences," *Journal of Personality and Social Psychology* 5: 162–174.

80. Wallston, B. (1973). "The Effects of Maternal Employment on Children," *Journal of Child Psychology and Psychiatry* 14: 81–95.

81. Weininger, O. (1972). "Effects of Parental Deprivation: An Overview of Literature and Report on Some Current Research," *Psychological Reports* 30: 591–612.

82. ——— (1975). "The Disabled and Dying Children: Does It Have to Hurt so Much?" *Ontario Psychologist* 7: 29–35.

83. Westman, J. C. (1972). "Effect of Divorce on a Child's Personality Development," *Medical Aspects of Human Sexuality* 6: 38–55.

84. Yarrow, L. J. (1961). "Maternal Deprivation: Toward an Empirical and Conceptual Re-evaluation," *Psychological Bulletin* 58: 459–490.

85. Yudkin, S. and Holme, A. (1963). *Working Mothers and Their Children* London: Michael Joseph.

Chapter 8

Birth Order (Ordinal Position)

1. Adams, B. N. (1972). "Birth Order: A Critical Review," *Sociometry* 35: 411–439.

2. Altus, W. D. (1965). "Birth Order and Scholastic Aptitude," *Journal of Consulting Psychology* 29: 202–205.

3. ——— (1965). "Birth Order and Academic Primogeniture," *Journal of Personality and Social Psychology* 2: 872–876.

4. ——— (1970). "Sex-Role Dissatisfaction, Birth Order, and Parental Favoritism," *Proceedings, 78th Annual Convention, APA,* pp. 161–162.

5. Dohrenwend, B. S. and Dohrenwend, B. P. (1966). "Stress Situations, Birth Order, and Psychological Symptoms," *Journal of Abnormal Psychology* 71: 215–223.

REFERENCES

6. Douvan, E. and Adelson, J. (1966). *The Adolescent Experience* New York: Wiley.

7. Eisenman, R., and Schussel, N. R. (1970). "Creativity, Birth Order, and Preference for Symmetry," *Journal of Consulting and Clinical Psychology* 34: 275–280.

8. Farley, F. H., Hatch, R., Murphy, P., and Miller, K. (1971). "Sibling Structure and Masculinity-Femininity in Male Adolescents," *Adolescence* 6: 441–450.

9. Havassy-De Avila, B. (1971). "A Critical Review of the Approach to Birth Order Research," *Canadian Psychologist* 12: 282–305.

10. Hilton, I. (1967). "Differences in the Behavior of Mothers toward First- and Later-Born Children," *Journal of Personality and Social Psychology* 7: 282–290.

11. Hollender, J. W., Duke, M. P., and Nowicki, S. (1973). "Interpersonal Distance: Sibling Structure and Parental Affection Antecedents," *Journal of Genetic Psychology* 123: 35–45.

12. Koch, H. L. (1956). "Sissiness and Tomboyishness in Relation to Sibling Characteristics," *Journal of Genetic Psychology* 88: 231–244.

13. Lasko, J. K. (1954). "Parent Behavior toward First and Second Children," *Genetic Psychology Monographs* 49: 97–137.

14. Longstreth, L. E. (1969). "Birth Order and Avoidance of Dangerous Activities," *Developmental Psychology* 2: 154.

15. Lunneborg, P. W. (1968). "Birth Order, Aptitude, and Achievement," *Journal of Consulting and Clinical Psychology* 32: 101.

16. MacDonald, A. P., Jr. (1969). "Manifestations of Differential Levels of Socialization by Birth Order," *Developmental Psychology* 1: 485–492.

17. Murray, C. (1971). "The Effects of Ordinal Position on Measured Intelligence and Peer Acceptance in Adolescence," *British Journal of Social and Clinical Psychology* 10: 221–227.

18. Nisbett, R. E. (1968). "Birth Order and Participation in Dangerous Sports," *Journal of Personality and Social Psychology* 8: 351–353.

19. Nowicki, S., Jr. (1971). "Ordinal Position, Approval Motivation, and Interpersonal Attraction," *Journal of Consulting and Clinical Psychology* 36: 265–267.

20. Nye, F. E., Carlson, J., and Garrett, G. (1970). "Family Size, Interaction, Affect, and Stress," *Journal of Marriage and the Family* 32: 216–226.

21. Oberlander, M. I., Frauenfelder, K. J., and Health, H. (1971). "The Relationship of Ordinal Position and Sex to Interest Patterns," *Journal of Genetic Psychology* 119: 29–36.

22. Oberlander, M., Jenkin, N., Houlihan, K., and Jackson, J. (1970). "Family Size and Birth Order as Determinants of Scholastic Aptitude and Achievement in a Sample of Eighth Graders," *Journal of Consulting and Clinical Psychology* 34: 19–21.

23. Sampson, E. E., and Hancock, F. T. (1967). "An Examination of the Relationship between Ordinal Position, Personality, and Conformity: An Extension, Replication, and Partial Verification," *Journal of Personality and Social Psychology* 5: 398–407.

24. Schooler, C. (1972). "Birth Order Effects: Not Here, Not Now!" *Psychological Bulletin*, 78: 161–175.

25. Sears, R. S., Maccoby, E. E., and Levin, H. (1957). *Patterns of Child Rearing* Evanston, Ill.: Row, Peterson.

26. Staples, F. R. and Walters, R. H. (1961). "Anxiety, Birth Order, and Susceptibility to Social Influence," *Journal of Abnormal and Social Psychology* 62: 716–719.

27. Stotland, E. and Dunn, R. E. (1963). "Empathy, Self-Esteem, and Birth Order," *Journal of Abnormal and Social Psychology* 66: 532–540.

28. Strodtbeck, F. L. and Creelan, P. G. (1968). "The Interaction Linkage between Family Size, Intelligence, and Sex-Role Identity," *Journal of Marriage and the Family* 30: 301–307.

29. Swanson, B. R., Massey, R. H., and Payne, I. R. (1972). "Ordinal Position, Family Size, and Personal Adjustment," *Journal of Psychology* 81: 53–58.

30. Uddenberg, N., Almgren, P. E., and Nilsson, A. (1971). "Birth Order and Sex of Siblings: Influence on Parental Identification," *Acta Psychiatrica Scandinavica* 47: 324–333.

31. Walker, C. E. and Tahmisian, J. (1967). "Birth Order and Student Characteristics: A Replication," *Journal of Consulting Psychology* 31: 219.

32. Warren, J. R. (1966). "Birth Order and Social Behavior," *Psychological Bulletin* 65: 38–49.

33. Wolkon, G. H. (1968). "Birth Order and Desire for and Participation in Psychiatric Posthospital Services," *Journal of Consulting and Clinical Psychology* 32: 42–46.

34. Zucker, R. A., Manosevitz, M., and Lanyon, R. I. (1968). "Birth Order, Anxiety, and Affiliation during a Crisis," *Journal of Personality and Social Psychology* 8: 354–359.

Religion

35. Adorno, T. W., et al. (1950). *The Authoritarian Personality* New York: Harper.

36. Allport, G. W. (1960). *The Individual and His Religion* New York: Macmillan.

37. Allport, G. W., Gillespie, J. M., and Young, J. (1953). "The Religion of the Post-War College Student," In *The Adolescent: A Book of Readings,* ed., J. M. Seidman. New York: Dryden Press.

38. Dittes, J. E. (1971). "Religion, Prejudice, and Personality," In *Research on Religious Development,* ed. M. P. Strommen. New York: Hawthorn Books.

39. Douvan, E. and Adelson, J. (1966). *The Adolescent Experience* New York: Wiley.

40. Grinder, R. E., ed. (1963). *Studies in Adolescence* New York: Macmillan.

41. Keene, J. J. (1967). "Religious Behavior and Neuroticism, Spontaneity, and Worldmindedness," *Sociometry* 30: 137–157.

42. Lambert, W. W., Triandis, L. M., and Wolf, M. (1959). "Some Correlates of Beliefs in the Malevolence and Benevolence of Supernatural Beings: A Cross-Societal Study," *Journal of Abnormal and Social Psychology* 58: 162–169.

43. Moberg, D. (1971). "Religious Practices," In *Research on Religious Development,* ed. M. P. Strommen. New York: Hawthorn Books.

44. Putney, S. and Middleton, R. (1961). "Rebellion, Conformity, and Parental Religious Ideologies," *Sociometry* 24: 125–135.

45. Ranck, J. G. (1955). "Some Personality Correlates of Religious Attitude and Belief." Unpublished doctoral dissertation, Columbia University.

46. Rohrbaugh, J. and Jessor, R. (1975). "Religiosity in Youth: A Personal Control against Deviant Behavior," *Journal of Personality* 43: 136–155.

47. Schofield, M. (1965). *The Sexual Behavior of Young People* Boston: Little, Brown.

REFERENCES

48. Whiting, J. W. M. and Child, I. L. (1953). *Child Training and Personality* New Haven: Yale University Press.

49. Yinger, J. M. (1971). *The Scientific Study of Religion* New York: Macmillan.

Sex Differences

50. Maccoby, E. E. and Jacklin, C. N. (1974). *The Psychology of Sex Differences* Stanford, Calif.: Stanford University Press.

Television

51. Bogart, L. (1972–73). "Warning: The Surgeon General Has Determined that TV Violence Is Moderately Dangerous to Your Child's Mental Health," *Public Opinion Quarterly* 36: 491–521.

52. Chaffee, S. H., McLeod, J. M., and Atkin, C. K. (1971). "Parental Influences on Adolescent Media Use," *American Behavioral Scientist* 14: 323–340.

53. Comstock, G. A. and Rubinstein, E. A., eds. (1972). *Television and Social Behavior:* Vol. 1: *Media Content and Control* Washington, D.C.: Government Printing Office.

54. ——— (1972). *Television and Social Behavior:* Vol. 3: *Television and Adolescent Aggressiveness* Washington, D.C.: Government Printing Office.

55. Eron, L. D., Lefkowitz, M. M., Huesmann, L. R., and Walder, L. O. (1972). "Does Television Violence Cause Aggression?" *American Psychologist* 27: 253–263.

56. Feshback, S. and Singer, R. D. (1971). *Television and Aggression* San Francisco: Jossey-Bass.

57. Friedrich, L. K. and Stein, A. H. (1973). "Aggressive and Prosocial Television Programs and the Natural Behavior of Preschool Children," *Monographs of the Society for Research in Child Development* 38: No. 4.

58. Hoffman, M. L. and Hoffman, L. W., eds. (1964). *Review of Child Development Research* New York: Russell Sage Foundation.

59. Liebert, R. M. and Baron, R. A. (1972). "Some Immediate Effects of Televised Violence on Children's Behavior," *Developmental Psychology* 6: 469–475.

60. Liebert, R. M., Neale, J. M., and Davidson, E. S. (1973). *The Early Window: Effects of Television on Children and Youth* New York: Pergamon.

61. Lyle, J. and Hoffman, H. R. (1972). "Children's Use of Television and Other Media," In *Television and Social Behavior,* ed. E. A. Rubenstein, G. A. Comstock, and J. P. Murray. Vol. 4: *Television in Day-to-Day Life: Patterns of Use.* Washington, D.C.: Government Printing Office, pp. 129–256.

62. ——— (1972). "Explorations in Patterns of Television Viewing by Preschool-Age Children," In *Television and Social Behavior,* ed. E. A. Rubenstein, G. A. Comstock, and J. P. Murray. Vol. 4: *Television in Day-to-Day Life: Patterns of Use.* Washington, D.C.: Government Printing Office, pp. 257–273.

63. Maccoby, E. E., Wilson, W. C., and Burton, R. V. (1958). "Differential Movie-Viewing Behavior of Male and Female Viewers," *Journal of Personality* 26: 259–267.

64. Osborn, D. K. and Endsley, R. C. (1971). "Emotional Reactions of Young Children to TV Violence," *Child Development* 42: 321–331.

65. Schramm, W., Lyle, J., and Parker, E. B. (1961). *Television in the Lives of Our Children* Stanford, Calif.: Stanford University Press.

66. Wotring, C. E. and Greenberg, B. S. "Experiments in Televised Violence and Verbal Aggression: Two Exploratory Studies," *Journal of Communication* 23: 446–460.

Family Themes

67. Ackerman, N. W. (1958). *The Psychodynamics of Family Life* New York: Basic Books.

68. Burgess, E. W. (1926). "The Family as a Unity of Interacting Personalities," *Family* 7: 3–9.

69. Fisher, S. and Mendell, D. (1956). "The Communication of Neurotic Patterns over Two and Three Generations," *Psychiatry* 10: 41–46.

70.———— (1958). "The Spread of Psychotherapeutic Effects from the Patient to His Family Group," *Psychiatry* 21: 133–140.

71. Haley, J. (1962). "Family Experiments: A New Type of Experimentation," *Family Process* 1: 265–293.

72. Handel, G. (1962). "A Study of Family and Personality." Unpublished doctoral dissertation, University of Chicago.

73. Handel, G., ed. (1967). *The Psychosocial Interior of the Family: A Sourcebook for the Study of Whole Families* Chicago: Aldine Publishing.

74. Handel, G. and Hess, R. D. (1956). "The Family as an Emotional Organization," *Marriage and Family Living* 18: 99–101.

75. Hess, R. D. and Handel, G. (1959). *Family Worlds: A Psychosocial Approach to Family Life* Chicago: University of Chicago Press.

76. Mendell, D. and Fisher, S. (1956). "An Approach to Neurotic Behavior in Terms of a Three-Generation Family Model," *Journal of Nervous and Mental Disease* 123: 171–180.

77. ———— (1958). "A Multi-Generation Approach to Treatment of Psychopathology," *Journal of Nervous and Mental Disease* 126: 523–529.

78. Rosenzweig, S. and Cass, L. K. (1954). "The Extension of Psychodiagnosis to Parents in the Child Guidance Setting," *American Journal of Orthopsychiatry* 24: 715–722.

79. Rosenzweig, S. and Isham, A. C. (1947). "Complementary Thematic Apperception Test Patterns in Close Kin," *American Journal of Orthopsychiatry* 17: 129–142.

80. Sohler, D. T., Holzberg, J. D., Fleck, S., Cornelison, A., Kay, E., and Lidz, T. (1957). "The Prediction of Family Interaction from a Battery of Projective Tests," *Journal of Projective Techniques* 21: 199–208.

81. Strodtbeck, F. L. (1954). "The Family as a Three-Person Group," *American Sociological Review* 19: 23–29.

82. Vogel, E. F. and Bell, N. W. (1960). "The Emotionally Disturbed Child as the Family Scapegoat," In *A Modern Introduction to the Family,* ed. N. W. Bell and E. F. Vogel. Glencoe, Ill.: Free Press.

INDEX

261

INDEX